QUESTIONS &
ANSWERS

Constitutional and Administrative Law

QUESTIONS & ANSWERS SERIES

Company Law

Constitutional and Administrative Law

Conveyancing

Criminal Law

EC Law

Employment Law

English Legal System

Equity and Trusts

Evidence

Family Law

Land Law

Landlord and Tenant

Law of Contract

Law of Torts

Wills, Probate and Administration

Other titles in preparation

QUESTIONS &
ANSWERS

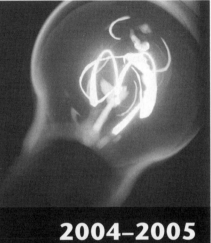

2004–2005

Constitutional and Administrative Law

THIRD EDITION

Richard Clements

LL B (University of Sheffield), LL M (University of London)

Jane Kay

LL B, LL M (University of Birmingham), MA (Brunel University)

OXFORD
UNIVERSITY PRESS

OXFORD

UNIVERSITY PRESS

Great Clarendon Street, Oxford OX2 6DP

Oxford University Press is a department of the University of Oxford.
It furthers the University's objective of excellence in research, scholarship,
and education by publishing worldwide in

Oxford New York

Auckland Bangkok Buenos Aires Cape Town Chennai
Dar es Salaam Delhi Hong Kong Istanbul Karachi Kolkata
Kuala Lumpur Madrid Melbourne Mexico City Mumbai Nairobi
São Paulo Shanghai Taipei Tokyo Toronto

Oxford is a registered trade mark of Oxford University Press
in the UK and in certain other countries

Published in the United States
by Oxford University Press Inc., New York

The moral rights of the authors have been asserted

Database right Oxford University Press (maker)

First published 1997
Second edition 2001
Reprinted 2002
Third edition 2004

British Library Cataloguing in Publication Data

Data available

British Library Cataloging in Publication Data

Data available

ISBN-13: 978-0-19-927086-6

ISBN-10: 0-19-927086-4

3 5 7 9 10 8 6 4

Typeset by RefineCatch Limited, Bungay, Suffolk
Printed in Great Britain by
Ashford Colour Press Ltd, Gosport, Hants.

Contents

Preface

Since the second edition in 2001, the Labour government's programme of constitutional reform has gathered pace. The implications of the Human Rights Act 1998 continue to be worked out in the British courts, whereas devolution to Scotland and Wales has, as yet, proved relatively unproblematic. The Freedom of Information Act 2000 is not fully in force, but the abolition of the office of Lord Chancellor and the creation of a Supreme Court, to replace the judicial role of the House of Lords, seem imminent. At the moment of writing an appointed, rather than an elected House of Lords is planned and electoral reform seems further away than ever.

Our thanks are due to our 'willing victims', the students upon whom we have tested earlier versions of these questions in examinations, assignments and tutorials. As is usual, any remaining errors in the book remain the responsibility of the authors alone.

Richard Clements
Jane Kay
November 2003

Table of Cases

Table of Statutes

material used and how the argument is structured and then you should be able to do it for yourself.

Read essay questions carefully, they can often be misunderstood. Identify the main topic first. Do not, as one author once did, mistake a question on Crown privilege for one on the royal prerogative! They are not at all the same thing. Often rather dense and obscure quotations are used, followed by 'Discuss'. Do not worry if you have never seen the quotation before, never heard of the author and do not understand it. Once you have identified the area, try to work out the main ideas involved and then try to talk about them. A question like the following might seem intimidating, but in reality it is not hard.

> The short explanation of the constitutional conventions is that they provide the flesh which clothes the dry bones of the law; they make the legal constitution work; they keep it in touch with the growth of ideas.
> Sir Ivor Jennings.

Discuss.

It is obviously about constitutional conventions! It indicates that only a small part of the constitution is law, 'the dry bones', much of it is convention. They are 'dry bones', because if we only looked at the law we would get a very misleading impression of the constitution. Without conventions the constitution would be unworkable. The student could give examples. 'The growth of ideas' bit indicates that conventions are flexible and change as politics and society change. Again, give examples!

Many students find problem questions in constitutional and administrative law a bit easier. Again the first thing to do is to identify the main topics that the problem focuses upon. Be warned: it is possible to 'disguise' areas quite easily in this subject. Then you identify the main legal points raised. They should often trigger cases in your memory. Do not worry if you cannot remember the exact name, still include them in your answer.

Whether you are writing an essay or a problem answer it is always best to do a rough plan first, listing the main points that you intend to cover. For a problem you might also include a list of the main cases. For an essay you would need not just cases, but authors' opinions and examples.

If you have done some work and have some basic knowledge there is nothing of which to be frightened. It does not matter if you are not sure that you have the right answer. In this subject there usually is no right answer.

Some students are concerned about whether they can express strong political views. Two points can be made. First it depends upon whether the question is asking for a fairly factual account or is asking for a view. A public order problem on the Criminal Justice and Public Order Act 1994 is asking you to apply the law to the facts supplied. An essay on the same area might ask you to express an opinion on whether this is a good or bad piece of legislation. Secondly, when putting forward a point of view you must have a proper argument supported by evidence. If you are asked for an opinion on the way in which European Community law has affected the traditional doctrine of the supremacy of Parliament, do not express the view that you hate all things European and that you dislike the way 'foreigners' are taking over this country! Instead, show that you are aware of the case law on this subject, both British and European and, in a really good answer, are aware of why the law has evolved in that way.

As in all legal subjects there are not any real short cuts to success but we hope that this book can convince you that constitutional and administrative law is not quite as intimidating as you thought.

not specifically mentioned. Students should also be able to discuss at least one other theory of the rule of law.

- **The law must authorise all government action.**

- **Equality before the law.**

- **The common law protects individual liberty.**

- **The supremacy of Parliament.**

- **The judiciary and the executive.**

- **The Human Rights Act 1998.**

ːǭː **Suggested answer**

The idea of the rule of law was not invented by Dicey, but he popularised it in the late nineteenth century. His book, *Introduction to the Study of the Law of the Constitution* (1885) can be seen as a strong defence of the English constitution when compared with the constitutions of other countries, particularly those with written constitutions. De Smith states that, 'His ideas . . . were very influential for two generations; today they no longer warrant detailed analysis' (*Constitutional and Administrative Law*, 1998). It is true that Dicey's ideas went out of fashion for a time, but they have now come back into favour, particularly with senior members of the judiciary. So, once again, they require detailed analysis.

It is often said that Britain has an 'unwritten constitution', meaning that it is not contained in one document and much of it has no formal legal status. Dicey argued that not only did this not matter, but in fact it was a positive advantage. In Britain there was a long tradition of respect for individual liberty and democracy. This tradition was upheld in our constitutional arrangements. For short it could be called the rule of law. Dicey summarised it under three main principles.

His first principle concerned the rule of law and discretionary powers. No person could be punished or interfered with by the authorities unless the law authorised it. Put another way, all government actions must be authorised by the law. This contrasted the situation in England with a country where there were no rules. In the latter, the government could do as it pleased and there would be no legal controls over its activities. Examples would be imprisonment when someone had broken no law, or the lack of any trial before punishment.

Dicey also felt that governments should not possess wide discretionary powers. The classic example of these ideas was *Entick v Carrington* (1765) 19 St Tr 1030 where the courts declared that the Secretary of State could not order the search of Entick's house, because there was no law that authorised such searches. The court would not accept arguments of 'state necessity' or that there was one law for government activities and another for ordinary people.

Dicey's second principle has the resounding title of 'equality before the law'. This held that the government and its officials should not have any special exemptions or protections from the law. He did not like the French system where government activities were dealt with by separate administrative courts. These he considered to be too partial to the government and inferior to ordinary courts of law.

The final principle concerns individual rights. The English constitution respects personal liberty. There is no need for a Bill of Rights because civil liberties are respected anyway. The courts protect them in their decisions by developing the common law in a way that respects individual liberty. Parliament legislates on particular problems. In contrast, Bills of Rights are documents which promise all sorts of rights. These promises are so general and capable of so many meanings that they are meaningless. Again the Bill of Rights might not be respected by the government and might be unenforceable.

Dicey's theory is open to many objections. Some might say that these ideas are so vague and wide ranging that they have no real meaning. As de Smith states: 'The concept is one of open texture; it lends itself to an extremely wide range of interpretations.' He also said: '. . . everyone who tries to redefine it begins with the assumption that it is a good thing, like justice or courage'. Some might say that his theory is so obvious that it is not worth stating it. Of course the government must obey the law and the courts enforce it in a modern constitutional system. R. F. V. Heuston ('The Rule of Law' from *Essays in Constitutional Law*, 1964) claims that Dicey misunderstood French administrative courts. They are not biased in favour of the government and they do at least as well, if not better, in controlling the government as the English courts. Separate 'public law' or 'constitutional' courts are the normal arrangement in continental Europe. E. Barendt ([1985] *Public Law* 596) argues that Dicey also misunderstood the nature of written constitutions. Although in 1885 Bills of Rights might just have been pious declarations that no one could enforce, nowadays most countries that have them possess sophisticated enforcement mechanisms.

The main criticism of the rule of law is that it fails to deal with the supremacy of Parliament. If Parliament legislates in a way that is contrary to the rule of law, it is still the law and there is nothing that the courts can do about it. Statutes can annul inconvenient court decisions. For instance, the War Damage Act 1965 reversed *Burmah Oil* v *Lord Advocate* [1965] AC 75, where the House of Lords ordered the government to pay compensation to Burmah Oil for the wartime destruction of its oil installations. Statutes also grant government officials some immunities from legal action, e.g., the Crown Proceedings Act 1947. Some Acts of Parliament grant the government wide and uncontrolled discretionary powers, e.g., the Deregulation and Contracting Out Act 1994. Dicey claimed that Parliament would protect our liberties and restrain the government. Perhaps that was true in 1885, but nowadays the government of the day controls Parliament through its majority and can nearly always get its own way.

- Conventions are enforced by peer pressure, public opinion or personal morality.

- Conventions evolve over time.

☿ Suggested answer

In all constitutions, even those that are written, like that of Canada, various practices or ways of doing things that are not strictly provided for in the constitution grow up over the years. These practices can harden and become the accepted way of doing things. Then they can be called conventions. In *Re Canada* (1982), although the written Canadian constitution did not require it, it was the convention that the consent of the Canadian provinces had to be obtained before changes were made to the constitution. In the UK, a country without a written constitution, conventions are particularly important.

In the late nineteenth century the famous constitutional writer, A. V. Dicey, drew attention to the role of conventions in the UK. He believed that most of the UK constitution and many of its most important parts consisted of conventions. This did not mean that there were no rules, merely that a lot of the rules were not legal ones. As he put it in, *Introduction to the Study of the Law of the Constitution*, 1885:

> The other set of rules consist of conventions, understandings, habits or practices which, though they may regulate the conduct of several members of the sovereign power, of the Ministers, or of other officials, are not in reality laws at all since they are not enforced by the courts. This portion of constitutional law may, for the sake of distinction, be termed 'the conventions of the constitution', or constitutional morality.

If we only look at the legal rules of the constitution we gain a seriously misleading impression. Legally, the Queen may refuse the Royal Assent to a parliamentary Bill. By convention she always agrees, taking the advice of Her Majesty's government. Legally, the Queen chooses the Prime Minister, but by convention it is always the person who can command a majority in the House of Commons. Legally the Queen chooses her own ministers, but by convention they are chosen by the Prime Minister.

Conventions are clearly not the law because, as in the above examples, they sometimes contradict the strict legal position. The courts take judicial notice of the existence of conventions and sometimes they can even influence their decisions, but the courts cannot enforce conventions because they are not law. In *Attorney-General* v *Jonathan Cape* [1976] QB 752 there is an interesting discussion of the various conventions relating to Cabinet secrecy, but the court cannot enforce them, only the law, which was breach of confidence in that case. In *Madzimbamuto* v *Lardner-Burke* [1969] AC 645 the court observed that there was a convention that the UK would not legislate for Rhodesia without that colony's consent. This could not stop the UK Parliament from legislating in breach of the convention if it chose.

There are many examples of convention. It is probably impossible to make a complete list. The office of Prime Minister and the existence of the Cabinet are conventional only. Ministers are accountable to Parliament and responsible for the actions of their civil servants. There are detailed 'rules' governing things like gifts to ministers and their financial interests, which have been written down in a booklet, *The Ministerial Code*. Parliament meets every year, but the Bill of Rights 1689 only says that it should meet 'frequently'.

The problem with all these conventions is that it is hard to decide which ones definitely exist and which are just everyday politics. Sir Ivor Jennings recommended a three stage test in, *The Law and the Constitution*, 1959. First, we must look for the precedents; how often and how consistently has this practice been observed before? Secondly, did the actors in the precedent believe that they were bound by the rule? In other words, did they believe that they had some sort of obligation to follow the precedent? Thirdly, there must be a reason for the rule. In other words, the convention must fit in with our general ideas of the constitution like democracy, accountability etc. This test works well with some of the major conventions. We know that the Queen always gives the Royal Assent because there are thousands of examples of her doing so. A Monarch has not refused since 1708 to give the Royal Assent. It seems clear that she feels that she has no choice in the matter. The reason is that a hereditary Monarch should abide by the wishes of the democratic government. With other proposed conventions such as when a minister should resign this test does not work so well. This gives rise to many doubts about conventions generally.

Conventions are continually changing. Up until 1902 a Prime Minister could come from the House of Lords. Since then they have always come from the Commons. Up until 1992 a new Speaker came from the governing party. In that year the Labour Opposition's Betty Boothroyd was elected, but in 2000 Michael Martin was elected Speaker. He was from the Labour party who formed the government, but he was not the government's 'choice'. This evolution of convention leads to uncertainty. Although we can say what happened last time a situation occurred, we cannot be absolutely certain that the precedent will be followed next time. As an editorial in *Public Law* in 1963, pp. 401–2, put it: 'so let us delete those pages in constitutional text books headed conventions, and talk about what happens and why what happened yesterday may not happen tomorrow'.

Conventions are called rules but they do not look much like rules. They are often vague and imprecise. No body deliberately creates them, unlike an Act of Parliament. It is not necessary for a court to rule upon whether they exist or not. In many cases, despite the efforts of writers like Jennings, it is hard to say whether a convention exists or not.

rules and the members need to know who has the power to take decisions or take actions. So what is the purpose of a constitution? A constitution is there to limit the power of those who govern and if necessary protect the individual citizen from them. It is there to ensure that those who run the State do not behave in an *arbitrary* manner. They must act according to the rules and procedures and not just persecute a citizen for no good reason. For example, a government official could not just say to someone 'I do not like you, you cannot live in this country.' Instead there must be laws about nationality, immigration and the right to a fair trial. A constitution provides for these things, but just as importantly it would also state who has the power to do what. Who can make laws, is there a Head of State, is there a Prime Minister and who has the real power to decide?

Nearly every country in the world, apart from the United Kingdom, New Zealand and Israel, has a written constitution. The idea of having a special constitutional document came into vogue at the end of the eighteenth century with the United States of America obtaining its independence from Britain and the French Revolution overthrowing the rule of King Louis XVI. Generally countries adopt a written constitution when there is a dramatic break with the past and there is a need to make a fresh start with a new system of government. Gaining independence and revolution, as with the USA and France above are often the occasions to adopt a constitution, as is recovery after a war, such as France in 1946. England was in fact one of the first countries to have a written constitution with Oliver Cromwell's 'Instrument of Governement' in 1653, after he had overthrown and executed Charles I. It only lasted, however, until 1660, when the old system of royal government was restored. Since then the British system of government has changed out of all recognition, but it has changed gradually and there has never been such a drastic break with the past that either politicians or the people have wanted a written constitution.

Every country has a different constitution and this also applies to the written variety, so it is only possible to give some examples of what might be in such a constitution. Some might be quite short, like that of the USA and just state the general principles, while others, like that of India, might be extremely long and go into great detail. Most written constitutions have superior status to the ordinary law and therefore many countries, particularly in Europe, make a big distinction between Constitutional Law, known as Public Law and Private Law. Many countries have specialist courts to deal with Public Law issues, separate to the private law courts. This system is not known in Britain, because without a written constitution, there is not a clear-cut distinction between Public Law and Private Law.

Many written constitutions have a clear statement of the 'values' of that country. For instance the constitution of the USA starts with the words 'We the People of the United States . . .' and, among other things proclaims the 'Blessings of Liberty'. The United Kingdom has no such statement so we have to rely on writers like the nineteenth-century Dicey, for statements of constitutional values.

A written constitution would often lay down a special procedure under which the constitution can be changed. For example, Article V of the US Constitution stipulates that two-thirds of both Houses of the Congress or two-thirds of the legislatures of the States can propose amendments to the Constitution. This has to be ratified by the legislatures of three-quarters of the States. In the Republic of Ireland, a Bill passed by both Houses of Parliament, a majority of the votes in a referendum and the assent of the President amends the Constitution. In contrast, there is no special procedure to change any part of the UK constitution.

Written constitutions will often detail the federal structure of a country, outlining the powers of each State or province and the powers of the central or federal government. The unification of once independent 'countries' to form a federal state is often the reason for adopting a written constitution and occurred in the United States of America, Canada, Australia, Nigeria, Malaysia and Germany, to give just a few examples. The United Kingdom, as the name suggests, is a union of once separate countries, but it is not federal. Instead, the Parliament of the UK, which sits at Westminster, retains full legislative supremacy. It has recently granted considerable self-government to Scotland, in the Scotland Act 1998, to Northern Ireland in the Northern Ireland Act 1998 and some powers of self-government to Wales in the Government of Wales Act of the same year. The UK Parliament can, however, just as easily repeal those Acts and regain full powers to govern Scotland, Northern Ireland and Wales. There is no written constitution to stop the sovereign Parliament of the UK doing this.

Many written constitutions contain a list of 'Rights', to which the citizen is entitled. Often, as in the USA and Germany, they are constitutionally protected and cannot easily be taken away, by the executive or legislature. The UK has a Bill of Rights from 1689, but that was more designed to reduce the power of the King rather than to grant individual rights. We now have the Human Rights Act 1998, which gives the European Convention on Human Rights some effect in UK law. Section 3 of this Act, however, carefully preserves the supremacy of Parliament. UK courts cannot strike down primary legislation, which is incompatible with human rights, and Act of Parliament can still restrict human rights.

Most written constitutions would contain some sort of 'organisation chart' of government and would explain whether there was a President or Prime Minister, or both, and what their powers were, who had the power to legislate, who appoints the judges, etc. There is no equivalent in the UK, as the system of government has just evolved over the centuries. The Head of State is the Queen, which is a matter of ancient common law, and there is no law that says that there has to be a Prime Minister. The existence of a Prime Minister is just a matter of 'convention' or non-legal custom.

In fact the UK Constitution can be found in a number of sources. Acts of Parliament are important and many are of constitutional significance such as the Act of Settlement 1700 and the European Communities Act 1972. As we have seen above, more and more of the UK Constitution is being incorporated into Acts of Parliament. These can be very important changes, for example the Scotland Act 1998 restored a Parliament to Scotland, the Human Rights Act 1998 makes human rights directly enforceable in UK courts for the first time and the House of Lords Act 1999 abolished the right of most hereditary peers to sit in the House of Lords. This indicates that nothing is permanent in the UK Constitution, everything can change. Cases can also be important sources of the constitution. For example, the House of Lords reaffirmed the principle of the supremacy of Parliament in *Pickin* v *BRB* [1974] AC 765, but a few years later had to moderate it to take account of membership of the European Community in *Factortame (No. 2)* [1991] 1 AC 603. Unlike many of the countries with a written constitution, the UK does not have a Supreme or Constitutional Court that rules on constitutional issues. All legal cases, constitutional or not, go to the same court system.

Historic documents, such as the Magna Carta (1215) and the Bill of Rights (1689) are important for establishing constitutional principles, such as the idea that the King or Executive does not have unlimited power, but these documents do not have the special, formal legal status of a written constitution.

A lot of the UK Constitution is not legal at all and consists of constitutional conventions, which were defined by Dicey in his The Law of the Constitution as: 'conventions, understandings, habits or practices which, although they may regulate the conduct of the several members of the sovereign power . . . are not in reality laws at all since they are not enforced by the courts.' (p. 24 10th edn 1959). Much of the most important parts of the constitution can be found in convention, such as the existence of the Prime Minister, the Cabinet, ministerial responsibility, accountability to parliament and how the considerable legal powers of the Queen are exercised by ministers in her name. Constitutional conventions are not legally enforceable (*Attorney-General* v *Jonathan Cape Ltd.* [1976] QB 752) and are constantly changing. For example, in June 2003, the Prime Minister abolished the Lord Chancellor's Department, as part of a ministerial reshuffle and replaced it with the Department of Constitutional Affairs.

This is supposed to be the major advantage of an unwritten constitution, its flexibility and its ability to change. By contrast, as we have seen, it can be difficult to change a written constitution. On the other hand, if everything can change, as it can with the UK constitution, it can lead to a lot of confusion and both members of the government and the ordinary citizen can be uncertain what is the true constitutional position. Some think that Prime Ministers and the governments that they lead have too much power and can take away any right by just using Parliament to pass an Act or by merely changing a convention. However, even in countries with written constitutions, that document is unlikely to reveal the full constitutional position. For instance in the USA, the Supreme Court has the power to strike down legislation which is incompatible with the constitution. That power is not found in the constitution, but in a case: *Marbury* v *Madison* 1803 1 Cranch. 137. Under Article II of the US Constitution, the President needs the consent of the Senate to agree treaties, but a practice has grown up of making 'Executive Agreements' with other countries, which does not require Senate approval. The difference between a written and unwritten constitution is not as great as some suppose, because it is not possible to write down everything in a document that will be valid for all time. Much of the UK constitution is in Act of Parliament anyway and that is increasingly the position today, as this essay has tried to show. Every country has different constitutional arrangements and those of the UK just reflect its individual history of being one of the oldest unified States in the world.

Further reading

Barnett, H. *Constitutional and Administrative Law*, 4th edn (Cavendish, 2002), chs 1, 2, 4 and 5.

Bradley, A. and Ewing, K. *Constitutional & Administrative Law*, 13th edn (Longman, 2003), chs 1, 2, 5 and 6.

de Smith, S. and Brazier, R. *Constitutional and Administrative Law*, 8th edn (Penguin, 1998).

Munro, C. *Studies in Constitutional Law*, 2nd edn (Butterworths, 1999), chs 1, 3 and 9.

Parliamentary supremacy

Introduction

This chapter covers the most important and controversial aspect of the present UK constitution, and one which is very likely to appear on any examination paper. Although it is possible for a question to be set which concentrates on the traditional doctrine, and an example of such a question is given here, most examiners will set a question on the effect of membership of the European Union on parliamentary supremacy. Two examples are given, in the form of an essay and a problem question. The principal difficulty which students experience in answering such questions lies in distinguishing between the attitude of European Community law, as laid down by the European Court of Justice, and the attitude of English law, as shown by the English courts. Only precedents from the English courts should be cited as authority for what English law actually is. Whether this complies with European Community law is a separate issue, and may not always be relevant, depending on the terms of the question asked.

Q Question 1

What is meant by the term parliamentary supremacy? What are its implications in matters other than those raised by Britain's membership of the European Union?

Commentary

This question requires the student to demonstrate a general understanding of the theoretical basis of parliamentary supremacy and its effects. Because it specifically excludes the problems arising from membership of the EU, which are dealt with in a subsequent question, the student can concentrate on some of the other issues which have attracted attention, such as the ability of Parliament to impose special procedures for the passage of later legislation. In many examination papers, this type of question will include discussion of the EU; the student should assume that the EU is meant to be discussed if it is not, as here, expressly excluded.

- Only Parliament can make a law, which can be on any subject.

- Any law made by Parliament will be obeyed by the courts.

- Today's Parliament can expressly repeal any law passed by a previous Parliament.

- An inconsistent later Act will impliedly repeal an earlier Act.

- But this may not apply to constitutional legislation.

⚲ Suggested answer

In most states, the validity of any law can be traced back to a written constitution, which forms the basis of the organisation of the state. But in the UK, once the origin of a legal rule is traced back to an Act of Parliament, there is no further document by which the validity of that Act can be determined. Instead, the lawyer is forced simply to assert the proposition that an Act of Parliament is law, because Parliament has the power to enact laws. Why Parliament has that power is an interesting historical and political question, but the lawyer is generally happy to accept the existence of Parliament's power as unquestioned and unquestionable.

The historical origins of parliamentary supremacy lie in the gradual development of the understanding that changes to the law required not merely the personal decision of the Monarch, but the 'advice and consent' of the representatives of Lords and Commons, formally assembled in the two Houses of Parliament. This understanding was challenged in the seventeenth century, but was confirmed once and for all by the Bill of Rights 1689, Art 1:

> That the pretended power of suspending of laws, or the execution of laws by regal authority without consent of Parliament is illegal.

From this point, the creation of new law has been a power possessed by Parliament alone.

But what was not clear was whether there were any restrictions or limits on that power. During the seventeenth century there were suggestions that any Act of Parliament which was unreasonable, repugnant or impossible would be declared invalid by the courts. These suggestions were heavily influenced by the philosophy of natural law, by which human law is judged against the standards set by an ideal, God-given law. With the decline of this philosophy and the growth of positivism, such sentiments were no longer expressed, and, as Parliament was not in any case interested in enacting unreasonable legislation, the courts were happy to accept the validity of any Act passed by traditional parliamentary procedure. Parliament was to be treated as the supreme law-maker.

The most celebrated statement of parliamentary supremacy is that of Dicey;

> that Parliament has the right to make or unmake any law whatever; and further that no person or body is recognised by the law of England as having a right to override or set aside the legislation of Parliament.

It received judicial confirmation in *Madzimbamuto* v *Lardner-Burke* [1969] 1 AC 645, where Lord Reid said:

> It is often said that it would be unconstitutional for the UK Parliament to do certain things, meaning that the moral, political and other reasons against doing them are so strong that most people would regard it as highly improper if Parliament did these things. But that does not mean that it is beyond the power of Parliament to do such things. If Parliament chose to do any of them, the courts could not hold the Act of Parliament invalid.

It is clear that Parliament can do, and has done, many things which in other countries might be regarded as unconstitutional. It may break international law; see *Mortensen* v *Peters* (1906) 8F(J) 93. It may legislate retrospectively; see War Damage Act 1965. It may order people to be detained without trial; see the Anti-Terrorism, Crime and Security Act, 2001.

It is virtually impossible to imagine any circumstances (other than a breach of EC law) where the UK courts would refuse to accept the validity of an Act of Parliament properly passed. Further, the courts will not involve themselves in questions relating to the way in which the legislation was passed. In *British Railways Board* v *Pickin* [1974] AC 765, the respondent alleged that a private Act of Parliament had been passed only after Parliament had been misled by the appellants. But the court upheld the validity of the Act, stating that it would be for Parliament itself to investigate any defects in the procedure.

There remains, however, one disputed area. Can Parliament bind its successors? The orthodox view is that it cannot. The Parliament which is supreme is the current Parliament, so it has the power to repeal the legislation of any previous Parliament. Normally such repeal is expressed in the later Act. But if, through inadvertence or caution, Parliament simply enacts something inconsistent with an earlier Act, the courts will treat this as an implied repeal of the earlier Act by the later. In *Ellen St Estates Ltd* v *Minister of Health* [1934] 1 KB 590, the Court of Appeal rejected an attempt to argue that the Housing Act 1925 should be read subject to inconsistent provisions in the Acquisition of Land Act 1919. The 1925 Act impliedly repealed those provisions.

What is the origin of this rule that Parliament cannot bind its successors? If it is regarded as a rule of common law, then logic would suggest that, like all other rules of common law, it would be subject to alteration by Act of Parliament. But, as Wade argued in his 1955 article, 'The Basis of Legal Sovereignty', if the rule is regarded as the rule of recognition, on which the whole basis of constitutional legality rests, it is not like other common law rules, and nothing short of a legal revolution could change it. Any attempt by an Act of Parliament to change the basis on which Acts of Parliament are treated as law is doomed to failure. But, in various contexts, the issue of Parliament's ability to bind its successors has arisen and given rise to legal and academic debate.

The first concerns grants of independence to former colonies, which are given legal effect by an Act of Parliament stating that Parliament will no longer legislate for the country in question. Could such an Act be repealed? Legal theory suggests that it could, but, as was pointed out in *British Coal Corporation* v *R* [1935] AC 500, that has no relation to realities. The independent state would take no notice of any attempt to revoke its independence without its consent. It appears though that the UK courts would feel themselves bound to obey the express terms of the UK statute. But no such issue is ever likely to arise in practice, so this remains a theoretical problem only.

There have been some differences of opinion between Scottish and English lawyers over the status of the Acts of Union 1707, various provisions of which were stated to be unalterable. It is argued that as the Acts were the work of the then separate English and Scottish Parliaments, they could not be repealed by the UK Parliament which replaced them and which owes its very existence to those Acts. In fact some of the 'unalterable' provisions have been altered, without successful legal challenge in Scotland or England. It is conceivable that any attempt to alter such fundamental matters as the status of Scots law or the nature of the Church of Scotland would be rejected, at least by the Scottish courts. But again, no such change could ever be imagined, so no legal ruling will ever be needed.

The question which has given rise to most debate is whether Parliament could prescribe special procedures for the passing of future legislation which could be made binding on future Parliaments. There is nothing to prevent Parliament creating special procedures; for example, the Northern Ireland Act 1998, s. 1 requires the holding of a referendum before any legislation to remove Northern Ireland from the UK. But this so-called constitutional guarantee derives its validity from the 1998 Act, which could itself be repealed without a referendum. Would it be possible to prevent this by stating in an Act that the Act itself could not be repealed without a referendum?

There is a school of thought that Parliament would in fact be bound by such a provision regulating the manner and form of future legislation. This would enable the partial entrenchment of legislation, by requiring referenda or special majorities before laws, for example protecting civil rights or devolving power, could be repealed. The contention is supported by reference to various Commonwealth cases, such as *Attorney-General for New South Wales* v *Trethowan* [1932] AC 526, *Harris* v *Minister of the Interior* 1952 (2) SA 428, and *Bribery Commissioner* v *Ranasinghe* [1965] AC 172. But in all these cases, the requirements as to the manner and form of future legislation were contained in the original UK statutes by which independence was granted, and it logically followed that these requirements could not be changed by the actions of a non-sovereign legislature. The problem in applying these precedents to the UK Parliament is that it would have to limit itself, rather than being subjected to external constitutional constraints.

In *Thoburn* v *Sunderland City Council* [2002] EWHC 195 Admin, [2002] 4 All ER 156,

Laws LJ confirmed the orthodox view that Parliament 'cannot stipulate as to the manner and form of any subsequent legislation' and could therefore repeal any previous legislation. However, he went on to suggest that the courts had begun to recognise a special category of constitutional statutes, those which created fundamental constitutional rights. These statutes, he said, could not be impliedly repealed. If Parliament wished to repeal them, it would have to use express, unambiguous words. Otherwise the courts would assume that Parliament intended the constitutional rights to be protected, even against later statutes. Which statutes are 'constitutional' in this sense? Laws LJ suggested some examples: the Bill of Rights 1689, the Acts of Union 1707 and the Human Rights Act 1998.

This interesting suggestion would provide a means by which the courts could retain the traditional theory of parliamentary supremacy while offering some protection to individual rights. It would retain the right of Parliament to deal with war, terrorism or other emergencies unhindered by the courts, while ensuring that any such legislation would have to be politically acceptable. It remains to be seen whether this new interpretation of parliamentary supremacy is adopted.

Q Question 2

What impact has British membership of the European Communities had on the doctrine of parliamentary supremacy?

Commentary

The issues raised by this question are likely to be central to any constitutional law course. Students must be careful to discuss this question in the light of case law, not the often ill-informed pronouncements of politicians. There have now been enough cases to enable definite answers to be given to most issues, but the exact boundaries to the courts' obedience to EC rather than UK law remain uncertain and therefore debatable. The student will need to explain the general doctrine of parliamentary supremacy, but there is no need to go into detail about the other complex issues which would arise in a more general question.

- By EC law, EC law has supremacy over national law.

- By English law, the law passed by Parliament has supremacy.

- These principles are contradictory, but can be reconciled as follows.

- Any UK law passed before 1972 can be impliedly repealed by the ECA 1972.

- Any UK law passed after 1972 will, if possible, be interpreted so as to comply with EC law.

- The *Factortame* cases ruled that UK laws passed after 1972 inconsistent with EC law will not be enforced by the UK courts.

- The ECA 1972 can be expressly repealed, but not impliedly repealed.

⋮Ọ⋮ Suggested answer

When Britain joined the EC, concerns were expressed in many quarters about the constitutional implications. In particular, how could EC membership be reconciled with the traditional doctrine of parliamentary supremacy? In states with a written constitution, it was generally possible to spell out the implications of EC membership by an appropriate constitutional amendment. But because the British constitution is unwritten, no such process was available. All that Britain could do was to pass the European Communities Act 1972, by the same procedure as for all other statutes and with, prima facie, the same legal force as all other statutes, leaving many unanswered questions.

According to Dicey, 'no person is recognised by the law of England as having a right to over-ride or set aside the legislation of Parliament'. This doctrine forms the very basis of the British constitution with the effect that the current Parliament can pass any legislation it wishes, including legislation to amend or repeal, expressly or by implication, legislation passed by an earlier Parliament. Although there has been considerable academic debate about possible exceptions to this power, and possible methods of entrenching legislation, the orthodox view accepted no limits on Parliament's authority.

But, before Britain ever joined the EC, the European Court of Justice had established, in *Costa* v *ENEL*, Case 6/64, [1964] CMLR 425, that Community law was to prevail over incompatible national law. The doctrine of direct effect obliged national courts to give effect to rights arising under Community law, regardless of any national law to the contrary. No doubt, in an ideal world, no national law inconsistent with the state's EC obligations would ever be enacted. But in the real world, it was all too likely that a state would enact such legislation, whether by inadvertence, or in the hope that the inconsistency would not be noticed or challenged. The particular problem faced by the British legislators was to find some way to instruct the courts to give effect to Community law in preference to Acts of Parliament whenever passed.

It was straightforward to provide, in s. 2(1) of the European Communities Act 1972, that all rights arising under the EC Treaties were to be given effect in preference to pre-existing UK law. The orthodox doctrines of express and implied repeal authorised that. But the real problem concerned legislation passed after 1972 which was inconsistent with EC law. This was dealt with in s. 2(4) of the 1972 Act, which provides that legislation passed, or to be passed in the future, should be construed and have effect subject to the rule laid down in s. 2(1), that is, that effect must be given to EC rights. This was reinforced by s. 3(1), which instructed the courts to decide any issues of

Community law 'in accordance with the principles laid down by, and any relevant decisions of, the European Court of Justice'. This would include the principle of the supremacy of EC law laid down in *Costa* v *ENEL* (1964).

The 1972 Act therefore appeared to provide the courts with an instruction that they should obey Community law, but left unresolved the question of what would happen if different instructions were provided in a later Act of Parliament. Leaving aside for the moment the issue of an express instruction to breach Community law, what if an Act passed after 1972 contained provisions inconsistent with Community law? By the traditional methods of interpretation, where provisions in an earlier Act are inconsistent with a later Act, the earlier Act is impliedly repealed; see *Ellen St Estates Ltd* v *Minister of Health* [1934] 1 KB 590. It could therefore be argued that any Act passed after 1972 could impliedly repeal the European Communities Act, so that the phrase 'legislation passed or to be passed' would be read with the proviso 'except this new Act'. This would leave the UK in breach of its obligations under the EC Treaties. How could the courts avoid this?

The solution, for many cases, was found in the long-standing rule of statutory interpretation that, where legislation is passed to implement the UK's international obligations, any ambiguity should be construed so as to comply with those obligations rather than conflict with them. This rule, taken with the express wording of s. 2(4) of the 1972 Act, has been treated by the courts as a clear instruction to interpret any UK legislation passed to implement EC law in such a way to ensure that there is no discrepancy between them. In *Garland* v *British Rail Engineering* [1983] 2 AC 751, the court preferred the interpretation of the Sex Discrimination Act 1975 which was consistent with Article 119 (now 141), EC Treaty, to the interpretation which created conflict between them. The courts have been willing to use purposive methods of interpretation rather than traditional literal methods to ensure compliance with EC law. In *Pickstone* v *Freemans plc* [1989] AC 66, and *Lister* v *Forth Dry Dock* [1990] 1 AC 546, the courts went far beyond literal interpretation, even implying extra words into a regulation in order to ensure that EC law was complied with. This approach has proved to deal satisfactorily with all cases where UK legislation is passed in order to incorporate EC directives and Treaty provisions into UK law.

A different problem was posed by the decision of the European Court of Justice in *Marleasing*, C-106/89, [1992] 1 CMLR 305, that all national legislation, whenever passed, should be interpreted in the light of EC law, in order to give effect to rights even if they did not have direct effect. The UK courts had earlier refused, in *Duke* v *GEC Reliance Ltd* [1988] AC 618, to interpret UK statutes passed in 1970 and 1975 in the light of a 1976 directive, on the grounds that that could not possibly have been Parliament's intention; the rules stated in the statutes were unambiguously in conflict with the directive. But in *Webb* v *EMO Air Cargo (No. 2)* [1995] 4 All ER 577, the House of Lords without debate interpreted an ambiguous 1975 Act to give effect to a 1976 directive, just as the European Court of Justice decision required. There remains considerable uncertainty in both UK and EC law as to just how far a national court is supposed to go in rewriting its existing laws under the guise of interpretation, but the UK courts seem willing to follow the instruction given by the 1972 Act.

The above cases, being treated as issues of statutory interpretation and the reconciling of apparently contradictory rules, managed to avoid the fundamental problem of a direct clash between EC law and a statute passed after 1972. In *Macarthys Ltd v Smith* [1979] 3 All ER 325, Lord Denning expressed the view that, in such a situation, it would be the court's duty to give effect to EC law. But the issue did not arise in an unavoidable form until the *Factortame* cases, C-213/89, [1990] 3 CMLR 375 and C-221/89, [1991] 3 CMLR 589. These concerned an apparent clash between the EC laws forbidding discrimination on grounds of nationality and the Merchant Shipping Act 1988 which imposed discriminatory rules on fishing boats. When Factortame challenged the application to them of the 1988 Act, they asked for an interim injunction suspending the Act, pending a reference to the European Court of Justice. English law would not permit such a suspension as it would clearly breach Dicey's formulation of parliamentary supremacy, but the European Court of Justice held that EC law could require it. The House of Lords were therefore faced with the ultimate choice: to obey the 1988 Act, as the newest statement of Parliament's intentions, or to obey the 1972 Act and enforce EC law. The House of Lords chose to obey the 1972 Act and awarded the injunction. In effect, the 1972 Act was held not to be subject to the doctrine of implied repeal. All legislation passed after 1972 has a proviso implicitly contained within it — 'unless EC law provides otherwise'. The European Communities Act 1972 was treated by the courts as having an exceptional status, but perhaps not a unique one. In *Thoburn* v *Sunderland City Council* [2002] EWHC 195 Admin, [2002] 4 All ER 156, Laws LJ suggested that other 'constitutional' statutes might share this protection against implied repeal.

The European Communities Act 1972 can, however, be expressly repealed, and if that happened, EC law would lose its effect within the UK in the eyes of the UK courts. Such a withdrawal from the EC would be facilitated by the provisions of the European Constitutional Convention, under discussion in 2003, which for the first time provides a method by which a state can leave the EC. Parliament's supremacy would be restored to its Diceyan form by the repeal.

It is interesting to consider the effect of an express enactment, short of a complete repeal of the European Communities Act 1972, stating that some particular provision was to prevail over any EC rule to the contrary. Given that the 1972 Act would still be in force, would the courts follow that or the later Act? In *Macarthys Ltd* v *Smith* (1979) Lord Denning suggested that in such a case, unlikely though it was, the courts would have to obey the new statute as the expression of the current will of Parliament. Any such legislation would provoke a political crisis as between Britain and the EC, and no doubt applications would be made to both British and European courts. But it would be most uncomfortable for the British courts to do anything other than follow the expressed wishes of Parliament and government, leaving it to those political institutions to solve what would be in essence a political problem.

In conclusion, it can be argued that the UK Parliament, through its power to repeal the 1972 Act, or legislate expressly contrary to it, does retain its ultimate supremacy, in spite of the fact that, in its daily operation, it is now constrained by Community law. The courts have in effect taken Parliament at its word as expressed in 1972, and will continue to do so until expressly instructed to the contrary. Any other decision would have led to the courts provoking clashes with Community law. It is right that the ultimate decision as to whether Community law should continue to have force in the UK should rest with the UK Parliament.

Q Question 3

Under Article 12, EC Treaty, it is forbidden for Member States to discriminate on grounds of nationality. Consider the following situations in the light of that provision and the doctrine of Parliamentary supremacy.

(a) Brunelli, an Italian railway engineer, applied for the post of chief engineer with the Great West Railway Co. But he was informed that, under a statute passed in 1850, only British citizens were eligible for that post.

(b) Because of concerns about public safety, the UK Parliament passed an Act in 2001 establishing a register of practitioners of alternative and complementary therapies. Only persons with appropriate qualifications can be registered. Erik, a qualified Swedish aromatherapist, applied to be registered. But his application was rejected on the ground that he was not a British citizen.

(c) As a result of an influx of Spanish waiters, the UK Parliament passed the Waiters (Control) Act 2002, which provides that no restaurant may employ more than one Spanish waiter. As a result, Manuel, Jose and Pablo, who used to work at the El Cordobes restaurant in Bristol, have all been dismissed.

(d) Because of recent poor performances by the English football team, the Football Association has asked the UK Parliament to pass a law restricting the number of footballers from other EU states who can play for English league clubs, regardless of any EU law to the contrary.

Commentary

This is a reasonably straightforward question, each section of which raises a different combination of issues. As with any question on the interrelationship of EU and English law, it is important to distinguish between the two different perspectives which these laws offer. The point of EU law on which this question is based is a simple one, an Article of the EC Treaty which is known to have vertical and horizontal direct effect. You can therefore deal with it in a few words, leaving the bulk of your answer to address the English law.

Remember that decisions of the ECJ provide authority for what Community law is, and what English law should be, but only decisions of the English courts can give authoritative rulings on what English law actually is. The most difficult and interesting issues arise when the two laws seem to produce differing, even conflicting answers. A good answer will give both perspectives, before offering an opinion on whether they can be reconciled, or, if they are in conflict, which will prevail. Where the answer is uncertain, it will not matter so much which conclusion you reach, but more how good an argument you can produce.

- **Remember to distinguish between EC and UK perspectives.**

- **Acts passed before 1972 can be impliedly repealed by the ECA.**

- **Try to find a compatible interpretation for Acts passed after 1972.**

- **By EC law, EC law prevails; *Factortame* accepts this for UK law too.**

- **An attempt to exclude an EC law is of uncertain effect.**

:ǿ: Answer

This question raises a variety of issues about the interrelationship of EC and English law.

(a) Looking at this situation first from the perspective of EC law, it is clear that to discriminate against Brunelli on the ground that he is not a British citizen is a breach of Article 12, EC Treaty. That Article has direct effect, so that Brunelli is entitled to enforce his rights in the English courts, most appropriately by an action for a declaration. As far as English law is concerned, the 1850 statute contradicts EC law. But s. 2(1) of the European Communities Act 1972 provides that rights under the treaties must be recognised and enforced. This means that the 1972 Act impliedly repeals any statute which is inconsistent with it, such as the 1850 Act. There is therefore no contradiction between EC and English law, both of which recognise Brunelli's rights.

(b) Again Erik will have no difficulty in establishing that, under EC law, it is unlawful to discriminate against him on grounds of his nationality. As far as English law is concerned, however, matters are a little more complex. The European Communities Act 1972 pre-dates the 2001 statute and so, on the orthodox interpretation of Parliamentary supremacy, the 2001 Act should prevail insofar as it is inconsistent with the earlier Act. See *Ellen Street Estates* v *Minister of Health* [1934] 1 KB 590. Are the two statutes inconsistent? It has long been established that statutes should, where possible, be interpreted so as to comply with, rather than contradict, the UK's international obligations. In cases such as *Garland* v *British Rail Engineering* [1983] 2 AC 751, the courts have applied this principle to ensure that English law is interpreted so as to comply with EC law. In *Webb* v *EMO Air Cargo (No. 2)* [1995] 4 All ER 577, the House of Lords was prepared to accept this principle whether or not the Act was intended to implement EC law. If, therefore, it is possible to interpret the 2001 Act so as to comply with EC law, that is the interpretation which the courts will adopt. As the 2001 Act appears to be silent on the issue of nationality, and speaks only of appropriate qualifications, there would be no difficulty in interpreting it to cover any citizen of the EC with appropriate qualifications, not just UK citizens. Erik would therefore be able to seek judicial review of the registrar's refusal.

(c) The dismissal of Manuel, Jose and Pablo is clearly unlawful from the perspective of EU law. They would be entitled to complain to the European Commission, which can take proceedings against the UK under Article 226 of the EC Treaty. But to obtain personal redress, they will need to bring an action for unfair dismissal against their employer in a UK industrial tribunal. Their problem arises from the fact that the Waiters (Limitation) Act 2002 was passed after the European Communities Act 1972, and is clearly inconsistent with it. Nor is it possible to find an interpretation of the 2002 Act which would be consistent with EU law. If the normal principles of Parliamentary supremacy were applied, the 2002 Act would impliedly repeal the 1972 act on this particular issue.

However, the 1972 Act s. 2(4) states that statutes 'passed or to be passed' are to be given effect in accordance with Community law. This seemed to instruct the UK courts to obey Community law, including the principle of supremacy of EC law over national law, laid down by the ECJ in *Costa* v *ENEL*, 6/64, [1964] CMLR 425. It was not clear what the UK courts would do when such a direct clash between English and EC law arose, until the case of *Factortame Ltd* v *Secretary of State for Transport (No. 2)* [1991] 1 AC 603. In that case, the House of Lords accepted that the European Communities Act 1972 s. 2(4) had incorporated the principle of the supremacy of EC law into English law, and that this would prevail over any later statute that appeared to be inconsistent with it. It would therefore appear that Manuel, Jose and Pablo can rely on their rights under EC law and that these will prevail over the 2002 Act. They will therefore succeed in their claim for unfair dismissal.

(d) Such an Act would clearly be a breach of EU law, and might attract an action by the European Commission under Article 226. But it is not entirely clear what its effect would be in the eyes of the English courts. If the statute were to be merely inconsistent with EU law, then, as in the *Factortame* case described above, the English courts would give effect to the instruction contained in s. 2(4) of the European Communities Act 1972 and hold that the statute should not be applied so as to breach EU law.

But what if such a statute expressly included a clause requiring the English courts to disregard any EU law to the contrary? In *McCarthys Ltd* v *Smith* [1979] 3 All ER 325, Lord Denning stated that the courts in such a situation should obey the will of the current Parliament, in accordance with the traditional doctrine of Parliamentary Supremacy. There is no doubt that Parliament could, if it wished, repeal the European Communities Act 1972 entirely, so it must be able to repeal it in part also. Such a repeal would have to be an express repeal, but a deliberate repudiation of the EU law on this issue would have that effect. The consequence of this would be a political crisis in relations between Britain and the EU, which could only be resolved by political negotiation. No such case has ever arisen, and as Lord Denning said, it is unlikely to happen, which is why the answer to such a question is likely to remain uncertain.

Further reading

Bradley, A. and Ewing, K. *Constitutional & Administrative Law*, 13th edn (Longman, 2003), chs 4 and 8.

Bradley, A. 'The Supremacy of Parliament,' in J. Jowell and D. Oliver (eds) *The Changing Constitution*, 4th edn (OUP, 2000).

Craig, P. 'Britain in the EU', in J. Jowell and D. Oliver (op cit.)

Munro, C. *Studies in Constitutional Law*, 2nd edn (Butterworths, 1999), chs 5 and 6.

The royal prerogative

Introduction

The title 'royal prerogative' seems rather quaint, ancient and irrelevant to the modern constitution. If the ordinary person has heard of it at all it summons up images of the Queen, ceremonials and obscure customs like the Queen's right to whales, sturgeons and swans on the river Thames. This gives an extremely misleading impression. The royal prerogative in fact contains some of the most important powers of government: foreign affairs, defence and justice. Munro defined it as: 'those attributes peculiar to the Crown which are derived from common law, not statute and which still survive' (*Studies in Constitutional Law*, 1999, 159).

Despite the 'royal' the Queen is not in fact the person who takes the decisions. Although, legally, powers under the prerogative belong to the Queen, by convention they are actually exercised by Her Majesty's government, often by the Prime Minister personally. The main issue that has concerned constitutional lawyers is how this power can be controlled. Questions on the subject, which would usually be essays, generally reflect this concern.

Often the questions concern judicial control, or more specifically judicial review of the prerogative. The most important case here is *Council of Civil Service Unions* v *Minister for the Civil Service* [1985] AC 374. Students often make the mistake of just learning this one case and then are stumped for anything else to talk about. There are other cases! There are not many of them, but it is important to know them well in order to answer questions on this area. They would include *Attorney-General* v *De Keyser* [1920] AC 508, *Burmah Oil* v *Lord Advocate* [1965] AC 75, *R* v *Home Secretary ex parte Northumbria Police Authority* [1987] 2 WLR 998, *Blackburn* v *Attorney-General* [1971] 2 All ER 1380 and *R* v *Home Secretary ex parte Bentley* [1993] 4 All ER 442.

Sometimes questions also concern parliamentary control over prerogative acts. For this the student also needs some knowledge of how parliamentary accountability works (see **Chapter 5**).

The most interesting constitutional question is, in what circumstances might the Queen resume her legal powers and take prerogative decisions once again? This can also be seen as an issue of control. It is thought that the Queen could, in certain circumstances, dismiss a government which was behaving 'unconstitutionally' by abusing her prerogative powers.

Questions on this area overlap with conventions in **Chapter 2** and the position of the Prime Minister in **Chapter 6**.

One of the widest prerogatives that exists is the Crown's power to conduct foreign affairs. The Crown's decisions in this area are unchallengeable as are some of its actions.

Q Question 1

'As De Keyser's case shows, the courts will inquire into whether a particular prerogative power exists or not, and, if it does exist, into its extent. But once the existence and the extent of a power are established to the satisfaction of the court, the court cannot inquire into the propriety of its exercise.'

Lord Fraser in *Council of Civil Service Unions* v *Minister for the Civil Service* [1985] AC 374.

Discuss.

Commentary

This is the commonest question on the royal prerogative and a quite well-used quotation. Note, in particular, that the question does not confine itself to *Council of Civil Service Unions*, i.e., the *GCHQ* case. The only disconcerting feature of this quotation is that it says the opposite of what the law is generally supposed to be. Some students find this more than off putting! The key to it is that Lord Fraser is explaining what the law used to be *before* the *GCHQ* case. A student with a good knowledge of the case might know that. Otherwise just be confident and discuss judicial review of the prerogative.

- Prerogative is the common law power of the Crown.

- The courts decide the existence and the extent of a prerogative power.

- Some prerogative powers can be judicially reviewed: GCHQ.

- High policy is not judicially reviewable.

- Prerogative powers that affect the rights of the individual subject may be reviewable.

☼ Suggested answer

The royal prerogative is the remains of royal power. Munro describes it as: 'those attributes peculiar to the crown which are derived from common law, not statute, and which still survive . . .' (*Studies in Constitutional Law*, 1999, 159). Because they are the powers of the Crown it was thought for a long time that they enjoyed the same legal immunities as the Queen and could not be reviewed by the courts. The

House of Lords had made this clear in cases like *Chandler* v *DPP* [1964] AC 763 and *Gouriet* v *UPW* [1978] AC 435. This was despite trailblazing dissents by Lord Denning, notably in *Laker Airways* v *Department of Trade* [1977] QB 643 and even Lord Devlin in *Chandler* had expressed some doubt. To Lord Denning prerogative powers were government powers just like statutory powers and if they were abused they should be controlled.

Despite this the courts had always been able to exercise some sort of control over prerogative. Since as early as the *Case of Proclamations* (1611) 12 Co Rep 74, they have claimed the right to decide whether there was adequate precedent for the prerogative claimed to exist. This gives the courts more power than is commonly realised because the precedents are often unclear. For instance in both *A-G* v *De Keyser's Hotel* [1920] AC 508 and *Burmah Oil* v *Lord Advocate* [1965] AC 75 the court decided that, although the government could seize and even destroy, a person's property in order to defend the realm, compensation must be paid. The right to compensation was not clearly established in the older cases but the court thought it appropriate. As late as 1987, the courts recognised that there was a prerogative of maintaining the peace of the realm in *R* v *Home Secretary ex parte Northumbria Police Authority* [1987] 1 WLR 998.

In 2001 the courts of Australia accepted that there was still a prerogative power to expel aliens in *Ruddock* v *Vadarlis* (2001) 66 ALD 25. What is certain though is that the courts will not recognise a 'new' prerogative for which there is no historic precedent. As Diplock LJ said in *BBC* v *Johns* [1965] Ch 32 at 79: 'It is 350 years and a civil war too late for the Queen's courts to broaden the prerogative'.

De Keyser (1920) had, however, made clear that the courts could not go beyond deciding whether prerogative still existed or not. Judicial review of the prerogative was finally allowed in *Council for Civil Service Unions* v *Minister for the Civil Service* [1985] AC 374. Lord Fraser gave a number of reasons for the change of heart in his judgment. The chief one was that the Queen was not personally involved in the use of the prerogative so that the court would not be questioning her legal immunity. He also noted that the courts had already judicially reviewed the decisions of a tribunal created under the royal prerogative in *R* v *Criminal Injuries Compensation Board ex parte Lain* [1967] 2 QB 864 and a prerogative court, that of the coroner in *A-G of Duchy of Lancaster* v *Overton Farms Ltd* [1982] Ch 277. With the development of judicial review in the last 30 years there was no reason nowadays to distinguish between statutory and prerogative powers.

All five House of Lords judges agreed that *some* prerogative powers could be judicially reviewed. It is unclear though *which* prerogative powers would be subject to judicial review. All their lordships agreed that a minor use of the prerogative such as, in this case, the conditions of service of civil servants could be reviewed. Lords Fraser and Brightman thought that this was possible because it was only a delegated use of the prerogative. An Order in Council gave the minister for the Civil Service power to alter civil servants' conditions of service. The Order in Council itself could not be reviewed but the minister's decision under it could. Prerogatives like control of the armed forces and foreign policy 'were unsuitable for discussion or review in the law courts' (Lord Fraser, 398).

The other three judges, Lords Scarman, Diplock and Roskill felt that only some prerogatives could be reviewed. It depended upon its 'subject matter'. Only the lower level, non-political uses of the prerogative could be considered by the courts. Decisions on matters like national security, also involved in this case, had to be left to the executive government. Only they had the information upon which to make a decision. Lord Roskill supplied a handy list of prerogatives that had to be left to government and were unreviewable: treaties, defence, mercy, honours, the dissolution of Parliament and the appointment of government ministers. Lord Diplock thought that they should also consider the effect that the prerogative act had on the private rights and expectations of citizens.

The views of Lords Scarman, Diplock and Roskill seem to have been followed: it is the subject matter of the prerogative that indicates whether or not it can be reviewed. In *R.* v *Ministry of Defence, ex parte Smith and Others* [1995] 4 All ER 427, it was held that the policy of dismissing homosexuals from the military could potentially be judicially reviewed. This was not a challenge to the disposition of the armed forces. Similarly, in *R. (on the application of Abbasi and Another* v *Secretary of State for Foreign Affairs and Secretary of State for the Home Department* [2002] WL 3145052, a British national, Abbasi, was held at Guantanamo Bay and argued that the Foreign Office had a duty to intervene on his behalf with the US government. The court declined to interfere, but conceded that judicial review would be available if the Foreign Office decision was irrational of defeated legitimate expectations.

Bearing this in mind it is perhaps not very surprising that, even after the *GCHQ* case, successful judicial reviews of the prerogative have been rare. *R* v *Foreign Secretary ex parte Everett* [1989] AC 1014 concerned the refusal to renew Everett's passport. The court followed the reasoning of Scarman, Diplock and Roskill in *GCHQ* and stated that they could not review the prerogative when it concerned matters of 'high policy'. This case did not concern weighty questions of foreign policy and also affected the rights of the individual. It was therefore susceptible to judicial review, but on the facts the court concluded that there had not been a breach of natural justice.

In *R* v *Home Secretary ex parte Bentley* [1993] 4 All ER 442 the court was prepared to ignore the previous case law, including the obiter dicta of Lord Roskill in *GCHQ*, and permit judicial review of the prerogative of mercy. The Home Secretary had misunderstood his legal powers when taking his decision and was asked to reconsider. In contrast the Privy Council declined to follow *Bentley* in *Reckley* v *Minister of Public Safety (No. 2)* [1996] 1 All ER 562.

The most recent case appears to be *R* v *Home Secretary ex parte Fire Brigades Union* [1995] 2 All ER 244. There the Home Secretary wanted to alter the prerogative based

Criminal Injuries Compensation Scheme. He was not permitted to do so, because a statute based scheme had replaced it under the Criminal Justice Act 1988, Successive Home Secretaries had failed to bring these provisions into force. The House of Lords ruled that the Home Secretary had failed to consider bringing the statutory scheme into force and had therefore defied the will of Parliament. This case is therefore not really a review of the prerogative but of a statutory power.

Lord Fraser was stating the law as it existed before the *GCHQ* case. The judgment in that case purported to change this law. In reality little has changed. Many areas of the prerogative are still regarded as non-justiciable and successful cases, like *Bentley*, look likely to remain rare.

Q Question 2

'The principal convention of the British Constitution is that the Queen shall exercise her formal legal powers only upon and in accordance with the advice of her Ministers, save in a few exceptional situations.'

De Smith and Brazier, *Constitutional and Administrative Law*.

Discuss.

Commentary

This is the sort of question that many students of constitutional law dislike! At first glance it is unclear what area of the syllabus it concerns. The student who looks a little longer might think that it is about convention. It is, in a way, but only about a very specific group of conventions: those that surround the role of the Queen. The point about the question is that the Queen nearly always acts on the advice of her ministers. The student would need to give examples of the situations where this happens. Even more importantly the student would need to be aware of the situations in which it is thought that the Queen could say 'No' to her ministers. A knowledge of actual incidents where this had happened would be essential for this question. Lastly, the question raises the issue of constitutional control. Should the Queen take a more active role in controlling the excesses of government?

- **Does the Queen still have the right to make a personal choice?**

- **The Queen has the right to be consulted, the right to encourage and the right to warn.**

- **In a 'hung Parliament' the Queen can become involved in the choice of Prime Minister.**

- **If the Prime Minister acts unconstitutionally, the Queen may dismiss him.**

⭑ Suggested answer

Old cases like *The Case of Proclamations* (1611) made a distinction between the ordinary and absolute prerogatives. The ordinary prerogatives were areas in which the Queen had no personal discretion. Nowadays she would merely act on the advice of her ministers. The absolute prerogative covers areas where the Queen has a choice. Usually this is thought to involve only the award of some honours such as the Order of the Garter. It is possible, though, that in some other situations the Queen still might have a choice.

It is accepted that the Queen does have the right to express a view to her ministers upon how her prerogatives are used. Bagehot put it that the Queen has 'the right to be consulted, the right to encourage, the right to warn' (*The Law of the Constitution*, 1867). Somewhat more recently, these principles were restated in a letter to *The Times* on 27 July 1986 by the Queen's Press Secretary, Sir William Heseltine. There had been some press coverage claiming that the Queen disapproved of some of the policies of the Prime Minister, Margaret Thatcher. The letter said that the Queen 'was entitled to have opinions on Government policy and to express them to her chief Minister'. However, the Queen was 'bound to accept and act on the advice of her Ministers'. Importantly the letter concluded by reminding us that discussions between the Queen and her ministers are confidential. It is difficult therefore to know for certain whether the Queen, or any previous Monarch, has ever gone beyond expressing a forceful opinion. That is allowed as long as the government has the final say.

Some examples are clear. The Sovereign has not refused assent to an Act of Parliament since 1708. Even that was on the advice of her ministers who did not like what Parliament was proposing. George V expressed the view that he could refuse assent to an Irish Home Rule Bill in 1914. He would do this to 'avert a national disaster' but there was 'no such evidence'.

Conventionally the Prime Minister chooses his or her government. George VI is recorded as having expressed a preference for certain ministerial appointments such as Ernest Bevin as Foreign Secretary. There is nothing particularly remarkable about this. As we saw above the sovereign is entitled to express an opinion in such matters. George VI also expressed opinion on matters such as whether the prerogative of mercy should be extended to persons sentenced to death. Again there is nothing unconstitutional about 'advice'.

If the Queen actually made a personal choice as to who should become Prime Minister it would be very controversial. She would be accused of political favouritism. Usually there is no decision for the Queen to make. There is a clear result from a general election and the leader of the majority party is called upon to form a government. If there is a 'hung Parliament', as was quite common earlier this century, matters are by no means so clear.

In 1916 the country was ruled by a coalition led by the Liberal leader, Asquith. The war was going badly and he resigned. The King sent for Bonar Law, leader of the second largest party, the Conservatives. Bonar Law could not form a government. This put the King in a difficult position. Would he have to make a personal choice? Instead George V hosted a conference of the party leaders and Lloyd George, another Liberal, emerged as the Prime Minister.

A somewhat similar process used to occur when the Conservative party were in office and their Prime Minister resigned. Before 1965 that party had no system for electing a leader. The King or Queen would consult party notables and a new Prime Minister would 'emerge'. This last occurred in 1963 with the selection of Sir Alec Douglas-Home. It is thought that the Monarch would sometimes express an opinion on the merits of a particular candidate, e.g., Lord Halifax instead of Winston Churchill in 1940, but there is no suggestion that the Monarch took the final decision.

The most controversial incident of this type occurred in 1931. Ramsay Macdonald was Prime Minister in the first Labour government. He was convinced that it was in the national interest to reduce public expenditure, in particular unemployment benefit. His own party would not accept this. The leaders of the other parties agreed with Macdonald. Macdonald offered to resign but the King did not accept his resignation. Instead George V consulted the leaders of the other parties. They advised that Macdonald should stay and form a 'national government'. Macdonald took this advice and won a resounding victory at a general election later in the year. Ironically he ended up as the Labour Prime Minister of a largely Conservative government. Subsequently George V has been criticised for playing too active a part in the choice of Prime Minister. Presumably the King did what he did on the advice of the other party leaders and because he thought that it was in the national interest. The electorate seems to have approved.

It is similarly thought that the sovereign could refuse the Prime Minister's request for a general election. In a letter to *The Times* on 2 May 1950 the King's Private Secretary said that refusal could be justified if three conditions are satisfied. First the existing Parliament was able to carry on, secondly a general election would be detrimental to the national economy and thirdly another Prime Minister with a working majority could be found. Although there are Commonwealth examples, in South Africa in 1939 and Canada in 1926, there are no modern British examples. The crucial element justifying the Monarch's refusal would seem, again, to be the national interest.

The most spectacular example of the sovereign resuming an active role would be the dismissal of the Prime Minister. This last occurred in 1834 when William IV dismissed Lord Melbourne. In 1975, however, the Governor-General dismissed the Prime Minister of Australia, Gough Whitlam. The Senate was refusing to agree to his budget because of illegal ministerial misbehaviour in procuring overseas loans. The Prime Minister recommended that there should be an election of the Senate only. The Governor-General refused and dismissed him from office. A Governor-General acts in the name of the Queen and exercises her powers. It is not thought that the Governor-General consulted the Queen in this incident. The Gough Whitlam affair shows that the Queen has the power to dismiss a Prime Minister if he or she is behaving 'unconstitutionally'. The problem in Britain, with its unwritten constitution is, what is unconstitutional? Trying to evade the correct parliamentary procedure and to continue governing without a majority to pass legislation seem to be the 'crimes' of Whitlam.

So what we have is a rather varied series of incidents, both in Britain and the Commonwealth. It does seem that the King or Queen claims the right to protect the 'national interest' even if it is against the wishes of the majority party. The big problem is that opinion upon what is in the national interest can vary. The rarity of incidents of royal interference indicates that Kings and Queens have, rightly, been very cautious about when it is appropriate to interfere.

Q Question 3

The United Kingdom and Fantasia are in dispute about possession of an island called Lackland which has been ruled by the UK for the last 200 years. Fantasian troops occupy the island and a British force is sent to remove them. No formal declaration of war is made, but the British Crown takes a number of actions. The Crown withdraws the passports of some British citizens resident in Fantasia who, in the opinion of the Crown, are helping the Fantasian invasion forces. Further, Fantasian citizens resident in the UK are arrested and expelled. A number of British owned and registered ships are requisitioned, without compensation, for military use. In Fantasia the British forces occupy and also destroy properties belonging to both Fantasian and British citizens.

The British action is successful and a peace treaty is concluded between the UK and Fantasia. Among other provisions, it stipulates that neither country accepts any liability for loss or damage inflicted during the hostilities. No British legislation is enacted to give effect to the treaty within the UK, as it is not thought necessary.

A number of British and Fantasian citizens are aggrieved by the actions taken against them during the hostilities and seek a legal remedy.

Advise them.

Commentary

The royal prerogative also extends to foreign affairs. The Crown has wide powers at its disposal, which in the older cases were largely unchallenged by the courts. In more modern cases, the courts have been more sceptical and more inclined to protect the rights of the individual.

If we examine the question closely it should give a number of clues as to the prerogatives involved and the cases that need to be considered. War and the deployment of troops, the issue of passports, the expulsion of aliens and the confiscation of property at home and abroad should all ring bells in your memory. The effect of treaties upon domestic law should be fairly straight-forward, now that we are familiar with European Community law and the Human Rights Act 1998 giving effect to the European Convention on Human Rights. Act of state is lurking in there somewhere. To most students it is a nightmare, but it is important to realise that it is not at all clear from the cases what it is. Cleverer people than you have tried in vain to define it!

It is usually easiest with problem questions to consider each event as it arises by going through the problem line by line. This tactic is certainly best in this example.

- **The war prerogative is unchallengeable in the courts.**

- **The prerogative to issue passports is reviewable.**

- **Aliens may be expelled under the prerogative.**

- **The prerogative allows the requisition of property, with compensation.**

- **Act of state is unchallengeable in the courts.**

- **The treaty-making prerogative is unchallengeable.**

:Q: Suggested answer

The declaration and conduct of war is one of the established royal prerogatives. It is most unlikely that a court would entertain any challenge as to whether the war was justified or troops should be sent: *Chandler* v *DPP* [1964] AC 763. This was confirmed by *CCSU* v *Minister for the Civil Service* [1985] AC 374 (the *GCHQ* case) where, in particular, Lord Roskill listed war as one of the prerogatives that was beyond the control of judicial review. This does not, however, mean the Crown can do as it pleases, as we shall see.

It was once thought that the prerogative to grant, replace or withdraw passports was unchallengeable. After the *GCHQ* case this changed. In *R* v *Foreign Secretary ex parte Everett* [1989] AC 1014 the Court of Appeal held that the Foreign Secretary's refusal to renew a passport was subject to judicial review for Everett had a right to natural justice. In this situation though, this case might be distinguished. Taylor LJ stated that matters of high policy, were not justiciable. War is one of those matters of high policy, so it is possible that the courts might refuse to intervene here. In *GCHQ* itself, a similar matter of high policy, namely national security, overrode the requirement of natural justice. Also, as in *Everett*, applicants might be thought to be unworthy and in its discretion the court might refuse a remedy.

The expulsion of enemy aliens has been held to be an unchallengeable prerogative matter; *Netz* v *Chuter Ede* [1946] Ch 224. In the famous case of *R* v *Bottrill ex parte Kuechenmeister* [1947] KB 41 it was held that the Home Secretary could intern an enemy alien. What is more, only the Home Secretary could decide when the war was over! That too was a matter of royal prerogative. Even in peace-time the courts of Australia upheld a prerogative power to expel aliens in *Ruddock* v *Vadarlis* (2001) 66 ALD 25. In our case though, war is formally declared and the Home Secretary would probably act under immigration legislation rather than the royal prerogative. At the time of the first Gulf war some Iraqi nationals were threatened with deportation. The courts were at least willing to look at their cases, although they decided that they could not investigate an issue of national security; *R* v *Home Secretary ex parte Cheblak* [1991] 2 All ER 319. Since then however, the European Court of Human Rights has ruled in *Chahal* v *UK* (1997) 23 EHRR 413 that the courts should be able to review such government decisions based on national security. So in any subsequent cases the *Cheblak* approach should be taken a stage further. The British courts still seem unwilling though to investigate governments claims to protest national security, as seen in *R* v *Shayler* [2003] 1 AC 247 and *Rehman* v *SSHD* [2001] 3 WLR 877.

The requisitioning of a British subject's property is certainly allowed in wartime. Compensation, however, must be paid; *Attorney-General* v *De Keyser's Royal Hotel* [1920] AC 508.

According to *Burmah Oil* v *Lord Advocate* [1965] AC 75, when British owned property abroad is destroyed for wartime purposes compensation must also be paid. This seems to be confirmed by *Nissan* v *Attorney-General* [1970] AC 179, when British forces requisitioned and damaged a hotel in Cyprus. The House of Lords confirmed that this action did not qualify as an act of state and therefore Nissan might have a remedy. Act of state was here defined as an action of government policy which should not be considered by the courts. To use the American phrase, it is non-justiciable. The case law seems to make a distinction based upon the nationality of the victim. Act of state cannot be committed against a British citizen. Nissan was a British citizen and so had his remedy in a British court. Actions in Fantasia that harm Fantasian citizens are almost certainly an act of the state as held in the old case, *Buron* v *Denman* [1848] 2 Ex 167 where the Royal Navy destroyed Spanish property in Africa, acting upon clear government policy to stamp out the slave trade. This can be contrasted with *Johnstone* v *Pedlar* [1921] 2 AC 262 where the property of a US citizen was confiscated within the UK. This was not an act of state. The true ratio of this case is hard to define. Can an act of state be committed in the UK? It seems that it cannot be committed against the citizen of a friendly country, here the USA. However *Johnstone* is interpreted, it certainly does not apply to the citizens of a country with which the UK is at war and acts committed in that foreign country.

It is clear that the conclusion of a treaty is an unchallengeable act in the British courts; *Blackburn* v *Attorney-General* [1971] 2 All ER 1780 confirmed in *R* v *Foreign*

Secretary ex parte Rees-Mogg [1994] 1 All ER 457. It is also clear, though, that the treaty cannot affect legal rights within the UK unless it is given statutory force. Statutory rights are unaffected; *Laker Airways* v *Department of Trade* [1977] QB 643. So too are rights derived from common law such as trespass and negligence; *The Parlement Belge* [1879] 4 PD 129. The latter point was confirmed in *Littrell* v *USA No. 2* [1994] 3 All ER 203.

In conclusion, the British citizen affected by these 'wartime actions' has a fairly good chance of some kind of legal remedy. The removal of passports may, however, be more difficult to challenge. The Fantasian citizens do not have much hope. Unless the Human Rights Act 1998 produces a dramatic change of attitude they are likely to be defeated by the old argument of act of state or the modern one of national security.

Q Question 4

'Behind the phrase "royal prerogative" lie hidden some issues of great constitutional importance, which are insufficiently recognised.'

Munro, *Studies in Constitutional Law.*

Consider whether you agree with this statement.

Commentary

This sort of question is often disliked by students, which is why we included it! It is obviously about the royal prerogative but to answer it properly requires knowledge of other areas of the syllabus. These would include elements of **Chapter 2** on the nature of the constitution and **Chapter 5** on accountability to Parliament. Be warned, it is extremely dangerous to revise for a constitutional examination just by looking at, say, four topics and hoping that they will come up. Many constitutional questions spread across several areas.

This particular question draws upon elements of questions 1 and 2 in this chapter and is really about the large amount of government power hidden behind the prerogative and the lack of adequate controls over it. The answer is an example of a fairly one-sided argument.

- Prerogative powers are used by the government of the day.

- These contain some of the most important powers of government.

- Many of these powers are ill-defined.

- Judicial review of some prerogative powers is now possible: *GCHQ* case.

- Judicial review of matters of high policy is not possible.

- Parliament has limited control over the use of prerogative powers.

;Ọ̈; **Suggested answer**

The phrase 'royal prerogative' makes many people think of the Queen, but that would be highly misleading. It is true that the royal prerogative is the remaining legal powers of the Crown. As De Smith put it 'those inherent legal attributes which are unique to the Crown.' (*Constitutional and Administrative Law*, 1998). In reality, though, the Queen has very little to do with the matter. By convention these powers are exercised in the Queen's name by Her Majesty's government. It is true that, by convention again, the Queen must be consulted and, as Bagehot put it, has 'the right to be consulted, the right to encourage, the right to warn' (*The Law of the Constitution*, 1867). In fact, though, the royal prerogative is today merely the power of the government.

Many of the central and most important government powers lie within the royal prerogative. They include the conduct of foreign affairs, defence and national security, claims to territory, maintaining the peace, the running of the civil service, mercy and pardon, some aspects of immigration and the honours system.

A problem with these ancient powers is that it is often unclear what exactly they allow the government to do. Occasional legal challenges require the courts to attempt to clarify which powers still exist. For instance, in *Attorney-General* v *De Keyser* [1920] AC 508 historical research was needed to discover the circumstances in which the Crown could requisition property in wartime. No really clear answer was obtained, so that when a similar point came up again in *Burmah Oil* v *Lord Advocate* [1965] AC 75 there was still doubt. As late as 1987 a 'new' prerogative power could emerge in *R* v *Home Secretary ex parte Northumbria Police Authority* [1987] 2 All ER 282 which stated that the government has the power to maintain peace in the kingdom. This is a prerogative in addition to all the government's statutory powers. The problem with it is, that it is very wide and vague. Could the government imprison people without trial if it claimed that it was keeping the peace of the realm? To take a roughly similar example, the government has the responsibility of protecting national security as recognised in the *GCHQ* case [1985] AC 374. What exactly is national security and what exactly is the government allowed to do to protect it? There are no clear answers to these two questions particularly, as it seems from the *GCHQ* case, that the courts will be satisfied, on very little evidence, that the government is protecting national security.

In the *GCHQ* case the House of Lords at last said that they could control how the royal prerogative was used by means of judicial review. Control on the basis of illegality, irrationality and procedural impropriety is anyway quite limited but, leaving that aside, all their lordships agreed that some government prerogative powers lay outside the control of the courts. Lords Fraser and Brightman felt that they could only consider delegated use of the prerogative. They could look at the minister's decision but not the Order in Council itself. The politically controversial prerogatives had to be left to the government and Lord Roskill provided a list of these: treaties, defence, mercy, honours, the dissolution of Parliament and the appointment of government ministers.

If we consider cases both before and after *GCHQ* we can see that the courts are in fact very reluctant to interfere with government prerogative decisions. In *Chandler v DPP* [1964] AC 763 the deployment and armament of troops was outside the control of the courts. A decision by the Attorney-General to take legal action or not was unchallengeable; *Gouriet v UPW* [1977] 2 WLR 310. The decision not to renew a passport was, in theory, reviewable; *R v Foreign Secretary ex parte Everett* [1989] AC 1014, but in reality the courts agreed with the government's policy not to renew the passports of wanted criminals. Taylor LJ considered that the courts should not look at 'high policy' executive decisions, but could look at lower level decisions affecting the rights of individuals. The court continued this approach in *R (Abbasi) v Foreign Secretary* (2002) WL 31452052. Abbasi, who was detained by the USA at Guantanamo Bay, wanted the British government to intervene on his behalf. The court refused to tell the government what to do, but maintained that such decisions were potentially reviewable. A more successful case is *R v Home Secretary ex parte Bentley* [1994] 4 All ER 442. The court disagreed with the Home Secretary's decision not to grant Bentley a posthumous pardon. As Bentley had been executed over 40 years before the decision is of little practical significance, particularly as the courts have declined to follow it in subsequent cases; (*Reckley v Minister of Public Safety (No. 2)* [1996] 1 All ER 562).

The courts have often justified their approach by saying, in cases like *Chandler* and *Gouriet* that the proper body to control the use of these highly political powers is Parliament. It is true that Parliament can remove prerogatives as in the Bill of Rights 1689 and the Treasure Act 1996. Acts of Parliament also supersede equivalent prerogative powers and the government must use the statutory power rather than the prerogative one; *De Keyser*. The courts have also held that the government must not ignore the will of Parliament when statutory powers have replaced a prerogative, but have not yet been brought into force; *R v Home Secretary ex parte Fire Brigade Union* [1995] 2 All ER 244. However the government usually controls what Parliament does and it is inconceivable that the legislature would be allowed to remove or restrict an important prerogative power against the government's wishes.

By the conventions of our constitution, ministers are accountable for their actions to Parliament. This would include actions under the prerogative. By long standing practices many prerogative areas are hidden from the view of Parliament. Since 1955 successive governments have refused to answer MPs' questions on the Prime Minister's advice to the Queen, the grant of honours, mercy in death sentences and the appointment of bishops, judges and Privy Councillors. Similarly, governments may refuse to answer questions on many defence issues such as arms sales, issues of national security and confidential relations with foreign states. The Parliamentary

Commissioner for Administration is also prevented from investigating many of the same areas and also personnel matters in the civil service.

On 20 October 2003 the Public Affairs Select Committee of the House of Commons announced that they would like to bring three of the most important prerogatives: armed forces, treaties and passports, under statutory control. This seems an excellent idea, but it is hard to see any government willingly complying.

Further reading

Barnett, H. *Constitutional and Administrative Law*, 4th edn (Cavendish, 2002), ch 6.

Bradley, A. and Ewing, K. *Constitutional & Administrative Law*, 13th edn (Longman, 2003), ch 12.

Loveland, I. *Constitutional Law, Administrative Law and Human Rights*, 3rd edn (Butterworths, 2003), ch 4.

Munro, C. *Studies in Constitutional Law*, 2nd edn (Butterworths, 1998), ch 8.

Parliament

Introduction

In any constitutional law course, the subject of Parliament is likely to be central. But courses vary greatly in the balance struck between the political and legal aspects. In a course where political issues are given prominence, one would expect to find examination questions about the defects of the electoral system, the powers of back-bench MPs or the reform of the House of Lords. More strictly legal topics would include parliamentary privilege or the legislative process. This chapter includes questions of both types.

Questions addressing possible reforms will be popular with examiners. To answer such questions well, the student who has already formed strong opinions must be careful to marshal the arguments in favour of their opinion and counter the arguments against, not just deliver a vehement oration more suitable for a party manifesto! The student who has no such opinion will need to adopt one for the purpose of answering the question. It is excellent practice for would-be lawyers to develop arguments for or against a proposition, disguising the fact that they are indifferent to it.

Q Question 1

Explain how the following voting systems work and consider their respective advantages and disadvantages as methods of electing a national parliament:

(a) First-Past-The-Post

(b) Party List

(c) Additional Member System.

Commentary

This is a pretty straightforward question with the only real difficulty being remembering correctly the differences between the different voting systems. For a start then, your answer must accurately describe the systems, highlighting the differences between them. A good answer would then, as required, go on to explain what is good and bad about each system.

It is better if you back up your arguments with evidence, such as examples of what each system could produce. I have taken nearly all my examples from various British elections, but you could equally well take your examples from the experiences of other countries. The question does not actually say that it is referring to the United Kingdom or to the House of Commons, because it is not unusual for questions in Public Law to be a little vague. The way to deal with this is to state clearly, in the introductory paragraph, how you intend to interpret the question, which is what I have done.

A conclusion is always a good idea. My conclusion is that reform seems unlikely at the moment. Other possible conclusions are to say which system you like the best and why. For example, you might argue that First-Past-the-Post is best as it is most likely to secure strong government or you might prefer the Party List system as the best way of securing representation for all groups in society. The choice is yours as there are few 'right' answers in Public Law.

- **Under First-Past-the-Post a minority vote can elect a government.**

- **But First-Past-the-Post often secures a government with a majority.**

- **Party List secures proportional representation.**

- **Under Party List there are no constituency MPs.**

- **The Additional Member System combines Party List and First-Past-the-Post.**

- **AMS secures better representation for minority parties.**

- **AMS may lead to coalition government.**

:Q: Suggested answer

Most modern states now have a system of elections, which recognise universal suffrage. All adult men and women have the right to vote, so controversies over whether women or the working classes should have the franchise are now a thing of the past. Attention has, instead, turned to how an election can best reflect the wishes of the electorate, in other words, the different voting systems that are available. More importantly this essay will focus upon what type of legislature and government the three different systems would produce. An electoral system might be ideal for securing representation for all social classes, minorities and geographical areas or it might be ideal for electing a government with an effective majority. The two aims might not be compatible. Although the question does not specifically say it, I intend to consider elections to the House of Commons of the United Kingdom Parliament.

(a) First-Past-the-Post, sometimes called the 'majoritarian' system, is the system traditionally used for elections to that House. The United Kingdom is divided up into 659 separate constituencies, each with a roughly equal electorate of around 70,000 voters. The electors in each constituency have one vote each, which they cast by writing an 'x' next to the name of their chosen candidate on the ballot paper. The winner is the candidate who receives the most votes. The candidate does not need an absolute majority over all the other candidates combined, say 35,001 in a typically sized constituency, but merely one more vote than their nearest rival. Usually a candidate only needs 20,000 to 25,000 votes and, sometimes, a lot less than that to win a seat.

That means that, in the average constituency, it is very likely that more electors voted for candidates other than the successful one. There lies the problem with this electoral system. Millions of votes are cast for unsuccessful candidates and those voters are unable to elect their choice. It is particularly hard for smaller parties, such as the Liberal Democrats, to win seats, because it is hard to secure enough votes in any one constituency. It is even harder to launch a new party and get into Parliament, as parties like the Greens have found. Often a General Election result can seem a distortion of the true wishes of the electorate. The last two elections seem to be a good example of this. In 2001 the Labour Party won 42 per cent of the vote nationwide, but secured 412 MPs, 63 per cent of the total. It is not impossible for the party with most votes nationwide to actually lose the election, as happened to the Labour Party in 1951 and the Conservatives in February 1974. The First-Past-the-Post system also seems to encourage a system where there is very little change. Only about twenty or so seats change party at an election and one of the two main parties, Labour and Conservative, has always formed the Government since 1945.

Those who support First-Past-the-Post would argue that stability is the main advantage of the system. Usually, it produces a Government with a substantial majority, who are able to implement the policies that they promised the electorate in their manifesto. The counting of the votes is also straightforward and reasonably quick. For the elector it is simple to vote with no complicated choices to make and the outcome is a constituency MP, with whom they can identify and to whom they can take their grievances.

(b) Party List is a very different system, which does not have separate constituencies, each with their own MP. Instead, electors vote for the party rather than an individual. Each party puts forward a list of candidates, hence the name, and seats are allocated in accordance with the number of votes. For example, if a party wins 40 per cent of the vote, it gains 40 per cent of the seats in the legislature and allocates its seats, as it chooses, to the candidates on its list. This 'proportional representation', which accurately reflects the wishes of the electors, is the main advantage of this system.

One list, for the whole country, would be unusual, except in small countries, so, usually, the country is divided into 'regions' and the parties present lists of candidates for each region. That was the system used in the UK's 1999 elections to the European Parliament. In those elections both the Green Party and the United Kingdom Independence Party, neither of whom have any representation in the UK House of Commons, secured MEPs. So, Party List can help small parties.

Opponents of Party List would argue that a multiplicity of small parties is a bad thing. Not only might it allow extremist groups to gain representation, but it could also mean that the Government would have to be formed from a coalition of two or more parties. Critics would argue that coalition governments are unstable and because the Government parties have to negotiate between themselves to decide on policy, either nothing gets done or all policies are compromises, that satisfy no one. Lastly, the individual con-stituency MP disappears, so the electors no longer choose their candidate and have no obvious person to whom they can take their grievances.

(c) The Additional Member System seems to be a happy compromise between First-Past-the-Post and Party List and has been used successfully in Germany for many years. The idea is very simple: some MPs are elected to represent individual constituencies under First-Past-the-Post and other MPs are elected under Party List and do not represent a constituency. So, as far as the elector is concerned, he/she has two votes, one for a candidate and one for a party. This system was used in the 1999 Elections for the Scottish Parliament and the Welsh Assembly. The effect in Scotland was that two of the smaller parties, the Scottish Nationalist Party and the Conservatives, did well from the Party List element of the system. The Conservatives only have one MP for a Scottish constituency in the House of Commons, but gained 18 MPs for the Scottish Parliament from the List.

In both Scotland and Wales the largest party, as in the House of Commons, is still the Labour Party, but because of the proportional element, they do not have an overall majority. The outcome, in both countries, has been a coalition government between the Labour Party and the Liberal Democrats. Some would argue that this is a good thing and has led to sensible, moderate policies such as the reintroduction of student grants and payment for the care of the elderly.

Opponents would argue that coalitions are undemocratic, because they are formed by bargaining between the political parties, which probably will not reflect the wishes of the electorate. For instance, in Scotland, the second biggest party, the Scottish Nationalists, were left out of Government. The two different types of MP, some with constituencies and some without may also, one day, cause disputes about relative workloads.

Despite these misgivings, the Additional Member System seems to be the most likely replacement for First-Past-the-Post, in elections to the Commons. In 1998, Lord Jenkins chaired a Commission into voting systems and concluded that the Additional Member System was the best option. In fact he proposed a refined version of it with Alternative Vote for the constituency elections. Whether these proposals will ever be implemented seems doubtful, as the Labour Government promised a referendum on voting reform in their 1997 manifesto, but not in 2001. Whatever the merits of voting reform, the decision to change is in the hands of politicians, who will only change to a system that favours their own party. So why would the Labour Party, who have done well through First-Past-the-Post in the last two elections, wish to change the voting system? If the result of the next General Election is close then the debate might reopen in earnest. We will have to wait until then.

Q Question 2

What changes have been made in recent years to modernise the procedures and operation of the House of Commons? Have these reforms made the House of Commons more effective? Are there further changes that you think would be desirable?

Commentary

The main element in your answer to this question will be a description of the changes made since the 1997 election, in accordance with the recommendations of the Modernisation Committee. But where a question uses a vague expression like 'in recent years' you can reasonably justify bringing in material from a longer period. What will make a good answer will be your assessment of the effectiveness of the House of Commons in the performance of its principal tasks, legislation and scrutiny of the executive. Recommendations from the Modernisation Committee are the best source for suggestions for further reform, but if you have ideas of your own, by all means bring them in too. It will not matter whether you choose to praise the reforms or criticise them, provided that you are able to support your remarks with appropriate examples.

- MPs' working conditions and sitting times.

- Publishing legislation in draft.

- Programme motions.

- Carrying over legislation between sessions.

- Prime Minister's Questions.

:Q: Suggested answer

The procedures of the House of Commons have often been criticised as archaic and inefficient. It is perhaps inevitable that because of its long history, the House of Commons is inclined to be backward looking; it is symbolic that when the Houses of Parliament had to be rebuilt in the nineteenth century, the architectural style chosen was medieval. But recent years have seen some significant changes to the way the House of Commons operates. These have been intended to improve working conditions for MPs as well as enabling it to perform its principal functions, legislation and scrutiny of the executive, more effectively. Much of the impetus for changes to the legislative process has come from governments, which are always trying to get substantial amounts of legislation through Parliament as smoothly as possible. Governments are, however, likely to be less enthusiastic about measures to improve scrutiny of the executive. Some long-standing criticisms of parliamentary procedures, such as the ineffective scrutiny of delegated legislation, remain to be addressed.

The first aspect that will be examined relates to the working conditions of MPs. Until relatively recently, MPs' work was seriously hampered by a shortage of office accommodation. Many had to share offices, and some had no office space at all. Now, with the opening in 2000 of Portcullis House, all MPs have an office usually with a room for a secretary and research assistant nearby. This is of particular value in dealing with the substantial volume of correspondence from constituents which MPs now receive. MPs are paid an allowance, now over £51,000 a year, towards their office costs. There is sometimes public criticism of this payment, but it is clearly essential for MPs wishing to perform their functions effectively to have appropriate assistance. The current allowance would cover the cost of employing two assistants, which is not an extravagant provision.

The change that has probably had the greatest impact on MPs working conditions concerns the sitting hours of the House of Commons. Traditionally, proceedings in the House of Commons Chamber did not begin until 2.30 in the afternoon, except on Fridays, when sittings began at 9.30 a.m. and ended by 3 p.m. to allow MPs to travel back to their constituencies for the weekend. Debates on legislation would not normally begin until 5 p.m. and would normally continue until 10 p.m., but on occasions late into the night. These hours were designed for the convenience of those MPs who had another occupation. Until well into the twentieth century, it was common for an MP to carry on a business or practise a profession, such as law, being in effect only a part-time MP. But this became less common as politics developed into a full-time occupation, which could no longer be combined with another profession. Constituencies demanded the exclusive attention of their MP and the amount of constituency business increased. In any case, meetings of select and standing committees were normally scheduled for mornings, and more MPs were involved in these.

As well as being outdated, these sitting hours seriously disrupted the private lives of MPs; it was impossible to enjoy a normal family life if one frequently had to be at the House of Commons until 10 p.m. or later. Particular difficulty was caused to women, especially those with young children, and it was widely believed that these hours contributed to the reluctance of women to stand for Parliament. The 1997 election saw the first significant increase in the number of women elected, albeit only to 120, and this increased the pressure for a change in the sitting hours. From 1999 Thursday sittings were brought forward to the morning and afternoon only, with Commons business ending at 6 p.m. From January 2003 a further experimental reform means that Commons business starts at 11.30 a.m. on Tuesdays and Wednesdays, ending at 7 p.m. It appears that opinions on the reform among MPs are divided. Those with homes and families in easy reach find the new hours a great improvement, but others find themselves left with isolated evenings. There may be political implications arising from the new hours. A government with only a small majority could be put under pressure by late night voting, and could be defeated if it let its MPs go home for the evening, whereas it is going to be much easier for the whips to keep enough MPs in Parliament to defeat the Opposition during the day.

There have also been adjustments to the arrangement of the yearly sessions, again partly to help MPs with families. There are half-term breaks in February and May, to coincide with school holidays. The House used often to sit throughout July, not returning until early October, after the party conferences. This gave the public the impression that MPs had excessively long holidays. From 2003 the intention is that the House will rise in mid-July and then return in early September, taking an extra break over the party conference season. This seems a more sensible arrangement and should produce a more rational spread of parliamentary business across the year.

Turning to the legislative process, there has long been criticism of the way the House of Commons examines legislation, or fails to do so. Even important laws may be rushed through without adequate scrutiny. The Anti-Terrorism, Crime and Security Act 2001 had only 16 hours scrutiny in the House of Commons, and was not amended at all in that time. It is true that the House of Lords, as is often the case, subjected that Act to much tighter scrutiny and forced the Government to accept significant amendments, but it should be for the elected House to take the lead in questioning legislation.

There have, however, been some welcome developments in the legislative process. It is now the practice of the Government to publish proposed legislation in draft form well in advance of its formal introduction, to allow both Parliament and public to examine and comment on it. For example, a draft Freedom of Information Bill was published in May 1999 for consultation purposes. Several committees in both Houses examined it and issued reports before the final version of the Bill was formally presented for first reading in November 1999. It is generally agreed that this early scrutiny is desirable and its use should be extended.

The timetable for passing legislation is always contentious. Governments, which feel they have a mandate for legislation, object to delays which they attribute to Opposition obstruction. The Opposition and backbenchers generally do not want their examination of Bills curtailed. The former practice was that discussion of Bills could only be curtailed by an allocation of time order, commonly known as a 'guillotine'. Such an order would only be made after a Bill had suffered delay in Committee, and would itself need a substantial and often acrimonious debate. From 2000 an experiment has been made with 'programme motions'. These give the Standing Committee considering a Bill a date for completing their deliberations, but empower it to allocate the time available between the various sections of the Bill. The use of these motions has led to a more rational and less contentious timetabling of legislative scrutiny, and it seems possible that over time they may replace the 'guillotine' completely.

One of the main reasons for the pressure on the parliamentary timetable is the rule that public bills must complete their passage through both Houses within one session. Any bill that is not so passed fails, and must start again from scratch next session. The Modernisation Committee recommended in 1998 that it should be possible for bills to be carried over from one session to the next. This would encourage governments to allow more thorough scrutiny and also spread the work of legislation more evenly across the session. This proposal was accepted, in spite of misgivings from the Opposition that it might make life too easy for the government. So far it has been used in respect of complex technical legislation and has been regarded as a useful innovation.

There have been other changes to parliamentary procedures. Soon after the 1997 election, Prime Minister's Question Time was moved from the traditional 15-minute Tuesday and Thursday afternoon slots, to 30 minutes on Wednesday afternoon. With the change in sitting hours, Wednesday lunchtime is now used. The intention was to allow for more extended and sober questioning, rather than the short and noisy performance of the past, but there is little noticeable difference. A further innovation has been the introduction of a parallel chamber for simultaneous debates, using a room in Westminster Hall. This has enabled backbenchers to raise more issues and provides the opportunity to debate select committee reports. This is again regarded as a valuable innovation.

Although many of the changes outlined above, and the removal of other arcane rules (like having to wear a hat to raise a point of order during a division!) have been welcomed, there remain many areas where further reform could be achieved. Many outside Parliament feel that the slow process of voting by walking through the division lobbies should be replaced by instant electronic voting. But MPs, who value the voting process as an opportunity to buttonhole a government minister, have rejected this. Some commentators suggest that the government's reforming zeal has diminished as they see the advantage in being protected from effective scrutiny by old procedures. The inherent conservatism of an institution which has existed for centuries is likely to leave many parliamentary procedures unaltered.

Q Question 3

At a recent general election, ten seats in the House of Commons were unexpectedly won by the 'Save the National Health Service' Party (SNHS). The newly elected MPs seek your advice as to the means available to them to try to influence government policy, especially on health issues.

Advise them.

Commentary

This question touches on a wide range of issues relating to the powers of back-bench MPs; the student should try to be reasonably comprehensive rather than just dealing with legislative processes or select committees. Although health issues are used as the example in this problem, no specialised knowledge of that subject is needed. A similar answer would serve if another area was identified. An awareness of political realities will enhance the answer, if it is combined with a good knowledge of the House of Commons' activities.

- Scrutiny of primary and secondary legislation.

- Private Member's Bill.

- Raising constituents' issues, asking PQs.

- Select Committees.

- Lobbying.

:Ọ: Suggested answer

The most important factor in determining how much the new MPs can influence the government will be the size of the government's majority. A government with a substantial majority, as long as its own supporters remain loyal, need not worry about the attitude of opposition parties. At the other extreme, a minority government will be dependent on the votes of other parties, which may be able to exact a high price in policy terms, even to the extent of insisting on places in a coalition government. But even where a government has a comfortable working majority, parliamentary procedures offer opposition and back-bench MPs a variety of opportunities for the exercise of influence, and a skilful use of such procedures will maximise their effect. Although government business generally has priority, the new SNHS Party MPs will find opportunities to make their presence felt in Parliament.

The largest single item in the House of Commons' timetable is the consideration of government legislation. The SNHS Party MPs may seek to speak in the second reading debate, but the party's greatest opportunity for influence will be achieved by getting one or two of its MPs onto the standing committees which subject bills to detailed scrutiny. This will provide the opportunity to propose amendments, though these will only succeed if they can attract the support of some government MPs; the government, provided that it has an overall majority in the House of Commons, will have a majority on each standing committee. Any amendments agreed to in committee can be reversed by the House of Commons as a whole at the report stage, but there is always the chance that the government will accept reasoned amendments in order to avoid delay in passing the legislation.

Other forms of legislation may provide opportunities for intervention. If a health authority were to promote a private Bill, that would give opportunities for backbench MPs to call for debates on the floor of the House, as well as participating in the quasi-judicial committee stages. There are various methods by which an MP can propose legislation, but most of these provide no real chance of success. To have the best chance of getting a Private Member's Bill debated and even enacted, the MPs should enter the annual ballot for the right to promote a Bill on one of the Fridays reserved for that purpose. Competition is very great; most backbenchers enter the ballot, whether or not they have a Bill ready to propose. If one of the SNHS MPs were to be successful in gaining a high place in the ballot, that would give an excellent opportunity to change the law. One important limitation must, however, be noted. Any bill requiring public expenditure, or the imposition of a tax, cannot be passed unless a money resolution is agreed, usually after the second reading. Only a government minister can move such a resolution. So there is no chance of the SNHS party procuring an increase in spending against the wishes of the government. In any case, all successful private members Bills need at least the benevolent neutrality of the government and preferably its tacit support. A modest measure, not involving public expenditure, would seem the most promising option for the SNHS party.

Some matters of health policy will also be dealt with by secondary legislation, but the opportunities for MPs to scrutinise this are not great. Although the most important statutory instruments may require the approval of the House of Commons, most do not and will become law unless a negative resolution is proposed and passed against them. There is a joint committee of Lords and Commons on statutory instruments which examines all instruments laid before Parliament, and has the power to draw matters of concern to the attention of the House, though not in respect of the substantive content of the instrument.

Apart from legislation, much of the House of Commons' time is spent on various forms of debate. Although most debate is at the government's initiative, there are a certain number of opposition days, when the opposition can choose the subject for debate. Most of these are used by the largest opposition party, but, by agreement, the SNHS may be allocated a half day to debate a subject of their choice. There have always been daily adjournment debates, with MPs' right to choose the topic being allocated by ballot. The opportunity for these debates has been greatly increased with the recent introduction of the parallel chamber in Westminster Hall. On Tuesdays and Wednesdays, ten slots are available for backbench MPs to debate issues, again chosen by ballot.

One of the most obvious ways for the SNHS Party MPs to make their presence felt is by asking parliamentary questions. To obtain maximum publicity, questions should be set for oral answer, often in an oblique form in the hope of surprising the minister with an embarrassing supplementary question. But MPs are subject to restrictions on the number of questions they can table, because of the likelihood of the system becoming clogged and, question time being strictly limited, only some 10 to 20 questions can be dealt with on any day. Any questions not reached are given a written answer, as are all questions where a written answer is requested. This procedure, while not attracting such immediate publicity as Question Time, is extremely useful as a means of obtaining information about the government's actions and policies.

In recent years, the departmentally related select committees have provided MPs with enhanced opportunities for scrutiny of the executive and the SNHS Party MPs would certainly hope to obtain a place on the Health Committee. Competition for places is intense and, while places are formally allocated by the Committee of Selection, in practice the party whips have a considerable influence over the allocation of places between parties. The government will have a majority on each committee, and the major opposition party will take the bulk of the remaining places, but determined lobbying by the SNHS MPs should secure them a place. Select committees do generally try to operate in a non-partisan way as far as possible, and are more likely to influence the government if they do so operate. The opportunities for questioning witnesses in public, and obtaining information from government and other sources make select committees an excellent forum for MPs to operate in. Of particular importance in the health field would be the right of the select committee to summon and question witnesses from health authorities and hospital trusts, rather than having to rely on questioning ministers and civil servants who are not directly involved in the provision of health care.

The SNHS Party MPs are likely to find themselves a focus for attempts to lobby the government and other authorities. The new restrictions, imposed as a result of the Nolan Committee report into standards in public life, forbid paid advocacy of any cause. Unpaid advocacy and the general making and facilitating of contacts — indeed the whole networking process — are going to be one of the most useful ways in which the SNHS Party MPs can help. Some groups of course prefer to operate as outsiders, believing that the inevitable compromises needed to 'make friends and influence people' are a betrayal of the cause. But others would argue that a voice closer to the internal workings of government will have more effect in practice than any amount of public protest.

In conclusion, there is a range of methods available to the new SNHS Party MPs to try to influence the government. While such a small group will have no substantial power, unless a combination of circumstances were to leave them holding the balance of power in a hung Parliament, they can, with political skill, make good use of the opportunities available to them. They may find the dominance of the major parties frustrating, and they will need to seek allies within those parties to achieve anything. But they will have opportunities, particularly to obtain information, which they would not have had but for their electoral success.

Q Question 4

What role do departmental select committees play in the scrutiny of the executive and how effective are they?

Commentary

This is a straightforward question whose answer will consist principally of a description of the committees, their structure, membership and operation. What will make a good answer is the assessment of their effectiveness. Issues such as government influence on the choice of members, cooperation from witnesses and government reaction to reports will all be relevant. As usual, it will not matter whether you choose to take a critical stance or a complimentary one, provided that you argue your case well and support it with appropriate examples.

- Membership.

- Power to summon witnesses and see records.

- Non-confrontational style.

- Assessing influence.

⚬ Suggested answer

The House of Commons uses select committees to perform tasks, such as investigation and scrutiny, which cannot be performed adequately in the Commons chamber. Only in committees can witnesses be questioned and evidence examined. The present system of departmental select committees dates from 1979, when it was agreed that there should be one select committee to examine the work of each government department and its associated agencies, boards and quangos. Originally, there were 12 such committees, but now there are 18. This increase is due to changes in the structure of government and an acceptance that even departments whose work was initially thought to be too sensitive to be subjected to this level of scrutiny, such as the Lord Chancellor's Department, should have a committee to examine them. It is therefore now the case that select committees cover the whole range of government activities.

Membership of select committees is confined to backbench MPs. There are usually 11 places on each committee though a recent Commons report suggested an increase to 15. Membership is proportionate to party strength, and it is accepted practice that the Opposition can hold the chair of some committees. Places are allocated by a committee of selection, which, it was hoped, would be independent of the party whips. But in practice each party puts forward its list of nominees, leaving the committees nothing to do. There were proposals in 2001 to replace the committee of selection by a more independent committee of nomination, but these were rejected. It is clear that the parties wish to retain control of nominations. That control, however, is not absolute. The membership of each select committee has to be approved by a vote of the House of Commons. Usually this is a formality, but in 2001, the House rejected the proposed membership of two committees, because the governing party had failed to renominate two popular and effective MPs to the chairs of those committees. This demonstration of backbench power, which led to the reinstatement of the two MPs, should serve as a warning to governments not to try to manipulate the membership in their favour.

A seat on a select committee is a highly sought after position. For newer MPs, it offers a means of making an impact; for more senior MPs, especially those who know that they will not be offered ministerial office, it offers an alternative career structure. MPs, once appointed, serve on the committee for the whole parliament unless they choose to resign, or are appointed to government or front bench opposition posts. MPs may have some expert knowledge before selection; the current membership of the Health select committee includes a doctor and a pharmacist. All MPs who sit on a select committee will acquire some level of expertise during their service.

Select committees have the power to send for persons, papers and records. Any individual, other than a member of either House of Parliament, may be formally summoned to appear, though in practice committees need do no more than issue an invitation, which will invariably be accepted. Many witnesses will indeed welcome the opportunity to give evidence before such a highly-regarded body. Others may be less co-operative; the brothers Kevin and Ian Maxwell declined to answer questions from the Social Security Committee about their late father's fraudulent use of pension funds, because they were facing criminal proceedings. The committees themselves have no coercive powers. All they can do is to refer the matter to the House of Commons, which has the power to punish those found to be in contempt, but is unlikely to be willing to do so except in an extreme case. No attempt was made to punish the Maxwells in this way.

Members of either House, including in particular government ministers, can only be invited, not summoned to appear. The government promised in 1979 that ministers would appear when invited, and they have complied with this, though it took four increasingly pressing invitations to persuade Mrs Edwina Currie to appear before the Agriculture Select Committee when it was investigating the incidence of salmonella in egg production. Although the House of Commons does have the power to force one of its members to attend a committee, such a power is never in practice going to be used against a government minister, as long as the government retains its overall majority. It is in any case always possible that the minister who willingly attends the committee meeting may be less than helpful in actually answering the questions.

The most interesting issues arise in relation to the appearance of civil servants before select committees. Traditionally, civil servants were not directly accountable to Parliament. Instead, they were responsible to the minister, who had to account to Parliament for their actions. But select committees can bypass the minister by calling the civil servants themselves to give evidence, creating an awkward, three-sided relationship between minister, official and committee. The government has issued, in successive versions, guidance for officials appearing before committees which, though it exhorts officials to be as helpful as possible, reiterates that they remain subject to the instructions of ministers in giving evidence. The guidance suggests that, where issues of the conduct or misconduct of officials are concerned, the official should suggest to the committee that the minister should give evidence instead. Some serious disputes have arisen where ministers have refused to permit particular officials to attend, instead appearing themselves or sending the permanent head of the department to give evidence. The Defence select committee had difficulty investigating the Westland affair because the relevant officials were not allowed to attend. Although the House of Commons could force officials to attend the committee, the government majority is unlikely to permit this, and the officials would be put in an impossible situation if they were ordered by the minister to remain silent. In such a situation, the committee is in practice helpless.

The guidance to officials also identifies various classes of material on which no information should be given to the committee without the minister's approval; these include advice given to ministers, confidential personal information, sensitive economic information and matters under international negotiation. While it is acceptable to assert that some matters are too sensitive to be discussed openly in committee, this list appears to cover some matters which would be of legitimate concern to an investigating committee.

Even more complex issues arise in relation to executive agencies which, while remaining part of government departments, are supposed to operate with a degree of autonomy. Although the government stated that the creation of these agencies was not intended to alter the arrangements for accountability, their existence has limited the scope for scrutiny through parliamentary questions, and increased the need for other methods of scrutiny to be developed. The government has accepted that, for matters concerning the day-to-day operation of an agency, the head of the agency is the appropriate witness to be called by a select committee, though reserving the minister's right to control the answers given. The select committee seems to be the best method available for parliamentary scrutiny of these agencies, and it is to be hoped that there will be further development of practice in this area.

The most striking feature of these committees is the ability of MPs from different parties to work together, symbolised by the fact that when hearing witnesses they sit together round a table, unlike the confrontational arrangement of the chamber of the House of Commons. Where possible, a consensus is reached and a unanimous report issued. There are some instances where party divisions have prevented this, but not so many as to diminish the effectiveness of the committees. Each committee can choose what topics to examine within its own remit; it will usually conduct one or two major investigations each session, as well as responding quickly to matters of immediate concern. The government has no direct control over the choice of topics and, while it may try to exert an influence behind the scenes, this has not prevented committees choosing subjects which have gravely embarrassed the government. Investigations like that into the Westland affair have lifted stones which the government would certainly prefer to have left unturned.

Although it is clear that select committees have the potential to enhance the powers of the back-bench MP to scrutinise government actions, it is very difficult to assess just how much impact they have had in practice. Some of their reports have been followed by statutory reform, but in most cases other pressures have contributed to persuading the government to act. A select committee report may simply be the last straw. The government has undertaken always to make a formal response to select committee reports; this does at least force the government to consider and justify its attitude to the issue. It is very difficult for a government to dismiss a unanimous select committee report out of hand; there is always the risk that the subject will arise again to embarrass the government.

It was never likely that the introduction of the reformed select committees would transform the House of Commons into as powerful a legislative chamber as the US Senate, before whose committees even the most powerful have to tremble. But the committees have succeeded in supplying back-benchers with a source of detailed information and in encouraging the development of expertise within Parliament. Their reports have given the public access to insights into the inner workings of government and the televising of their hearings shows the people that the House of Commons is not just a beargarden but is working on their behalf.

The existence of select committees has now become an established part of the parliamentary system. Their impact can perhaps best be assessed by trying to imagine the furore that would be caused, both inside and outside Parliament, by any attempt to abolish them.

Q Question 5

What recent developments have there been in the rules relating to the conduct of elections and election campaigns? Will these changes increase voter participation and improve the fairness of the electoral process?

Commentary

This question is typical of those asked when new laws have been passed, making subjects which may have been of little interest topical and exciting. Because this question refers to 'recent developments', there is no need to consider past history, except to explain what defects in the law led to the changes. The main bulk of your answer will inevitably consist of a description of the new laws. What will make for a good answer is an attempt to assess the merits of the reforms and to consider what might happen in the future. There is plenty of material available on this topic on the Electoral Commission's website, <http://www.electoralcommission.gov.uk> and, as so often in constitutional matters, it pays to read a broadsheet newspaper and keep a file of cuttings.

- **Registration of voters.**

- **Voting practices and places.**

- **Limits on party expenditure.**

- **Controls on fundraising.**

:Q̇: Suggested answer

In recent years, two issues relating to the conduct of elections have attracted concern. First, turnout of voters is often low even for parliamentary elections and is extremely poor for local and European elections. Secondly, the rules relating to election expenditure had become seriously outdated. Parties could, and did, spend as much money as they could raise on national campaigning and resorted to ever more questionable practices in the effort to raise money. Both these matters have been dealt with by recent legislation, but it remains to be seen whether changes in the law will be sufficient to bring about changes in the political climate.

We will examine first the issue of voter turnout. The basic requirement for participation in elections is that the name of the person must be entered in the electoral register maintained by the registration officer in each local area. An initial canvass of the area is made each October, with forms sent to each household, and checks made where forms are not returned. Although there is a legal obligation to complete the forms, some people do not. When the Poll Tax was in operation, many people deliberately kept themselves off the electoral register because, as a public document, it could be used by local authorities to track down defaulters. The completed register came into effect in February each year and remained in force for one year with no possibility of alteration. Because of people moving, the register rapidly became out of date. Anyone who had moved house during the currency of the register had either to return to their original area to vote or arrange a postal vote; many did not bother. The Representation of the People Act 2000 has addressed this problem by making it possible for the register to be amended during its year of operation. It will be possible, on moving house, to inform the registration officer of one's new address and so acquire the right to vote in one's new area. This is a useful amendment which should enable more people to vote.

A more general problem concerning the electoral register has been the requirement that the voter be 'resident' in the constituency on the qualifying date. The term 'resident' has been interpreted by the courts in a broad way. In *Hipperson* v *Electoral Registration Officer for Newbury* [1985] 2 All ER 456, it was held that the occupants of the peace camp at Greenham Common, who lived in tents on common land from which they could have been evicted at any time, counted as 'resident' there as there was evidence that their occupation was in practice stable. But for anyone without a residence of even such a precarious nature there was no possibility of registration. The homeless were in effect disenfranchised. The Representation of the People Act 2000 deals with this problem by allowing a person without a residence to be registered on the basis of a 'declaration of local connection', based on an address where they used to live, or even an address where, or near to where, they spend their time. This could be a hostel, a night shelter or a drop-in centre for the homeless. It will probably require considerable efforts by local authorities and voluntary organisations to get homeless persons to take advantage of these new rules. But it seems proper that the law should not place obstacles in the way of the exercise of the most basic democratic right.

The final issue relating to voter turnout is the most intractable; how to persuade people to bother to vote. In the general election of 2001, only about 59 per cent of the electorate voted, and in the European Parliament election of 1999, turnout was as low as 24 per cent. There are countries where voting is compulsory, but there is no enthusiasm for such a law in the UK. Instead, attempts are being made to make the process of voting easier. Traditionally, people have to vote in person, by visiting a polling station set up in a school, library or parish hall, on a Thursday, during the day. Postal and proxy votes were difficult to obtain. The Representation of the People Act 2000 allows local authorities to experiment with changes to these traditional practices for local elections, and many such experiments have taken place. These have included voting on different days and in different places, making postal votes more easily available and using all postal ballots. More radical experiments include allowing people to vote by telephone, text message, e-mail or through the internet.

All these experiments are being assessed by the Electoral Commission. So far, postal voting seems the most successful method for increasing turnout. In some local elections it has doubled the number of votes cast. But there remain concerns about the possibility of fraud, especially where new technology is used. The experience of the USA, where the result of the 2000 presidential election was disputed because of the deficiencies of electronic voting, is a warning. Further legislation would be needed before the procedures for parliamentary elections could be changed. It remains to be seen how successful any further changes are, but they are unlikely to overcome voter apathy completely.

We can now turn to the issue of electoral campaigning. The old rules on election expenditure, which were first introduced in 1883, were concerned to control local expenditure in individual constituencies. The candidates and their agents could spend only a limited amount of money on the election and accounts had to be kept. No one else could spend more than a nominal £5. These rules effectively stopped the bribery and corruption characteristic of nineteenth-century elections. But no rules governed national expenditure by political parties or others. In *R* v *Tronoh Mines* [1952] 1 All ER 697, it was held that campaigning by outsiders for or against a national party was permitted, provided no mention was made of individual candidates in individual constituencies. As a consequence of this lack of regulation, political parties have increased their expenditure on election campaigns dramatically. It is reckoned that in 1992 the Conservative Party spent £10 million and Labour £7 million, but that in 1997 both parties spent over £25 million. This led to two separate fears, first, that the results of elections were being distorted and, secondly, that the parties' find-raising activities almost amounted to selling political influence for money. These concerns led to the issue being referred to Lord Neill's Committee on Standards in Public Life. The committee reported in October 1998 and its recommendations have been implemented by the Political Parties, Elections and Referendums Act 2000.

The Act tackles the problems in three ways. First, it imposes controls on donations to political parties. The only permitted donors will be individuals registered to vote in the UK and companies and other organisations based in the UK. Foreign donations, a source of particular concern, will be banned. A new Electoral Commission will receive and publish details of all donations over £5,000, and inspect the accounts of all political parties. Secondly, the Act imposes limits on overall campaign expenditure by political parties; the maximum is just under £20 million for the year preceding Westminster elections, with proportionately lower maxima for European and regional assembly elections, and for referendum campaigns. Thirdly, the Act controls the expenditure of bodies other than political parties. This is in part a response to the judgment of the European Court of Human Rights in *Bowman* v *United Kingdom* (1998) 26–1 EHRR 1, where it was held that the old limit of £5 in a constituency was so low as to be an infringement of the right to freedom of expression. The Act permits any person or body to spend a sum up to £25,000 on election campaigns. But if it wishes to spend more than that, up to a maximum of just under £1 million, it must comply with the same rules as political parties concerning donations, accounts and records.

The most significant feature of those rules is the introduction of openness into an area where secrecy has been endemic. Parties and major donors will have to get used to the ideas that their financial dealings are open to public scrutiny. Whether this will make donors less willing to give is not clear. Many political donations, such as those from trade unions and companies, are already open, and some wealthy individuals make no secret of their support for particular parties. Adverse publicity is, however, likely to be attracted if donors subsequently appear to be obtaining favours from the party they supported. If donations to parties were substantially reduced, there might be a revival of the suggestion, put forward in 1976, that political parties should receive public funding, because they are an essential part of the democratic process. But the public probably feels that there are better uses to which public money could be put.

Whether the new rules will actually have an effect on the results of elections is doubtful. The Conservative Party spent more on its campaign in 1997 than ever before but that did not save it from heavy defeat, and the Liberal Democrats obtained more seats than in any post-war election in spite of relatively modest spending. But if the new funding rules help to reduce public cynicism about politics they will encourage more voters to participate in the electoral process and that is the main means of increasing its fairness.

Q Question 6

Consider the following situations in the light of the rules on parliamentary privilege.

(a) Giles, a back-bench MP, said during a debate in the House of Commons that the directors of the three largest UK fertiliser companies met together regularly to fix prices, in breach of both UK and EC law. The Minister of Agriculture asked Giles to send him further details of the accusation and also suggested that Giles inform the European Commission. Giles wrote to both the minister and the Commission from his parliamentary office. The managing director of one of the companies is threatening to sue Giles for defamation.

(b) A private member's Bill to outlaw fox-hunting is to be debated next week in the House of Commons. Reynard MP is the parliamentary consultant to the British Horse Society; he is paid £2,000 a year for his services, and has declared this in the register of Members' interests. He has been told by the Society that they will end his consultancy immediately unless he votes against the Bill. Animal rights activists have told Reynard that they will picket his home and his office unless he votes for the Bill.

(c) During a debate in the House of Commons on the decline in moral standards. Pecksniff MP accused Deadlock MP of fathering an illegitimate child. This accusation was false, and Deadlock was so annoyed that he punched Pecksniff in the voting lobby. The following day, the *Daily Broadsheet* published a report of the debate, including a mention of Deadlock's accusation. The *Daily Tabloid* published a front page article under the headline 'Deadlock in Love Child Scandal' not mentioning the rest of the debate.

Commentary

When dealing with questions on parliamentary privilege, it is important for the student to remember that there are two perspectives, that of the courts, and that of Parliament itself. These do not necessarily coincide; it is possible for the courts not to accept that a particular issue is protected by parliamentary privilege, even though that is how Parliament would regard it. The student should therefore take both points of view into account.

• Freedom of speech, absolute within Parliament, qualified outside.

• Controls over consultancy.

• Reporting parliamentary proceedings.

• Procedure for dealing with breach of privilege.

:Q: Suggested answer

(a) This problem is concerned with the fundamental privilege of Parliament, freedom of speech. This is protected by Article 9 of the Bill of Rights 1689, which states:

> That the freedom of speech and debates in Parliament ought not to be impeached or questioned in any place out of Parliament.

As a consequence, the courts have accepted that words spoken in the course of parliamentary proceedings are absolutely privileged. No action for defamation can be brought in respect of such words, not can they even be cited in court to support an action for defamation arising from words spoken outside Parliament, as in *Church of Scientology* v *Johnson-Smith* [1972] 1 QB 522. Giles can therefore face no legal action over what he said in the debate.

As for the letter written by Giles to the minister, the position here is less clear. If Giles had given the details orally in the course of the debate, this would be protected as a proceeding in Parliament. Does the writing of a letter count as a proceeding in Parliament? In 1957, the MP G. R. Strauss had written a letter to the minister outlining complaints from a constituent about an electricity board. The board considered the letter defamatory and threatened legal action, which the MP suggested might be a breach of privilege. The Committee of Privileges felt that the MP's letter was a proceeding in Parliament and should have the protection of absolute privilege, but the House of Commons disagreed and voted to dismiss the complaint of breach of privilege. Although suggestions have been made by various select committees that the position should be clarified by a formal extension of privilege to correspondence between MPs and ministers, no such ruling has been made.

Because correspondence is increasingly used by MPs as the best way of raising issues with a minister, parliamentary questions being reserved as the second line of attack, it can be argued that the absolute privilege should be extended. Indeed, MPs are now encouraged to deal with the new executive agencies directly by letter rather than by asking a question of the minister in the House of Commons. However, an MP's correspondence on official matters will have the protection of qualified privilege, and it can be argued that this is sufficient. Why should an MP be immune if he or she is maliciously passing false information to a government minister or official? But the reason for absolute privilege is that even the unfounded threat of legal action might operate to deter MPs from performing their proper function without fear or favour. Anything which reduces the effectiveness of MPs is undesirable.

As far as the letter to the European Commission is concerned, it would be difficult to argue that this is entitled to absolute privilege as a proceeding in Parliament, as EC institutions are completely separate from UK institutions. Giles would certainly be able to claim qualified privilege, however, so that he will be protected if he has acted without malice.

(**b**) Provided that Reynard has made a full declaration of his agreement with the British Horse Society, he will not be in breach of any rules by voting on the fox-hunting Bill, whether for or against. His problem is that two different groups are attempting to force him to vote in particular ways. It is a clear breach of privilege for any outsider to attempt, by bribery or threats, to influence an MP, and any such attempt would be subject to punishment as a contempt of Parliament, as well as possibly amounting to a criminal offence. But it is not clear how this rule relates to the practice of parliamentary consultancy. This issue was raised in 1947. W. J. Brown an MP, was appointed by a trade union to further its interests in Parliament, but when political disagreements arose between them, the union threatened to withdraw from the contract, causing Brown financial loss. The Committee of Privileges was concerned mainly with the propriety of the original contract and, having decided that it was proper, found no breach of privilege in the decision to terminate it. But they confirmed that any agreement which purported to bind an MP to behave, vote or speak in a particular way would be improper. In some later instances, the threat by a trade union to withdraw sponsorship from an MP has been classed as a breach of privilege. On each occasion the union withdrew the threat as soon as the issue of privilege was raised, and no punitive action was taken.

It therefore seems probable that any express threat from the British Horse Society, or any subsequent decision to withdraw sponsorship with immediate effect, would be regarded as a breach of privilege, though there would be nothing wrong with a decision to terminate the contract in due course in accordance with its terms. The Society might be satisfied to reflect that in any case, an MP is likely to feel inclined to support the causes for which he has accepted a consultancy. The new rules introduced as a result of the Nolan Committee report will, however, prevent Reynard from speaking during the debate.

Any physical action taken by the protesters may be a breach of the criminal law; an offence under the Public Order Act 1986, assault or criminal damage. Reynard's best course of action, if subjected to harassment, may well be just to call the police. But it will also be a contempt of Parliament to molest or threaten an MP. In the case of the *Sunday Graphic*, 1956, a newspaper was held to be in contempt when it published an MP's telephone number and incited its readers to ring him up and complain about his actions in Parliament. The House of Commons has the power to order an outsider to appear at the bar of the House to be reprimanded, but this power is rarely used. It is probable that, as happens if persons demonstrate in the public gallery, any protesters will be handed to the police to be dealt with.

(c) Because Pecksniff's statement was made during a debate, he is protected by the absolute privilege conferred by the Bill of Rights. Deadlock cannot bring any legal action against Pecksniff for defamation, even if Pecksniff knew the accusation was false. Only if he repeated the statement outside Parliament could Deadlock sue him. Deadlock could, however, refer the matter to the Speaker as a possible breach of privilege, if Pecksniff is abusing his parliamentary immunity; MPs have been reprimanded in such circumstances.

As far as the assault by Deadlock on Pecksniff is concerned, there are various possible consequences. Deadlock has apparently committed a criminal offence, possibly an arrestable offence as defined by s. 24 of the Police and Criminal Evidence Act 1984. Although MPs were once entitled to freedom from arrest, this no longer applies to criminal proceedings. Deadlock may therefore be arrested and charged with a criminal offence, and dealt with by the criminal courts in the same way as any other person. It is, however, possible for the House of Commons to exercise its right to regulate its own proceedings. It has from time to time had to deal with disorderly conduct by MPs. It may suspend the MP from the House for a time; the MP is not paid during that time and cannot take part in any of the House's activities. The ultimate sanction available against an MP is expulsion from the House, but this has only been used in extreme circumstances, such as conviction for a grave criminal offence, or gross contempt of the House. It is unlikely that Deadlock's behaviour would be regarded as justifying such an extreme sanction, though he would certainly be expected to apologise as was Ron Brown MP when in 1988 he damaged the mace during an overheated debate.

So far as newspapers are concerned, absolute privilege only extends, under the

Parliamentary Papers Act 1840, to material published by or under the authority of either House, such as Hansard. But a newspaper has qualified privilege for any fair and accurate report of parliamentary proceedings made without malice, as in *Wason* v *Walter* (1868) LR 4 QB 73. The report does not have to be verbatim to be protected. In *Cook* v *Alexander* [1974] QB 279, it was held that a parliamentary sketch, provided it was honest and fair comment, was entitled to qualified privilege. It therefore appears that the *Daily Broadsheet* may be able to claim qualified privilege for its report. The *Daily Tabloid*, however, is hardly in a position to assert that it is reporting parliamentary proceedings at all, let alone in a fair and accurate way. It will therefore be susceptible to an action in defamation, and cannot plead any privilege as a defence.

Q Question 7

If it is to fulfil the functions of a second legislative chamber, the House of Lords needs substantial further reforms.
  Discuss.

Commentary

Questions about reform of the House of Lords have become particularly topical with the removal of most of the hereditary peers under the House of Lords Act 1999 and the publication of the report of the Royal Commission chaired by Lord Wakeham. To answer this question adequately, it is necessary to identify the principal features of a second legislative chamber. This will establish the criteria against which the need for further reform can be judged. It will be easiest to use the proposals of the Wakeham Commission as the basis for discussing reform, but students are entitled, if they wish, to criticise those proposals and put forward other, perhaps more radical, suggestions. References to legislatures in other states, while not essential, will enhance the quality of the answer.

* **Representation.**

* **Selection or election.**

* **Checking the power of the House of Commons.**

* **Scrutiny of legislation.**

* **Scrutiny of the executive.**

:Q: Suggested answer

In most liberal democracies, the legislature consists of two chambers. Only in smaller states is a single chamber, or unicameral, legislature found to be effective. The respective powers of the two chambers will vary according to the constitutional structure of the state. In Britain, the House of Lords and House of Commons have developed over the centuries, and, as with much of the British constitution, their relationship is to be found in both statute and unwritten convention.

It is an essential element in any democratic state that the legislature should consist of representatives of the people. In a bicameral legislature, one of the main functions of the second chamber is to represent the people in some way which differs from the first chamber. In a federal state, such as Germany or the USA, the separate constituent parts of the federation will be represented in the second chamber. The US Senate consists of two senators from each state regardless of size. Even in non-federal states, such as France, it is common for the second chamber to consist of representatives of geographical areas.

The House of Lords, however, is in no sense a representative assembly. Historically, it consisted of the great noble and ecclesiastical landowners, who were entitled as individuals to privileged political power. The House of Lords Act 1999 removed all but 92 of the hereditary peers, and they too will lose their seats if and when further reform occurs. The life peers, who now form the bulk of members of the House of Lords, also sit as individuals not as representatives. The only members who could be described as in any way representative are the 26 Bishops of the Church of England and the Lords of Appeal.

How to make the House of Lords in some way representative was one of the principal issues addressed by the Wakeham Commission. It rejected what might appear to be the most obvious solution, having the second chamber directly elected by the people. The problem it identified is that, if the second chamber were elected at the same time as the House of Commons and in the same way, the result would be two identical chambers and an important constitutional safeguard would be lost. If it were to be elected by some other electoral system or at a different time, it could claim an equal or greater democratic legitimacy and challenge the dominance of the House of Commons, requiring a complete rethink of the relationship between the two Houses. Furthermore, an elected chamber would inevitably attract the same type of candidates as the House of Commons, principally career politicians, thus losing the diversity which has been viewed as one of the strengths of the unreformed House of Lords.

The Wakeham Commission therefore recommended that the reformed chamber should consist of a minority of regional members, elected by some form of pro-portional representation, and a majority of appointed members. These would be selected by an independent Appointments Commission, which would be instructed to ensure a political, social, gender and ethnic balance. The Wakeham Commission could reach no consensus on the size of the elected component. The majority suggested 87 out of the 550 members, but dissenters suggested as few as 65 or as many as 195.

Many commentators were critical of this proposal, preferring a wholly or at least substantially elected chamber. The Government, however, appeared to view it favourably. It established an appointments commission to select future cross-bench peers and, in a White Paper issued in November 2001, proposed that 20 per cent of the membership should be elected, using a Party List system on a regional basis, and the remaining 80 per cent appointed. This proposal was met with even more widespread criticism, particularly from Labour MPs, and was abandoned almost immediately. Instead, the Government established a Joint Committee of both Houses and asked it to come up with proposals. The Committee offered a range of suggestions, fully elected, fully appointed or a hybrid in various proportions, and called for a free vote in each House. The House of Lords chose a fully appointed house, but the House of Commons rejected all the options, including abolition. This left the Government with an apparently insoluble problem and it remains to be seen whether they will pursue reform any further or abandon their attempt. Perhaps if regional devolution becomes a reality, it may be possible to develop a meaningful structure for a new chamber based on representation of the nations and regions of the UK.

One of the principal roles of a second chamber is to act as a check on the first and a safeguard against the concentration of too much power in the hands of one institution. The powers of a second chamber vary in different constitutions from a mere power of delay to a complete veto. Under the Parliament Acts 1911 and 1949, the power of the House of Lords was reduced to a power to delay legislation introduced in and passed by the House of Commons for one year. It is significant that the House of Lords retains the power to reject any Bill to extend the life of the House of Commons, thus making the House of Lords a safeguard against any attempt to subvert democracy by postponing elections. The Wakeham Commission proposed that this should be strengthened by making it impossible to use the Parliament Acts procedure to amend the Parliament Acts themselves, as happened, controversially, in 1949.

For all other legislation, the House of Lords retains some power to act as a check on the House of Commons, because it is still necessary for a Bill to be passed in identical form by both Houses for it to become law in a single session. Because of its unrepresentative nature, the unreformed House of Lords was reluctant to reject legislation approved by the House of Commons. In particular, from 1945, the Conservative majority observed the so-called Salisbury convention, that it would not obstruct measures put forward by a Labour government in fulfilment of a manifesto commitment. But this has not prevented both Labour and Conservative governments having their legislation delayed by the House of Lords, and if such delays occur in the last year of a Parliament, the Bill is defeated. Since the passage of the House of Lords Act 1999, the remaining Conservative peers have announced that they no longer consider themselves to be bound by the Salisbury convention, and have defeated government legislation on several occasions. This is likely to increase the use of the Parliament Act procedure. In the longer term, the Wakeham Commission suggests that the reformed second chamber should retain, with only minor amendments, the existing powers of the House of Lords and should continue to act as a check on the House of Commons. If the second chamber were to be wholly elected, it would be justified in expecting greater powers, but giving it a power of veto would run the risk of creating legislative gridlock.

A third task performed by a second chamber is to share the onerous work of scrutinising legislation. Modern governments require the enactment of large amounts of increasingly complex legislation. In Britain, some 50 to 70 Acts are passed each year. It is an essential element in the democratic process that all legislation should be scrutinised by the legislature and that governments should have to justify their proposals in both substance and detail. Because legislation can be introduced in either House, it is common practice for some legislation, particularly non-controversial measures, to start its passage in the House of Lords where detailed scrutiny can be given, thus saving time in the over-pressed House of Commons.

The House of Lords has been considered to play a very useful role in the scrutiny of legislation, particularly since the introduction of life peers, who include experts in many fields; legal, medical, scientific, technical and ethical. Whereas in the House of Commons the intensity of the party struggle detracts from the technical scrutiny of legislation, members of the House of Lords may be able to take a more detached view ensuring that legislation, whatever its substantive merits, is well drafted and effective. Were the House of Lords to become a fully elected chamber, it is very possible that its performance of this function would be impaired, as the party struggle would intensify. A chamber in the form proposed by the Wakeham Commission, with its nominated members, should be at least as effective as the present House of Lords.

A fourth purpose which can be served by a second chamber is to assist in the scrutiny of the executive. Whether a government is fully accountable to both chambers will vary from state to state, but it is usual for both chambers to play a part in questioning the government and investigating its activities. In Britain the government is ultimately accountable to the House of Commons alone, through the convention of Ministerial Responsibility. But some members of the government will sit in the House of Lords, most government departments will be represented there, and members of the House of Lords can ask oral and written questions of them. The House of Lords also uses its power to set up select committees to scrutinise aspects of government behaviour, though there are no departmental select committees like those in the Commons. Were the House of Lords to be wholly elected, its members would expect a greater role in the scrutiny of the executive, but the Wakeham Commission's proposals do not envisage any major changes in the exercise of this function by its predominantly appointed chamber. For as long as the second chamber remains unelected, its role in the scrutiny of the executive can only be secondary.

By removing the hereditary peers, the government abolished a historical anomaly. But it has not turned the House of Lords into a fully representative chamber, nor do the Wakeham Commission proposals give the reformed chamber full democratic legitimacy. The Wakeham Commission's proposals are concerned rather to preserve those features of the House of Lords which have made it effective in practice, even if they are difficult to defend in theory. Few would argue that a second chamber is unnecessary, and its abolition without replacement would leave the House of Commons, and the government which controls it, in an excessively powerful position. There are good reasons for preferring even a partial reform to outright abolition, but there remain strong arguments for further reform.

Further reading

Bradley, A. and Ewing, K. *Constitutional & Administrative Law*, 13th edn (Longman, 2003), chs 9–11.

Jowell, J. and Oliver, D. *The Changing Constitution*, 4th edn (OUP, 2000), chs 10 and 11.

Munro, C. *Studies in Constitutional Law*, 2nd edn (Butterworths, 1999), chs 4 and 7.

Turpin, C. *British Government & Constitution*, 5th edn (Butterworths, 2002), ch 8.

Loveland, I. *Constitutional Law*, 3rd edn (Butterworths, 2003), chs 5–8.

Prime Minister and Cabinet

Introduction

These topics will be included in any constitutional law course, but are almost exclusively matters of convention, not law. This chapter includes what must be the classic question in this area, the relationship between Prime Minister and Cabinet. Questions on the Prime Minister's powers and the convention of Ministerial Responsibility can take the form of essays or problems. The basic material for these two types of answer will be similar, but it is always important when answering a problem question to focus the material on the actual question asked.

For all these questions, it is essential for the student to show familiarity with current political developments. A failure to refer to the current Prime Minister, whoever that is, will give the examiner the impression that you are not really aware of the significance of the subject you are studying.

Q Question 1

How far is it true to say that Britain has moved from a system of Cabinet government to a system of Prime Ministerial government?

Commentary

This is one of the classic subjects for debate in constitutional law, and there are as many opinions on it as there are commentators. The conclusion reached by the student is of much less importance than the quality of the arguments displayed. Because the question addresses change in the constitution, the student must show an awareness of historical developments. It will also be desirable for the student to make comparisons between different Prime Ministers. Any reference to contemporary developments will impress the examiner, though the core of the answer can properly consist of the classic examples of Prime Ministers using their powers, or being prevented from doing so by their Cabinet.

- PM's powers derive from convention.

- Choosing members of government.

- Control of Cabinet and its committees.

- Downing Street staff.

☼ Suggested answer

When Bagehot wrote his classic study of the British constitution in 1867, he identified the Cabinet as the central controlling institution, the principal of the 'efficient' parts of the system. But when in 1963 Richard Crossman provided a new introduction to Bagehot's work, he wrote:

> The post-war epoch has seen the final transformation of Cabinet Government into Prime Ministerial Government.

Many commentators have agreed with him, particularly when describing the prime ministership of Margaret Thatcher. Others have pointed to her downfall as demonstrating that the fundamental nature of British government remains collective not individual. The Cabinet, if it so wishes, can still rule.

In the British constitution, both Cabinet and Prime Minister are creatures of convention. Their functions and powers are not defined by law, but have developed gradually in order to provide a form of government answerable to Parliament rather than to the Monarch. The Cabinet developed from the practice of government ministers meeting in private, in the absence of the Monarch, to agree on policies to be presented to Parliament. No legal rules defined which minister was to be regarded as most important. But the position of First Lord of the Treasury, with responsibility for government finance, inevitably made the holder first, or Prime, Minister.

Initially, the Prime Minister was described as 'primus inter pares' or first among equals. Although by the nineteenth century some Prime Ministers, such as Gladstone, were exercising a dominant influence, others, particularly if they sat in the House of Lords, were little more than chairmen of the Cabinet. In the present century, it has become an established convention that the Prime Minister must sit in the House of Commons and political practice now concentrates intense attention on the position of Prime Minister.

The Prime Minister's powers derive almost exclusively from convention and the Royal Prerogative, not from statute. Whether such powers are exercised by the Prime Minister alone, or by the Cabinet collectively, may be determined by established convention, but will often be a matter of political practice or expediency. Even conventions may change over time. The decision to ask the Monarch to dissolve Parliament and call a general election was at one time taken by the Cabinet, but since 1918 the Prime Minister has made that decision, after such consultation with colleagues as appears desirable at the time.

The initial creation of a new government provides the first illustration of the inter-relationship between the Prime Minister's powers and political practice. By convention, the Monarch calls on the leader of the party with a majority in the House of Commons to form a government. The new Prime Minister then has the power to select all the members of the new administration. The Cabinet is therefore of the Prime Minister's own choosing and could be expected to reflect his or her ideas. But in practice, the Prime Minister's choice will be constrained. Leading members of the party will expect important posts, preferably those which they shadowed while in opposition; former political favours may need to be repaid. The longer a Prime Minister remains in office, however, the more opportunity there is for the Cabinet to be reshaped according to the Prime Minister's real preferences. It is now accepted political practice for there to be frequent reshuffles; ministers whose performance is seen as inadequate, or who are not fully in sympathy with the Prime Minister's policies can be removed. The dismissal of ministers can, however, weaken a Prime Minister by providing a focus for party discontent, or even by being perceived as an act of desperation.

Once the government is formed, the Prime Minister has a decisive voice in the processes by which it operates. Because of the increasing complexity of modern government, meetings of the full Cabinet can deal with only a fraction of government business. The Prime Minister, who approves the agenda, can decide which matters are discussed there, and can keep controversial items off the agenda, though this will be subject to political constraints. Michael Heseltine resigned from the Cabinet when unable to raise the Westland affair there.

The Prime Minister, as chairperson of the Cabinet, can lead and control the discussion there. Because it is not the practice to take votes, the Prime Minister normally concludes discussion by summing up the sense of the meeting, which will be entered in the minutes. It is a matter of personal style whether the Prime Minister allows a genuine consensus to develop or attempts to dominate the debate. But no Prime Minister can be sure whether a Cabinet discussion will lead to the desired result. In the last resort, the Prime Minister cannot insist on the adoption of a policy against the wishes of the rest of the Cabinet.

The Cabinet forms the apex of a hierarchy of cabinet committees, sub-committees and working groups, and most government business will now be dealt with outside the full Cabinet. The Prime Minister now has considerable freedom in establishing and staffing such committees, and can, by careful selection, ensure that only those likely to favour his or her opinion are involved in the taking of the decision. Decisions made in a Cabinet committee are generally as final as those made in the full Cabinet, and ministers remain bound by collective responsiblity even if they were not party to the making of the decision. The existence of Cabinet committees used not to be publicly admitted, but since 1992 the identity and membership of several have been officially revealed. A Prime Minister may even avoid the use of such formal bodies and use wholly informal working groups to take sensitive decisions. Tony Blair is said to have met ministers individually to persuade them to support the invasion of Iraq, before any collective discussion. This clearly shows how the Prime Minister can exercise a dominating influence over the decision-making process, though the exclusion of ministers who feel they should be more involved may ultimately cause political problems. Robin Cook resigned over the invasion of Iraq and has since voiced frequent criticisms of Tony Blair's style of leadership.

The Prime Minister has a general responsibility for government policy and is therefore entitled to intervene in almost any aspect of the work of any department, subject only to the limits imposed by energy and enthusiasm. All Prime Ministers are expected to take a particular interest in economic and foreign affairs. Diplomacy is now conducted to a great extent by summit meetings, and the regular meetings of the European Council are the main focus for developments in the European Union. In other matters, a Prime Minister may allow departmental ministers to develop their own policies within an overall strategy, or may insist on involvement in all developments.

The Prime Minister has the assistance of a range of support services, including a Private Office, staffed by the most promising young civil servants, a Press Office, staffed by what are popularly known as 'spin doctors', and a Political Office staffed by members of their party. All recent Prime Ministers have engaged policy advisers from outside the civil service, though problems have arisen where these advisers are thought to have too much influence. Some commentators argue that, under Tony Blair, these support services have expanded to the point where they could be described as a Prime Minister's Department. In particular, the Cabinet Office, the government department which works most closely with the Prime Minister, now includes a large number of specialised units, such as the Social Exclusion Unit. There is now a Minister for the Cabinet Office. Perhaps the only reason why a Prime Minister's Department has not been created on an official basis is that it would be taken as ultimate proof that a system of Prime Ministerial Government had been established.

There can be no doubt that recent years have seen an increasing concentration of media attention on the Prime Minister. Surveys suggest that the Prime Minister gets more publicity than all the rest of the Cabinet put together. The broadcasting of Parliament, especially the regular televising of Prime Minister's Question Time, has created a perception that the Prime Minister is the government, whatever may be the reality. Elections are described as if they were a contest between party leaders, and it can be argued that elections give the Prime Minister a personal, not just a party, mandate. This strengthens the hand of a successful Prime Minister, but also increases the likelihood that a party's response to unpopularity will be to replace its leader. Even Margaret Thatcher's dominance after 11 years in office did not save her from that fate.

It is very difficult to envisage a return to the days when the Prime Minister was only first among equals. Even a Prime Minister who does not wish to dominate the government would find it impossible to reverse the popular perception of the dominant leader. There are very considerable powers available to a Prime Minister who wishes to make full use of them, and such a Prime Minister will overshadow the rest of the government as Tony Blair does. But the Cabinet remains as the forum in which fundamental issues have ultimately to be decided, and no Prime Minister can ignore or evade the objections of the majority there to the policies he or she wishes to pursue. There have been times when Britain has come very close to having a system of Prime Ministerial government. But the Cabinet remains among the efficient rather than the dignified parts of the Constitution. The picture drawn by Bagehot is still recognisable.

Q Question 2

Last year, Peter became Prime Minister when his party won a general election with a majority of 30 seats. He promised, during the election campaign, to provide a massive expansion of higher education. He has now decided that this can only be achieved if a special tax is imposed on graduates. He has discussed this privately with the Chancellor of the Exchequer, who agrees with the scheme. No other ministers have yet been informed, and several of them are likely to be critical of the plan.

What steps can Peter take to ensure that:

(a) the scheme is adopted as government policy;

(b) the necessary legislation is passed through Parliament;

(c) the public accepts the need for the new tax?

Commentary

This question is principally concerned with the powers of the Prime Minister, but it also includes material from other parts of the syllabus; particularly the legislative process. The extent to which material on pressure group activity and policy formation would need to be included would depend on whether the course takes such a political slant. The student will be expected to demonstrate a clear understanding of the conventions governing the Cabinet and of the legal rules governing the passage of legislation. The answer will be greatly enhanced by an awareness of political realities. Too often students' answers read as if this was an abstract theoretical problem, whereas it could easily happen in practice. Because this question is in the form of a problem, the answer should take the same form: do not answer it as if it were an essay.

- Policy adopted by Cabinet or Cabinet committee.

- Whips' control of party in Commons.

- Disputes between Lords and Commons.

- Influencing the media: 'spin'.

:Ọ: Suggested answer

The British Prime Minister has a considerable range of powers and means of influence available to ensure the adoption of his or her policies. Indeed, it is often argued that the British system of government has become one of Prime Ministerial government. But there are constraints on the Prime Minister's powers, and even determined Prime Ministers may find that they fail to ensure the adoption of their preferred policies.

(a) The most formal means available to have the scheme adopted as government policy is to have it agreed in a meeting of the Cabinet. This will ensure that all ministers are bound, by the convention of collective Cabinet responsibility, to support it in public, whatever their private misgivings. Any minister who feels unable to support the policy must, by convention, resign. It would be most unlikely in practice that any such matter would be raised in Cabinet without extensive prior consultations with the ministers directly affected, such as those at the Department for Education and Skills. To avoid a possibly embarrassing defeat, the Prime Minister is sure to take soundings generally among his colleagues, so that he can take the matter to Cabinet having already satisfied himself of a majority there.

Most issues are not, however, dealt with by the full Cabinet, because of pressure of business, but are instead referred to Cabinet committees. There are both permanent and temporary committees and sub-committees. Peter, as Prime Minister, selects the membership and remit of all these bodies. It would therefore be possible for him to refer this scheme to a committee whose membership was carefully selected to provide a majority in favour of it. The Chancellor of the Exchequer and the Secretary of State for Education and Skills would have to be members, but Peter would have a fairly free hand in selecting the other members. It would be to Peter's advantage to chair the committee himself, giving extra power to guide the discussion.

It is accepted practice that, if matters have been decided by a Cabinet committee, they will not be discussed again by the full Cabinet. Only if there is disagreement within the committee, or the matter proves to be one of extreme sensitivity, will it be referred up to a Cabinet meeting. It is therefore quite likely that this scheme could be adopted as government policy without the involvement of some members of the Cabinet, who will none the less remain bound by collective Cabinet responsibility. This gives rise to the possiblity that a minister who feels he or she is being bypassed may resign, thereby revealing splits in the Government which the Opposition can exploit. The resignation of Michael Heseltine over the Westland affair is an example of this. But it is only with the greatest reluctance that most ministers would take such a step, as resignation is often a path to political oblivion.

Once adopted as government policy, the scheme must be supported in public by all members of the government, down to the most junior Parliamentary Private Secretary. The civil servants in the Treasury and Department for Education and Skills will be instructed to prepare the necessary legislation and administrative procedures, instructions which they are bound to obey. Normally such a major proposal would be announced in the Queen's Speech at the opening of the next session of Parliament, but the government may propose legislation at any time.

Peter is justified in feeling that gaining the adoption of his scheme as government policy is the most important step in its progress.

(**b**) The next hurdle is the passage of the necessary legislation through Parliament. Because this is a measure affecting taxation, it will be introduced in the House of Commons, where the government has a comfortable majority. Peter need not therefore be particularly concerned about the attitude of the opposition parties; indeed, vehement criticism of the Bill by them may well encourage the loyal support of his own back-bench MPs.

The task of getting the legislation through lies with the whips, who must ensure a disciplined turnout of MPs to vote on the measure. After the formal introduction and first reading, the second reading provides the opportunity for the House of Commons to debate and vote on the principle of the Bill. Defeat at second reading will force the withdrawal of the Bill, but this is a rare occurrence. The whips will inform Peter in advance of potential revolts, and any measure likely to be defeated will be withdrawn for amendment before the government suffers the embarrassment of defeat. After second reading, the Bill will be referred to a standing committee for detailed examination. The government will have a majority on this committee proportionate to its overall majority, so it should have no difficulty in getting the Bill safely through this stage, though it may have to accept any amendments on which its own supporters insist. If the Opposition parties attempt to delay the bill by filibustering, the government can ask the House of Commons to pass a programme motion restricting the time allowed for discussion. Once the committee stage has been completed, the government will have to decide whether to accept any amendments made in committee, or to get them reversed by a vote of the whole House. Finally the vote on third reading will complete the Bill's passage through the House of Commons.

The whips' careful use of persuasion, cajolery and coercion will normally ensure the passage of all legislation to which the government is committed. But back-bench revolts have become more common in recent years, as it is no longer the convention that any defeat will force the government to resign. Only defeat on a vote of confidence, announced as such, will force a resignation, as in 1979. It is possible for a

Prime Minister to make a vote on a particular piece of legislation into a matter of confidence in order to demand his party's support, but this may be regarded as a sign of weakness not strength, forcing back-bench MPs to choose between their beliefs and their political survival.

The Bill will then be sent to the House of Lords, where a similar pattern of readings will be followed. Voting in the House of Lords is somewhat unpredictable because there are many cross-bench Lords without a fixed party allegiance. This Bill is likely to arouse the keen interest of those Lords interested in higher education, and the final result of the votes cannot be predicted. The House of Lords has shown itself more willing in recent years to reject government legislation and, since the removal of the hereditary peers, has announced that it will no longer observe the Salisbury convention, under which it would not obstruct legislation intended to fulfil manifesto commitments. It is therefore possible that the government may have to resort to the Parliament Acts procedure, as was done for the European Parliamentary Elections Act 1999. If the Bill were to contain no provisions except for the tax, it would be classified as a Money Bill, and the Lords could delay it for only one month. If, as is more likely, it contains other matters as well, the Lords can delay it for one session. On the other hand, the Lords may feel satisfied with amending the Bill, which will then have to return to the Commons. The government will then have to decide whether to accept the amendments or to try and persuade the Lords to concede. Only if the Bill has been passed by both Houses in identical form can it proceed to Royal Assent and become law within one session.

(c) In trying to get his scheme accepted by the general public, Peter's greatest asset is the opportunity to influence the media. The Prime Minister has a press office, which meets regularly with the journalists accredited to the Lobby to brief them on government business. All the arguments in favour of the scheme would be advanced and opposing arguments rebutted, and it could be expected that some at least of this material would find its way into the press. It is vital for any Prime Minister to cultivate good relations with the media but attempts to manipulate it have been subject to considerable criticism in recent years.

It is likely that this scheme will provoke many individuals to write to their MPs, especially as its effects will be felt most strongly by the articulate and educated. It will therefore be desirable for all MPs of the government party to be supplied with material suitable for explaining and justifying the scheme to their constituents, thus keeping both the MPs and their constituents happy.

It may be that the scheme will provoke protest and demonstrations from students, but these can probably be ignored and are as likely to turn public opinion in favour of the scheme as against it. This is particularly true where protests turn violent. Even the demonstrations against the community charge or poll tax played a limited role in forcing the government to abolish it. In the last resort, it must be remembered that there are as many as four years to go before the next general election. Even if the tax is unpopular Peter can reasonably hope that it will have ceased to be a matter of major concern by then.

The above discussion demonstrates clearly that, once a measure has been adopted as government policy, its chances of becoming law are very high. Very little government-sponsored legislation is rejected by Parliament, and public opinion can rarely be mobilised so as to prevent the government pursuing its policies. The greatest problems for the Prime Minister lie in getting the initial agreement of his or her colleagues, but even here the influence of a determined Prime Minister can be hard to resist.

Q Question 3

What is meant by the convention of individual ministerial responsibility? How has it been affected by recent developments in Parliament and government?

Commentary

The first part of this question is deceptively simple. Although it is possible to give a brief restatement of the traditional doctrine, that alone would not be sufficient. A deeper analysis is needed, identifying the difficulty in establishing how ministers are supposed to behave, with examples drawn, if possible, from recent practice. The second part of the question gives the student useful hints as to where to look for changes. In Parliament, the reform of select committees has made an impact. In government, changes to the structure and organisation of departments are making it increasingly difficult to apply the traditional doctrine.

- Government accountable to Commons.

- Questioning ministers.

- Questioning civil servants.

- Questioning Next Steps agencies.

☽ Suggested answer

Traditional constitutional doctrine states that each minister is responsible to Parliament for the work of his or her department. This is intended to ensure that government departments are ultimately accountable, through Parliament, to the electorate. Such accountability is essential in a democracy, and is an elaboration of the general accountability of the government as a whole to Parliament. It is well established that the ultimate sanction to enforce this is the power of the House of Commons to force a government to resign by passing a vote of no confidence in it. Similarly, a minister who loses the confidence of the House of Commons has to resign, though in practice, a Prime Minister who knew that a minister was facing defeat in such a vote would require an immediate resignation before any vote occurred. But how the doctrine operates in less extreme circumstances is more difficult to ascertain.

The classic instance used to describe the doctrine of ministerial responsibility is the Crichel Down affair. Civil servants in the Ministry of Agriculture refused to honour a promise made to a landowner when his land was compulsorily purchased for military use, that he or his heirs would be given the opportunity to repurchase the land when it was no longer needed. There was no suggestion of corruption or other gross impropriety; rather it was a plain case of maladministration. The minister was not directly involved, but when a critical report was published, he felt obliged to resign, being the person ultimately responsible. This course of action was praised as particularly honourable.

In the 40 years since then, it has become clear that this was not a typical example of the doctrine of ministerial responsibility in operation. Rather, it was the unpopularity of the government's whole agricultural policy which led to the loss of back-bench support for the minister. The only other example since then of a ministerial resignation for departmental, rather than personal fault is the resignation of Lord Carrington and his junior ministers from the Foreign Office when Argentina invaded the Falkland Islands. Here, the apparent misjudgments by the Foreign Office could be said to have cost many lives, making it infinitely more serious than the average case of faulty administration.

What then does the doctrine of ministerial responsibility amount to in normal circumstances? Its starting point is the right of MPs to question each minister about the activities of the department and the corresponding duty of the minister to answer. Ever since all Crown servants other than ministers were excluded from the House of Commons at the beginning of the eighteenth century, the minister has been the only person available for questioning. When government activity was much less, it was reasonable to expect ministers to know what was going on in their departments. But even as government activity increased, it remained the expectation that the minister should be able and willing, given reasonable notice, to answer questions on any aspect of the department's work. This provided one of the principal means by which an individual could seek redress for grievances, as the complainant in the Crichel Down affair eventually did. Many such grievances would be dealt with without publicity, and even those which did reach the floor of the House of Commons would conclude with an explanation, an apology and a promise of redress from the minister, without the issue of resignation even being raised.

From the 1960s onwards, other means of redress were developed, to supplement or even replace the traditional method. In 1967, the Parliamentary Commissioner for Administration, or Ombudsman, was introduced, providing an alternative course of action for an MP whose constituent was aggrieved by an act of maladministration.

As the PCA's reports and recommendations are almost always accepted in full by the government, and appropriate redress offered, there is no need to invoke the doctrine of ministerial responsibility, and no question of resignation is ever raised. The other development was the immense growth of judicial review, which provides a means of redress wholly outside the political process. A finding by the High Court that a department had acted ultra vires may provoke the Opposition to derision, but is not taken as a ground for threatening the minister's political survival. It is possible to imagine that in extreme circumstances, a judicial ruling could bring the minister's future into question. In the case of Re M [1994] 1 AC 377, it was held that government ministers could be punished for contempt of court; if such a punishment were ever imposed, the minister would surely be forced to resign.

It was stated above that one of the bases for the doctrine of ministerial responsibility was the fact that only the minister was present in Parliament to be questioned. That remains true for questions on the floor of the House. But select committees have the right to call civil servants to give evidence, and the departmental select committees use this right extensively. There can be problems; although the committee can in theory insist on the civil servant's presence, the minister may refuse permission and attend in person instead. In practice, the committee would have to be satisfied with that. Civil servants who do attend are expected to obey a memorandum of guidance from the Cabinet Office which restricts the answers they can give on sensitive issues. If they refuse to answer particular questions, the committee cannot force them to do so. In spite of these problems, it has become common to see civil servants appearing before select committees, and MPs are finding this form of scrutiny in some ways more satisfactory and effective than questioning the minister in the traditional way. No longer is the minister the only person who can be called to account by Parliament.

The development which is likely to have the greatest impact on the traditional doctrine of ministerial responsibility is the reorganisation of the government under the Next Steps programme. This was intended to improve the management and efficiency of the government, by converting those parts of the civil service which provide services to the public into separate agencies, each under the control of a chief executive. Ministers, assisted by a central core of civil servants, would lay down the general policy for each agency, leaving the agency to put that policy into operation.

Concern was expressed as to how these new arrangements could be reconciled with the traditional understanding of ministerial responsibility, especially as no institutional provision was made for any new form of parliamentary accountability. But some new procedures have developed. As agencies were established, ministers developed the practice of replying to parliamentary questions about the work of agencies by simply informing MPs that they had passed the matter to the chief executive, who would answer the MP by letter. MPs were concerned that this procedure provided inadequate scrutiny, in particular because such replies would be private. After a long campaign by MPs, such replies are published in Hansard, like written answers from ministers, making them matters of formal record. This does, however, carry the implication that the minister is not responsible or accountable for the operations conducted by the agency, as he or she would have been before the reorganisation.

To follow up a complaint relating to an agency, the MP has limited scope for raising the matter on the floor of the House. It is, however, possible for the chief executive of an agency to be called before a select committee, and this is becoming the normal practice where a large number of complaints are giving cause for concern. The Child Support Agency is an example where the relevant select committee conducted a thorough investigation. If there is direct accountability of the agency to Parliament by means of the detailed scrutiny by a select committee, the responsibility of the minister becomes almost irrelevant.

Major difficulties remain, however, in establishing accountability where matters fall between the clearly operational, with which the minister is not concerned, and the matters of high policy for which the minister alone remains accountable. The situation could become as difficult as that which used to exist in the nationalised industries, where ministers were not accountable for the day-to-day running of the industry, but were consistently interfering in what should have been managerial decisions.

In conclusion, it is clear that the shouts of 'Resign!' which greet any minister whose department has been at fault are little more than a traditional ritual. Crichel Down, far from being the typical example, is in fact unique. It is difficult to imagine any circumstances in which a minister would feel an obligation to follow that precedent in the absence of personal fault. It would perhaps be desirable if more attention were paid to improve the means by which Parliament scrutinises the executive directly, rather than trying to revive a doctrine which took shape in a more leisured age, when the minister read and even wrote his own despatches. The arrival of executive agencies may provide the opportunity for the development of new means of scrutiny, if Parliament wishes to perform this function more effectively.

Q Question 4

Consider the following situations in the light of the convention of ministerial responsibility.

(a) In his Budget speech, the Chancellor of the Exchequer announced his intention to impose VAT on books and newspapers. Twenty government back-bench MPs have told the whips that they will vote against this proposal, and if necessary against the whole Budget. The government's overall majority is 15.

(b) Julia, the Minister of Transport, proposed to the Cabinet that extra safety barriers be erected along all elevated sections of motorways, but her proposal was rejected on grounds of cost. Last week, 40 people died when a coach crashed off a motorway, an accident which the safety barriers would have prevented. Julia told Boot, a journalist, about the rejection of her proposal, and he has published an article blaming the rest of the Cabinet for putting lives at risk.

(c) Fred, the Foreign Secretary, informed the House of Commons two years ago that he would be adopting a new, ethical foreign policy. It has now been discovered that the Foreign Office has being negotiating for a year to surrender a small British colony to a neighbouring dictatorship. No information about this has ever been given to the House of Commons.

(d) Smith, a junior minister in the Department of Transport, crashed his car on the M4 motorway. PCs Ford and Austin attended the accident. Smith was breathalysed, but the result was negative. Smith was slightly injured as was his passenger Jones, a businessman whose financial dealings are currently under investigation by the Department of Trade and Industry. PCs Ford and Austin completed reports on the accident, but were then told by their superiors that instructions 'from on high' were to remove all records of it.

Commentary

This problem covers various different aspects of ministerial responsibility. The student's first task will be to identify and explain the particular facet of the convention that may apply in each case, being careful to describe and illustrate how the convention actually operates in practice. An awareness of political realities, and even a familiarity with the attitudes of the tabloid press, will be most useful.

- Loss of vote of confidence.

- Collective responsibility; 'all saying the same thing'.

- Individual responsibility for self and department.

- Personal misconduct.

⚪ Suggested answer

(a) The convention of ministerial responsibility requires above all that the government must have the confidence of the House of Commons. If it loses that confidence it must resign, either to be replaced by another government in which the House of Commons does have confidence or, more usually, to cause a general election. The issue raised in this problem is to identify the circumstances in which a government defeat in the Commons will be taken as an indication of such a fatal loss of confidence. It was thought at one time that any defeat on a major issue would demonstrate a loss of confidence and force the government's resignation, but over the last 20 years this has changed. It is clear that any defeat on a vote of confidence, moved as such by government or Opposition, will make the government resign. This occurred in 1979, when the Labour government lost a vote of confidence and immediately called a general election. This government could adopt the high risk strategy of making the vote on VAT into a vote of confidence, if it felt sure that this would force the 20 rebel back-benchers to support it. But if the 20 were to persist in their rebellion, the government would, if defeated, have no choice but to resign.

Defeat on one aspect of the Budget would not in itself force the government to resign; it would merely cause political embarrassment. In recent years, a government has been forced to rescind an increase in VAT on fuel, without any threat to its survival in office. Defeat on the entire Budget, however, presents a more complex problem. Traditionally, the votes on the Queen's Speech and the Budget were seen as being inherently votes of confidence, but it is not clear whether this is still the case. However, it can be argued that it is both a political and a legal necessity for the government to get its financial proposals accepted by the House of Commons. A Finance Act must be passed each year. Were the Budget to be rejected, the only way the government could survive would be to propose and have passed a vote of confidence, and then to introduce a new and acceptable Budget. This would be a political humiliation for the Chancellor of the Exchequer which he or she could hardly survive, but it would be possible for the government as a whole to claim that it retained the confidence of the House of Commons just enough to enable it to continue in office.

(**b**) The doctrines of collective ministerial responsibility and Cabinet secrecy require all ministers to support government policy and to refrain from revealing discussion in Cabinet. If a minister has a fundamental disagreement with the rest of the Cabinet, and is not prepared to accept government policy, that minister must resign. Robin Cook was considered to have acted in a principled way when he resigned because he could not support the invasion of Iraq without United Nations approval. There was criticism of Clare Short's failure to resign after expressing similar opinions.

But in reality, in most governments, differences of opinion between ministers will be publicly known and discussed in the media. This may be tolerated for a time, but eventually, as happened with Clare Short, the Prime Minister's patience with dissent will be exhausted. Of course, if Boot maintains the confidentiality of his conversation with Julia, and it may well be in his interests to do so in the hope of future revelations, it is unlikely that it could be proved that Julia is the source of the story. She may therefore get away with the breach of Cabinet secrecy.

It can be argued that it is not justifiable to describe collective ministerial responsi-bility as a convention, given that ministers do not appear to feel an obligation to suppress all feelings of dissent. Rather they will tread carefully and express their views in carefully coded language. But there is a recognition of the political reality that an openly divided Cabinet cannot hope to survive and few ministers will take a disagreement so far as to resign, or to express dissent so openly that the Prime Minister has no option but to dismiss them.

(**c**) According to the convention of individual ministerial responsibility a minister is accountable to Parliament for the activities of his department. This gives Parliament the right to question him and imposes on him an obligation to answer. The minister is the only person available for Parliament to question, at least on the floor of the House of Commons. If the minister cannot satisfy MPs, particularly those from his own party, he may lose the confidence of the House of Commons. In extreme circumstances, the House of Commons could force the resignation of a minister by passing a vote of censure against him.

It is spelled out, in both the Ministerial Code and in a resolution of the House of Commons, that a minister must not mislead Parliament. If it were to be shown that the Foreign Secretary had knowingly misinformed Parliament by, for example, denying that any such negotiations were taking place, that would be regarded as a grave offence and it is almost certain that Fred would have to resign. Giving Parliament misleading information by mistake may, however, be forgiven, if the minister admits the error as soon as it is discovered and apologises. For example, a junior Home Office minister assured the House of Commons that pregnant female prisoners were not kept fettered while in labour, having been given that assurance by civil servants. When it was discovered that the civil servants had been wrong, she apologised immediately to the House and the apology was accepted.

It is now considered acceptable for a minister to deny personal knowledge of and responsibility for purely operational matters within their department. Successive Home Secretaries have got away with denying responsibility for prison escapes. Could Fred deny all knowledge of the negotiations? They were of such importance and sensitivity that the Foreign Secretary either must have known or should have known if he were running his department effectively. His defence in these circumstances may be to assert that he has not actively misled Parliament, but has merely failed to keep MPs informed. The Scott Inquiry into Arms to Iraq revealed the widespread attitude in government that information should not be disclosed if at all possible, in spite of the implications for parliamentary scrutiny of the executive. What is particularly interesting about that affair is that those ministers who were found to have misled Parliament were protected by their Prime Minister and party. The vote on the Scott Inquiry was treated as a vote of confidence in the whole government. Back-bench MPs as usual fell into line behind the three line whip and the government ministers survived by one vote.

In this problem, Fred may claim that he has not really misled Parliament or that his failure to keep MPs informed was due to the delicacy of the negotiations, or that there is no real contradiction with the ethical foreign policy. Whether these excuses are acceptable will be determined in practice by the attitude of the Prime Minister and the party. If the government has a loyal majority in the House of Commons who are prepared to back him, Fred can ignore calls for his resignation from the Opposition. But if the government feels that public opinion needs a scapegoat, Fred may find himself sacrificed.

(**d**) Although personal misconduct by government ministers will generally lead to public and media criticism, it is unlikely that the mere fact that Smith has crashed his car would endanger his position, even in the Department of Transport. There is no suggestion that he is particularly culpable; he had not been drinking and no one has been seriously injured. Much more serious, however, is the question of why Jones was a passenger in his car. Any suggestion of financial impropriety is likely to be regarded by the public and media as very reprehensible, and various ministers have been forced to resign for such reasons.

In this problem there is the further suggestion that someone in authority is attempting to cover up what happened. If it were merely shown that the police and the Crown Prosecution Service had decided, in the exercise of their lawful discretion, not to prosecute Smith for any offence, there would be no problem. But removing police records is a serious matter, and any suggestion that there has been political interference in the legal process would provoke public outrage. If this were to become known, Smith, and any other minister involved, would be forced to resign, and so a scandal might endanger the whole government. A cover-up is always regarded as unforgivable, however minor the initial offence.

Further reading

Bradley, A. and Ewing, K. *Constitutional & Administrative Law*, 13th edn (Longman, 2003), chs 7, 13.

Turpin, C. *British Government & Constitution*, 5th edn (Butterworths, 2002), ch 7.

Loveland, I. *Constitutional Law*, 3rd edn (Butterworths, 2003), ch 9.

Woodhouse, D. *Ministers and Parliament* (OUP, 1994).

Hennessy, P. *The Hidden Wiring* (INDIGO, 1996), chs 3 and 4.

Q&A 7

The Human Rights Act 1998

Introduction

Although the Labour government that won the 1997 General Election had promised, in its election manifesto, to enact the European Convention on Human Rights into British law, the speed with which this was done took many by surprise. It instantly rendered out of date the debate, found in most public law textbooks, upon whether the UK should enact a modern Bill of Rights or not. Now we have adopted an existing human rights treaty, which will serve as a Bill of Rights and which came into force on 2 October 2000. In a sense this is nothing new, since the European Convention on Human Rights has existed since 1951. It was issued by the Council of Europe, *not the European Union*, which is a common mistake made not just by students, but by the media and even some judges as well! The UK was a founder member of the Council which was established, in 1949, to promote democracy, human rights and the rule of law in a Europe devastated by war. Britain played a leading role in drafting the Convention, but it was not then thought necessary to give it legal force in British law as it was considered that the rights protected in the Convention were already respected in this country.

Despite this, it was always possible to enforce the Convention on an international level. Any of the 45 Member States could bring a complaint of breach of human rights against any of the other members, alleging that that state had not respected the rights laid down in the Convention. This procedure is rarely used, but the Convention also allows individual 'victims' the right to bring a complaint against the state that they claim has infringed their human rights. Nowadays these complaints go directly to the European Court of Human Rights, which is an international court staffed by judges from the 45 Member States, sitting in Strasburg. (Note that this is not to be confused with the quite separate European Court of Justice, which is the court of the European Union and sits in Luxembourg.) The European Court of Human Rights will rule upon whether there has been any infringement of human rights and may order the offending state to award compensation to the victim. Member States, including the UK, have a very good record for obeying these judgments, which often mean that domestic law has to be changed. Over the years the European Court of Human Rights has decided over 1200 cases, which means that there is a fair amount of guidance upon what the Convention actually means in practice.

All that the Human Rights Act 1998 does is provide that the 'Convention rights' can be enforced in British courts. British legislation must be interpreted in a way which is consistent with the rights granted under the Convention. All public authorities must also act in a way which is compatible with the Convention. As 'public authorities' includes courts, this means that case law must be interpreted to 'take into account' the cases decided by the European Court of Human Rights.

So what would an examiner expect you to know about all this? At the very least you would need to know what the Human Rights Act actually says. It would also be helpful to know the procedure to make a complaint to the European Court of Human Rights, which has been mentioned above. Even after the Human Rights Act came into force this procedure still exists and someone dissatisfied with the British courts might choose to go there. Even more important, it is essential to have some idea of which rights are actually protected in the 'Articles' of the Convention and some idea of the major cases that tell us what those rights actually mean. A more difficult question is the discussion essay on what difference the Act and/or the Convention will make to the protection of rights in this country. Of course no one can know the answer to that yet, but armed with some *factual* knowledge about the Act, Convention and case law any student should be able to at least offer some sort of answer.

Q Question 1

The Government is alarmed by the activities of the Blue Party. A leading government minister has been assassinated and bombs have been exploded in various government offices. The Blue Party has not claimed responsibility for these acts, but the Government blames them. Parliament enacts a Suppression of Terrorism Act which (a) makes the Blue Party an illegal organisation, (b) makes members of it subject to arrest and detention (c) makes possession of Blue Party literature a criminal offence, and (d) allows the police to intercept the communications of suspected members.

The police intercept Joanna's telephone calls, because they suspect that she is a leading member of the Blue Party. Her house is searched and Blue Party literature is found. She and other suspected Blue Party members are detained in a disused army camp, which is unheated and where they are fed a diet of bread, water and porridge. Joanna is not allowed any letters in or out and she is not permitted to contact her family, friends or lawyer.

Advise Joanna upon whether her human rights have been infringed.

- Only a 'victim' may bring a Human Rights case.

- Human rights may be restricted to protect national security.

- The concept of proportionality.

- All restrictions on human rights must be prescribed by law.

- Only a court may deprive a person of their liberty.

- The right to a fair trial requires legal representation.

- In addition to using the Human Rights Act 1998, the victim may still complain to the European Court of Human Rights.

Commentary

This is obviously a problem question, which many students prefer, in that the 'answer' seems more clear-cut than in a discussion essay. The facts may seem rather fanciful, but all of them are inspired by real events that have occurred in the UK, although not all at the same time to the same person! The question is just a vehicle to help you spot the relevant cases and the appropriate Articles of the European Convention. For instance, telephone tapping should remind you of well-known cases like *Malone* v *United Kingdom* (1984) 7 EHRR 14 and Article 8, the right to a private life.

So is it just a question of spotting the 'clues' in the question and responding with the correct Article number or case name? Well no, just as in areas of the common law it is not enough just to recite information, you need to show that you understand it enough to apply it. So you would need to explain *why* you thought our example above was a breach of Article 8 and show how it resembled *Malone's* case. Also, this question is specifically asking *which* of Joanna's human rights have been infringed. It is not asking for an account of what is in the Human Rights Act, nor is it asking for the procedure by which applications are made to the European Court of Human Rights. You actually need to know what the Convention says and how it has been interpreted to answer this question.

☀ Suggested answer

It seems fairly clear that there have been infringements of the European Convention on Human Rights, in that the Suppression of Terrorism Act appears to restrict rights without sufficient justification. This is not, however, enough by itself, because neither the European Court of Human Rights nor the British courts deal in theoretical cases. Under Article 34 of the Convention and s. 7 of the Human Rights Act 1998, there must be a 'victim' of the breach of human rights, who is able to bring a case. There is no real definition of 'victim', but, for instance, in *Dudgeon* v *United Kingdom* (1981) 4 EHRR 149, the mere threat of prosecution and the intrusion into his private life was enough to make him a victim. Joanna has certainly been personally affected by the provisions of the Terrorism Act, so she would be able to pursue a case. So let us see to which infringements Joanna can point.

Making a political party illegal would seem to contravene Article 11, which guarantees the right to freedom of association. The rights in Articles 8 to 11 can, however, be restricted on various grounds. In Article 11.2 the restrictions most relevant to Joanna's case are 'the interests of national security or public safety, for the prevention of disorder or crime . . .'. It would be up to the British government to prove that there was, for instance, a threat to national security posed by the Blue Party. This approach can be seen in cases such as *Brannigan and McBride* v *United Kingdom* (1994) 17 EHRR 539, where the European Court of Human Rights accepted that there was a terrorist problem in Northern Ireland. In contrast, the English courts accepted that it was permissible under the Terrorism Act 2000 to require an alleged member of a terrorist organisation to prove that they were not a terrorist in *Attorney-General's Reference (No. 4 of 2002)* [2003] *The Times*, 1 April. This did not contravene the presumption of innocence under Article 6, nor Freedom of Expression under Article 10, even though it reverses the normal burden of proof. Under this approach, Joanna might have to prove that she was *not* a terrorist. So it looks as though Joanna might receive a different response, depending upon which court, European Court of Human Rights or English, from which she seeks a remedy.

Restrictions on rights must not be more excessive than the problem demands. Articles 8 to 11 have a fairly similar wording, as Article 11.2 has it: 'No restrictions shall be placed on the exercise of these rights other than such as are prescribed by law and are necessary in a democratic society . . .'. This is known as the concept of 'proportionality'. For example in *Tolstoy* v *United Kingdom* (1995) 20 EHRR 442, it was acceptable to have libel laws restricting freedom of expression under Article 10, because a restriction 'for the protection of the reputation or rights of others' is mentioned in Article 10.2. However, to give a jury the uncontrolled right to decide upon the level of damages, here £1,500,000 for a libel with very limited publication, went much further than was necessary to protect the reputation of the libelled person. So, it is submitted that it would be necessary for the government to prove that the Blue Party actually is a 'terrorist' organisation to justify banning it.

Any restrictions on rights must also be 'prescribed by law', as we have seen above. There must be clear and defined laws that the affected person can identify. As we shall see this has sometimes caused problems for the UK, but, here, the Suppression of Terrorism Act seems clear enough.

'Telephone tapping' is a good example of this. On the face of it, the interception of Joanna's telephone calls is a breach of Article 8, 'respect for correspondence', but as with Article 11 this right can be restricted on grounds such as 'national security', public safety', 'disorder or crime'. Again, the government would have to possess some evidence that listening to the calls of persons such as Joanna would actually help to prevent crime or protect national security. There would have to be clear laws to regulate the 'tapping' which has caused problems for the UK in cases such as *Malone* v *United Kingdom* (1984) 7 EHRR 14 and *Halford* v *United Kingdom* (1998) 24 EHRR 523, where Britain was found to have no laws regulating telephone tapping! The Suppression of Terrorism Act appears to have provisions governing this, but there is no mention of allowing the aggrieved person an 'appeal' to an independent authority, which was held to be very important in *Malone* v *United Kingdom*.

Search of the home, like telephone tapping, would also seem to contravene Article 8 as 'Everyone has the right to respect for his private and family life, his home and his correspondence'. However, as with telephone tapping, search can be made if there is a justification like crime or national security etc., there are clear laws regulating the matter and, very importantly, there is some sort of judicial protection, such as a judge or magistrate issuing a warrant; *Chappell* v *United Kingdom* (1990) 12 EHRR 1

Under the Terrorism Act 2000, the police have the power to search any pedestrian or vehicle on the street. There is no need for any suspicion of an offence or any warrant. The English courts upheld the legality of this in *R (Gillan)* v *Commissioner of Police for the Metropolis* [2003] *The Times*, 5 November. It is to be hoped that the UK courts would follow *Chappell* (ibid.) and treat the search of a home as a more serious intrusion into 'private life'.

Whether there is any justification for seizing the Blue Party literature is a different matter. Freedom of expression under Article 10 is deemed to be a very important right as stated in the well-known case of *Sunday Times* v *United Kingdom* (1980) 2 EHRR 245 and any restrictions would need to be carefully justified. The needs of 'national security' are not enough by themselves as shown in *The Observer and The Guardian* v *United Kingdom* (1992) 14 EHRR 153, if it is no longer 'necessary in a democratic society' to protect those needs. Even the fact that information, or a document, might reveal evidence of a crime may not be enough to justify disclosure or seizure as seen in *Goodwin* v *United Kingdom* (1996) 22 EHRR 123, where a journalist was allowed to protect his sources. The UK government would probably have to show that the 'Blue Party literature' was likely to contain evidence of specific crimes in order to justify seizure.

Detention without trial is a clear breach of Article 5.4 as the lawfulness of detention must be decided 'speedily by a court'. Even four days detention without access to the courts was deemed unacceptable in *Brogan* v *United Kingdom* (1988) 11 EHRR 117. The conditions in the disused army camp are also likely to be held a breach of the Convention. Article 3 states that: 'No one shall be subjected to torture or to inhuman or degrading treatment or punishment'. The treatment meted out to Joanna seems less severe than the beatings, 'wall-standing', deprivation of sleep and 'white noise' in *Ireland* v *United Kingdom* (1978) 2 EHRR 25 and these were held not severe enough to be 'torture', but only 'inhuman and degrading', a lesser category. Since that case, though, the European Court of Human Rights has ruled that generally poor standards for the detention of prisoners can be a breach of Article 3. A good example would be *Soering* v *United Kingdom* (1989) 11 EHRR 439, where the conditions on 'death-row' in US prisons were held to be 'inhuman and degrading'. The conditions in the disused army camp, although rather different to 'death-row' also seem unreasonably harsh and would probably breach Article 3.

Denying Joanna all contact with the outside world would seem to be a breach of Article 8.1 for 'Everyone has the right to respect for his private and family life, has home and his correspondence'. As we have seen, Article 8.2 allows some restrictions on this right for the prevention of 'disorder or crime' or 'national security', but it is hard to see how such an all-encompassing restriction could be proportional to any threat posed by Joanna's contact with the outside world. Although some restrictions on the correspondence of prisoners could be justified as in *Boyle and Rice* v *United Kingdom* (1988) 10 EHRR 425, it is clear that any interference that goes beyond a legitimate aim, such as the prevention of crime, is not acceptable; *Foxley* v *United Kingdom* (2001) 31 EHRR 637. Prevention of access to legal advice is also a serious infringement, not just of Article 8, but also Article 6, the right to a fair trial, because legal advice is an essential preparation in making a proper defence or preparing an action. Britain for instance has lost a number of cases, involving prisoners, on this point going back to *Golder* v *United Kingdom* (1975) 1 EHRR 524 and *Silver* v *United Kingdom* (1981) 3 EHRR 475. Even delay in access to a lawyer infringes Article 6 as in *Magee* v *United Kingdom*, (2001) 31 EHRR 35, so a complete denial of contact would clearly be unacceptable.

Although the facts of the question do not say so, it is possible that the UK government would have made a 'derogation', under Article 15, in these circumstances of a terrorist threat. This would enable a state to suspend some of the Articles of the Convention, but not the more fundamental human rights such as the 'Right to life' in Article 2, the prohibition of slavery in Article 4, the prohibition on retrospective laws in Article 7 or, relevant to Joanna's case, the 'Prohibition of torture' in Article 3. For instance, in *Brannigan and McBride* v *United Kingdom* (1994) 17 EHRR 539, it was permissible to detain terrorist suspects without trial, for a short period, because the UK had made a derogation from Article 5. In 2001 the UK government made a derogation to Article 5, in order to allow the detention of aliens, suspected of international terrorism, without trial under s. 23 of the Anti-Terrorism, Crime and Security Act 2001. The legality of this was upheld by the UK courts in *A & Others* v *Secretary of State for the Home Department* [2003] 1 AC 153. For this case to be followed though, the UK would have to produce evidence to the court that there was a 'public emergency threatening the life of the nation' and the court would have to be satisfied that the emergency justified the restrictions imposed upon human rights. On our facts there is no evidence that the Blue Party is actually responsible for the terrorist acts. Similarly, derogation does not mean that all human rights protections can be abandoned. In *Brannigan*, suspects were still allowed to contact their lawyers, but in contrast Joanna is not. Lastly, the state must keep the Secretary-General of the Council of Europe fully informed and there is no evidence that the UK has done this.

Joanna would need to commence any legal action in a British court, because Article 35.1 requires local remedies to be exhausted first. Although s. 3 of the Human Rights Act 1998 requires all British legislation to be interpreted in a way that is compatible with the Convention, it is difficult to see how this would be possible with the Suppression of Terrorism Act. All the Court could do is issue a 'Declaration of Incompatibility' and then it would be up to Parliament whether it wanted to amend or repeal the offending parts of the Terrorism Act.

From the few terrorist cases so far, it does not seem that Joanna would have much success in the UK courts, so after she has lost her case at first instance, she may as well petition the European Court of Human Rights. The European Court would certainly find in Joanna's favour, in view of the extensive breaches of the Convention we have discussed. Then the Council of Europe and other Member States would put pressure on Britain to release Joanna, if still detained, and repeal the Suppression of Terrorism Act. The court might order the UK government to pay her compensation as well for the injuries she has suffered.

Q Question 2

What effect has the Human Rights Act 1998 had upon English law?
  Discuss.

Commentary

Despite the Act only being in force for three years there has already been a torrent of court cases and a welter of academic opinion based on its provisions. A good structure for an answer is to go through the most important provisions of the Act and explain their effect. This is not very difficult to do and this is not a very long Act. A good answer though must refer to some of the case law. No student could possibly be familiar with all the cases, but textbooks and your lecturers will give you some guidance on the best examples. Another approach, but not the one taken by the example below is to look at the effect of the Act on just one area of the law. One could look at prisoners' rights; criminal trials, privacy, family law or whatever interests you. This is still an evolving area of law, so watch out for important new cases to give your examination answer something different from other students.

- A tradition of civil liberties in the past.

- Legislation must be interpreted in a way which is compatible with human rights.

- Courts may make a declaration of incompatibility.

- Judicial deference to the legislature and executive.

- It is unlawful for a public authority to act in a way which is incompatible with human rights.

- The Human Rights Act 1998 may also apply in private disputes.

:Ö: Suggested answer

The Human Rights Act 1998 came into force on 2 October 2000 and made it far easier to enforce the European Convention of Human Rights in British courts. There have already been a large number of court decisions that refer to the provisions of the Act. As we will see, although there have been inconsistencies, particularly in the lower courts, a trend of cautious application by the judges has begun to appear.

Before this Act Britain had a tradition of civil liberties, popularised by the late nineteenth-century writer, A.V. Dicey. Citizens did not have rights guaranteed by the constitution, but rather they had liberties, they could do anything that the law did not forbid. Judges would prevent governments taking actions for which they did not have legal power as in the classic case of *Entick* v *Carrington* (1765) 19 St Tr 1030. If any problems remained Parliament would enact legislation to deal with the matter.

Unfortunately, that is not always what happened. Sometimes judges would decide that public authorities, such as the police, could take action against a person, simply because there was no law to say that they could not, as in the telephone tapping case *Malone* v *Metropolitan Police Commissioner* [1979] Ch 344. This is the exact opposite of what Dicey said. Similarly, although Parliament sometimes passes Acts that add to the liberties and rights of the people, as in the Freedom of Information Act 2000, they can also legislate in a way that greatly reduces liberties and adds to the power of the police and similar agencies, as in the Regulation of Investigatory Powers Act 2000.

The United Kingdom has been a party to the European Convention of Human Rights since 1951. Even before the Human Rights Act 1998, the courts of this country could refer to the provisions of the Convention to help interpret ambiguous legislation: *R* v *Home Secretary ex parte Brind* [1991] 1 AC 696. The courts had also said that breaches of the European Convention would encourage them to judicially review a minister's decision and hold it to be unreasonable and therefore illegal: *R* v *Ministry of Defence ex parte Smith* [1995] 4 All ER 427.

The 1998 Act requires more of the courts. Section 3 states that:

> So far as it is possible to do so, primary legislation and subordinate legislation must be read and given effect in a way which is compatible with the convention rights.

The courts have held that this requires them to go much further than ordinary statutory interpretation, where the court might depart from the ordinary language of the statute to avoid absurd consequences. If necessary the judge could read words into a statute that were not there to ensure compliance with the Convention. As Lord Steyn put it in *R* v *A (Complainant's sexual history)* [2002] 1 AC 45:

> The techniques to be used would not only involve the reading down of express language in a statute but also the implication of provisions.

Section 43(1)(c) of the Youth Justice and Criminal Evidence Act 1999 forbids the questioning of a rape complainant about her previous sexual history. The court re-interpeted this to mean that the judge could allow such questioning, if to do otherwise would prevent a fair trial. Similarly, in *R v Offen* [2000] 1 WLR 253, the Court of Appeal looked at s. 2 of the Crime (Sentences) Act 1997, which says that a defendant should be given a life sentence if they commit two serious offences, unless there were 'exceptional circumstances'. The court took account of the European Convention and interpreted it to mean that a life sentence should only be imposed if the defendant was a serious risk to the public. So far a lot of the cases on the Human Rights Act have involved a consideration of the fairness or otherwise of criminal and, sometimes, civil trials, which is covered by Articles 5 and 6 of the Convention. If the court concludes that there is no breach of the Convention, as they often do, then the judges do not have to do any 'interpreting' under s. 3 and the existing law remains: *Poplar Housing* v *Donoghue* [2001] 3 WLR 183.

If there is a clear breach of a Convention Article and the courts cannot interpret the difficulty away under s. 3, the court has no power to declare the Act void. Such a power would conflict with the supremacy of Parliament so, instead, s. 4 allows the courts to make a 'declaration of incompatibility'. The court merely states that the Act of Parliament in question is 'incompatible' with human rights. Only the High Court and above can do this. Then it is up to Parliament to amend or repeal the offending Act, if Parliament chooses to do so. There is a special 'fast-track' procedure to do this under s. 10 of the Human Rights Act 1998, using delegated legislation. This was done after the declaration of incompatibility in *R (on the application of H)* v *London North and East Mental Health Review Tribunal* [2001] QB 1, where the court held that it was a breach of Article 5 to place the burden of proof on a restricted patient to show that he was no longer suffering from a mental disorder warranting detention. In fact, declarations of incompatibility have not been that common and it has not been unusual for a higher court to overturn the declaration of incompatibility made by a lower court, on the grounds that there is no breach of the Convention. Examples of this would be *Matthews* v *Ministry of Defence* [2003] 1 AC 1163, where Crown Immunity prevented a sailor suing the government and *Wilson* v *First County Trust (No. 2)* [2003] 4 All ER 97, where a lender was denied access to the courts. In contrast, the House of Lords made a declaration of incompatibility in *R (Anderson)* v *Home Secretary* [2002] 4 All ER 108, and said that the Home Secretary could not decide the minimum period that a murderer must stay in prison. This was not a fair trial under Article 6, because a trial should be conducted by a judge, not a politician. The government and Parliament have decided upon satisfactory legislation to implement this judgment in the Criminal Justice Act 2003.

In fact the courts have been rather cautious in their application of the Convention. Indeed, Richard Edwards has eloquently argued that a culture of 'judicial deference' has developed, in that judges can be reluctant to interfere with laws enacted by a democratically elected Parliament: 65 (2002) MLR 859. In *R v DPP ex parte Kebilene* [2000] 2 AC 326, a case involving the Prevention of Terrorism Act 2000, the Court of Appeal issued a declaration of incompatibility. The House of Lords disagreed that there was a breach of the Convention and Lord Hope observed that:

> In some circumstances it will be appropriate for the courts to recognise that there is an area of judgment within which the judiciary will defer, on democratic grounds, to the considered opinion of the elected body or person whose act or decision is said to be incompatible with the Convention.

In the far less politically charged *Brown v Stott*, which involved the question of whether a suspected drunk driver had to answer police questions, the Privy Council declined to find a breach of the Convention. Lord Bingham stated:

> Judicial recognition and assertion of the human rights defined in the Convention is not a substitute for the processes of democratic government but a complement to them. ([2001] 2 WLR 817 at 834).

Section 6 of the Human Rights Act 1998 makes it 'unlawful for a public authority to act in a way which is incompatible with a Convention right'. This combined with the succeeding ss 7 and 8, creates a new right of action and allows the 'victim' of a human rights abuse to sue and recover damages among other remedies. As yet it has not been much used and the courts have had some difficulty in deciding what is a public authority, as it is not defined in the Act. In *Parochial Church Council of the Parish of Aston Cantlow and Wilmcote with Billesley v Wallbank* [2003] 3 All ER 1213, the House of Lords ruled that although the Church of England had special links with central government and performed certain public functions, it was essentially a religious organisation and not a public authority. However, in *Regina (KB) v Mental Health Review Tribunal* [2003] 2 All ER 209, the court awarded damages to patients whose hearings had not been held speedily enough. It was held that the damages should equal those of the comparable tort, rather than the lower levels awarded by the European Court of Human Rights. The Court of Appeal, however, has since disagreed with this approach in *Anufrijeva v London Borough of Southwark* [2003] EWCA Civ 1406. There it was held that damages should be a last resort under the Human Rights Act 1998 and the scale of damages for maladministration should be modest.

A much-discussed question is whether the Human Rights Act applies to legal disputes between private individuals or just when a public authority infringes a person's human rights. Section 2 would suggest that the Act could apply to any legal dispute because it states that all courts and tribunals must 'take into account' decisions of the European Court and Commission of Human Rights, whenever a 'Convention' right arises. Also, under s. 6, the courts are themselves public authorities and bound to promote Convention rights. The UK courts have tentatively moved towards using the Convention in private disputes to reinforce claims that already exist in English Law.

In both *Hello!* v *Douglas* [2001] 2 All ER 289 and *Venables & Thompson* v *News Group Newspapers Ltd.* [2001] 1 All ER 908, Convention rights were used to reinforce claims for breach of confidence. The courts have not so far been willing to recognise completely new rights based on the Convention in disputes between private individuals. In *Wainwright* v *Home Office* [2003] UKHL 53, the House of Lords rejected a free-standing right of privacy.

In only three years, the courts have decided hundreds of cases that refer to the Convention, but this has not changed English law as much as might be expected. Most judges, particularly in the higher courts have taken a cautious approach. This was recognised by the House of Lords in *Bellinger* v *Bellinger* [2003] 2 AC 467, where their Lordships refused to recognise the marriage of a male to female transsexual to a man. They were aware that, unlike Parliament, they are not elected and may not represent the democratic wishes of the country. Besides they are not yet used to deciding so many cases dealing with complicated political, social and moral issues and prefer to leave it to the politicians in Parliament.

Q Question 3

What effect has the European Convention of Human Rights had upon the protection of civil liberties in English law?
    Discuss.

Commentary

At first sight this would seem a strange question, because it refers to the past and the Human Rights Act 1998 has only recently been brought into force. The United Kingdom has, however, been a party to the Convention since its beginning, in 1951, and the judgments of the European Court of Human Rights have already had a considerable effect upon English law. Not only has legislation been required, but the courts have adapted the common law to reflect the Convention. The Human Rights Act 1998 should just make this process easier.

The problem with writing an essay like this is that there are so many possible examples, and therefore it is difficult to know what to leave out. It is certainly unwise though to attempt an all-inclusive answer and it is better to be selective and carefully *plan* what you wish to write, concentrating on only a few themes.

* Petition to the European Court of Human Rights in Strasburg.

* Corporal punishment has been abolished.

* Discrimination against homosexuals has been reduced.

* Interference with communications is now regulated by statute.

- Release from prison is now decided by the courts.

- The fairness of criminal trials has been improved.

- Delays in the hearing of asylum and mental health applications have been reduced.

☼ Suggested answer

The European Convention on Human Rights came into existence in 1951, sponsored by the Council of Europe. It had been drafted with the help of British civil servants and the future Lord Chancellor, Lord Kilmuir, and it was intended to extend the same standard of protection of civil liberties that existed in Britain to other European states.

The UK has allowed the right of individual petition since 1966, which allows aggrieved individuals to bring a complaint against the UK. Over sixty successful cases have been brought against the UK and this has led to many changes in English law. The person who considers themselves a 'victim' of a human rights abuse petitions the European Court of Human Rights. They have six months in which to do this and they must first have 'exhausted domestic remedies'. In other words they must have done all that they reasonably could to pursue their case in the British legal system. Before 1998, the petition would be preliminarily investigated by the Commission of Human Rights, but now this is done by the Court itself. The Court issues 'final and binding' judgments, which will explain whether there has been any infringement of the Convention Articles. Although the Court may conclude that some of a states' laws are defective it does not give instructions upon how those laws should be changed. It is up to the state affected to abide by the judgment and make any changes to its laws that are necessary. Enforcement is by international pressure, the disapproval of the Council of Europe and other Convention states. That said, offending states nearly always comply with the judgments of the Court and Britain has a particularly good record in this respect. Let us consider some of the changes in English law precipitated by the European Court of Human Rights.

Corporal punishment, particularly of children, used to be an established part of British life. *Tyrer* v *United Kingdom* (1978) 2 EHHR 1, held that sentencing Tyrer to be 'birched' under Manx law was unacceptable as it was 'degrading treatment' under Article 3. This punishment had once been used in mainland Britain, but continued in use only on the Isle of Man and, although the British Crown controlled Man's foreign relations and adherence to treaties, it did not control the Isle's internal affairs. Hence Britain could not legislate directly to abolish 'birching'. Instead, a compromise was reached and such punishments were discontinued, although Manx law did not formally change until 1994.

Corporal punishment in schools also fell foul of the Convention, but this time it was Article 2 of the First Protocol, wherein the state must respect the philosophical convictions of parents when educating their children. In *Campbell and Cosans* v *United Kingdom* (1982) 4 EHRR 293, some parents objected to the possibility that their children might be beaten at school and this was held to be a breach of the above Article. The government was undecided upon how to react to this, as corporal punishment still seemed to enjoy public support. Could there be a system where some children could be beaten, if their parents agreed, while others could not, if their parents objected? Eventually, the House of Lords resolved the problem by amending the Education (No. 2) Act 1986 with a new s. 46, which had the effect of abolishing corporal punishment in state schools. Although not legally obliged to do so, most public schools have followed suit. So maybe a court decision can help to change public opinion. Lastly, *A* v *United Kingdom* (1999) 27 EHRR 611, throws doubt upon the extent to which parents can use physical force to discipline children. 'A' had been beaten by his stepfather with a garden cane, leaving visible bruising and, although the English courts had held that this was not actual bodily harm, the European Court of Human Rights held that this was a breach of Article 3. Legislation on this subject is unnecessary, as the British courts can simply take account of the ruling above when deciding domestic cases.

The European Court of Human Rights has also made number of important decisions on what we might loosely term sexual conduct, because a person's right to a private life is protected under Article 8 and cannot be restricted unless it is 'necessary in a democratic society'. *Dudgeon* v *United Kingdom* (1981) 4 EHRR 149 exposed an anomaly in British law, because whilst homosexual acts had been legalised in 'mainland' Britain as long ago as 1967, they remained a criminal offence in Northern Ireland. The European Court held this to be a breach of Article 8, as they could see no good reason for having such a law, and legislative reform swiftly followed in Northern Ireland. More recently the same issue resurfaced in relation to homosexuals serving in the armed forces, where 'buggery' was still a serious criminal offence and homosexual personnel were discharged from the service. Again, in *Lustig-Prean and Becket* v *United Kingdom* (2000) 29 EHRR 548, the European Court of Human Rights could see no good reason for such a restriction and, in response, the law in Britain was soon changed. The Court is consistent in its line that discrimination against homosexuals is not acceptable and in *ADT* v *United Kingdom*, (2001) 31 EHRR 33, where five men had been engaging in sexual activity, it held that the offence of 'gross indecency', which can only be committed between men, was a breach of Article 8. The different age of consent for men and women was eliminated in the Sexual Offences (Amendment) Act 2000, reducing the discriminatory aspect of this offence. Transsexuals have frequently questioned why British law refuses to recognise a change in sex, in cases such as *Rees* v *United Kingdom* (1987) 9 EHRR 56 and *Sheffield and Horsham* v *United Kingdom* (1999) 27 EHRR 163, among others. Finally, there was a successful case in *Goodwin* v *UK* (2002) 35 EHRR 18 and the law is to be changed in the Gender Recognition Bill 2004.

Article 8 has also proved useful to those who have wished to challenge unjustified government interference with their correspondence and other communications. The police had listened in to Malone's telephone communications. The English courts held that this must be legal, as there appeared to be no law against 'telephone tapping'; *Malone* v *Metropolitan Police Commissioner* [1979] Ch 344. Malone was more successful before the European Court of Human Rights, which held that this was a breach of his right to respect for his correspondence, because there were no laws to govern 'telephone tapping' and no 'appeal', hence no judicial control. Parliament responded by passing the Interception of Communications Act 1985, which brought in a system of warrants, appeals to a tribunal and supervision by a Commissioner. This Act did not regulate the use of other listening devices, which was exposed in *Khan* v *United Kingdom*, (2001) 31 EHRR 1016, where the police had attached a listening device to a house. At the time there was no legal regulation of police 'bugging', and Khan was unsuccessful in having the evidence, obtained by the listening device, excluded in an English court; *R* v *Khan* [1996] 3 All ER 289. This practice, of placing listening devices, is now legally controlled in the Regulation of Investigatory Powers Act 2000.

Article 8 has also caused problems for Britain in a long series of 'prison cases', starting with *Golder* v *United Kingdom* (1975) 1 EHRR 524, which involved a prisoner's right to communicate with his solicitor and ended with a general right to correspond with the outside world in *Campbell* v *United Kingdom* (1993) 15 EHRR 137. These rulings led to the abandonment of the automatic censoring of prisoner's mail.

The UK courts have also made a great number of decisions on the fairness of criminal trials. In *R* v *A (No. 2)* [2002] 1 AC 45, the Home Secretary stated that the complete exclusion of questioning about a rape complainant's previous sexual history could sometimes lead to an unfair trial. Similarly, in *R* v *Offen* [2000] 1 WLR 253, it was held that jailing an offender for life, who had committed two serious offences, was only justified if the offender was a danger to the public.

Similarly, there have been many cases where judges have been critical of delays and inefficiencies in the asylum system that infringe upon the applicant's human rights, as in *R (Anufrijeva)* v *Home Secretary* [2003] 3 All ER 827. Changes have also occurred in Mental Health Review Tribunals. In *R (H)* v *MHRT, North and East London Region* [2001] QB 1 the House of Lords did not accept that a patient had to prove that he no longer suffered from a mental disorder in order to obtain release. This reversed the burden of proof, and is unacceptable under Article 5. Delays in Mental Health Review Tribunal hearings also contravene the same Article: *R (KB)* v *Mental Health Review Tribunal* [2003] 2 All ER 209.

Judges, however, have not been so brave in the big 'political' cases. They have declined to overturn the detention without trial of alleged international terrorists in *R. (A)* v *Home Secretary* [2003] 2 WLR 564.

The right of the Home Secretary to decide upon the release of life prisoners has been removed by a series of judgments in the European Court of Human Rights and the UK courts. As a 'politician', he does not satisfy Article 6.1 of the European Court of Human Rights, which requires trial 'by an independent and impartial tribunal established by law'.

The process began when the European Court of Human Rights decided that it was not acceptable for the Home Secretary to decide upon the release on parole, or recall from parole of discretionary life prisoners in *Thynne, Wilson and Gunnell* v *UK* (1991) 13 EHRR 666. Both the courts of the UK, in *R.* v *Home Secretary, ex parte Venables and Thompson* [1998] AC 407 and the European Court of Human Rights, in *T* v *UK and V* v *UK* (2000) 30 EHRR 121, objected to the Home Secretary setting the 'tariff' or minimum period of detention for juveniles convicted of murder.

The culmination was in *R (Anderson)* v *Home Secretary* [2002] 4 All ER 1089, where the House of Lords declared that the Home Secretary's role in fixing the tariff and deciding upon the prisoner's release, was incompatible with human rights. The law has now been changed in the Criminal Justice Act 2003.

The decisions of the European Court of Human Rights have already had a major impact upon civil liberties in this country. The UK courts have just begun exploring human rights and are feeling their way towards what it is acceptable for the courts to do and what they must leave to Parliament.

Further reading

Barnett, H. *Constitutional and Administrative Law*, 4th edn (Cavendish, 2002), ch 19.

Bradley, A. and Ewing, K. *Constitutional & Administrative Law*, 13th edn (Longman, 2003), ch 19.

Bailey, S., Harris, D. and Jonci, B. *Civil Liberties Cases and Materials*, 5th edn (Butterworths, 2001), ch 1.

Edwards, R. Judicial Preference under the Human Rights Act 65 (2002) MLR 859.

Freedom to protest

Introduction

This is sometimes known as the law of public order. There are a number of criminal offences involved so, occasionally, it is treated as part of a criminal law syllabus. It, however, concerns a very important civil liberty, that of protest against the government or other powerful bodies, so historically it has been an important constitutional law issue. How far may the citizen lawfully go to indicate their dislike of government? According to the British tradition of civil liberties citizens may protest in any way that they want, as long as they do not break the law.

The Human Rights Act 1998 introduced Article 11, the right of peaceful assembly into UK law, but as yet, this has made little difference.

To study this subject we need to know, fairly accurately, which laws may be broken. Problem questions are common in this area. All that you need to do is to identify which laws may have been broken or offences committed. Many students find essay questions more demanding: you have to have a point of view, argue it and marshal evidence to support it. You may be asked whether you think that there is sufficient liberty to protest or whether you approve of the Criminal Justice and Public Order Act 1994 for example.

There is a lot of duplication in the laws on this area. The old common law such as breach of the peace remains. Added to this was the Public Order Act 1936. Some of that Act still remains although much of it was replaced by the Public Order Act 1986. On top of that the Criminal Justice and Public Order Act 1994 creates additional criminal offences and police powers. It is perfectly possible for the same set of facts to give rise to liability under several different laws. The more one looks at a public order problem the more offences one can see. Under examination conditions this is not a problem, time will limit what you can identify. If it is an essay you have to be sensible about what you are going to cover. Select material to support your argument.

If you are considering a problem question only deal with the legal issues raised by the facts. For instance, if you are given a set of facts indicating fairly minor public disturbances it is unlikely that you would be expected to consider riot. A reasonably high level of violence would indicate riot.

Q Question 1 Public Order

Twelve members of the 'No Abortion Campaign' are protesting on the pavement outside an abortion clinic on Eastby High Street. They are displaying placards with the words 'No to abortion' and speaking to each woman who enters the clinic asking her to consider whether she is 'doing the right thing'.

The owner of the abortion clinic summons the police and PC Kent arrives. She stands on the pavement observing the 'No Abortion Campaign' members, but takes no action.

Then 20 members of a group in favour of abortion, Women's Choice, arrive and start shouting at the 'No Abortion Campaign' members, insulting them and telling them to leave. Three of the members of Women's Choice throw stones, breaking the windows of the clinic.

PC Kent asks the 'No Abortion Campaign' members to leave, which they unwillingly do. They march half a mile down the High Street to the railway station.

PC Kent, together with other police officers who have joined her, arrest the 12 members of the 'No Abortion Campaign'.

Advise the 'No Abortion Campaign' on whether they have committed any public order offences and whether the police actions are legal.

Commentary

This is a fairly standard sort of problem question on public order law. What you have to do is to identify and discuss possible offences that might have been committed and consider the police's powers to control public protest. The question asks you to confine yourself to public order law, so do not stray off into ordinary criminal law and consider things like criminal damage. Nor is it necessary to consider civil matters such as nuisance. Your answer will be quite long enough and complicated enough just confining yourself to public order law! This area of law has many overlapping provisions and some contradictory case law. A good answer will make sense of this law by applying it to the problem and trying to come to a conclusion. Reasoned conclusions show that you understand the law. There are twelve members of the No Abortion Campaign, 20 members of Women's Choice and three women throw stones. This is not just chance, as numbers of participants are important in public order law and give the student a clue as to which area of law they should be considering.

The Human Rights Act 1998 means that the European Convention on Human Rights is now relevant to this area of law, in particular Article 10, which provides for Freedom of Expression and Article 11, which provides for Freedom of Assembly. This is actually helpful, because court decisions on these Articles are helping to clarify what English Law on public order should be.

- **The police have discretion.**

- **Wilful obstruction of the highway.**

- Threatening, abusive or insulting words or behaviour.

- Immediate unlawful violence or to provoke immediate use of unlawful violence.

- Likely to cause harassment, alarm or distress.

- An assembly of 20 or more persons in a public place open to the air.

- Riot is 12 or more persons present together using or threatening unlawful violence for a common purpose.

- Violent disorder is 3 or more people present together using or threatening unlawful violence.

- Breach of the peace is an act or threat of violence against a person or their property in their presence.

- The organiser of a procession must give the police six day's notice.

:Q: Suggested answer

There are a number of public order offences that could have been committed by both the 'No Abortion Campaign' and Women's Choice and also a number of powers that PC Kent could have used to control the developing situation. According to *R* v *Chief Constable of Devon and Cornwall, ex parte The Central Electricity Generating Board* [1982] QB 458, the police have discretion on how they use their public order control powers. They are not obliged to arrest for crimes or to use their powers to disperse protesters. This was confirmed by the more recent *R* v *Chief Constable of Sussex, ex parte International Trader's Ferry Ltd.* [1999] 1 All ER 129. The opposite is not, however, the case, the police cannot arrest for something that is not a crime, nor prevent lawful protest.

A gathering on the pavement has been held to be obstruction of the highway in *Arrowsmith* v *Jenkins* [1963] 2 QB 561. It is still the offence of wilful obstruction, even if there was no intention to obstruct and even if no one was actually obstructed. The highway is for passage and repassage and purposes incidental to that movement. The European Court of Human Rights has ruled, in *Platform Arzte fur das Leben* (1988) 13 EHRR 204, that there is a right to hold meetings in a public place. A case more favourable to the 'No Abortion Campaign' is *DPP* v *Jones (Margaret)* [1999] 2 AC 240, where the House of Lords held that a small protest on a roadside verge, near Stonehenge, was not an obstruction of the highway. Lord Irvine, the Lord Chancellor, thought that a right of peaceful assembly on the highway might exist and that the common law should develop to conform to Article 11 of the European Convention, which gives a right of peaceful assembly. The 'No Abortion Campaign's' protest is certainly peaceful and quite small in number, so it is probably not obstruction of the highway.

They also do not seem to be committing any offences under the Public Order Act 1986. They are not using 'threatening, abusive or insulting words or behaviour' nor are their signs 'threatening, abusive or insulting' and there are no threats of violence, so there is no offence under s. 4 of the Act. Even the lesser offence in s. 5, where it is enough for 'disorderly behaviour' to be likely to cause 'harassment, alarm or distress' is not committed. *DPP* v *Clarke, Lewis, O'Connell & O'Keefe* [1992] Crim LR 60, also involved a protest outside an abortion clinic, but the protesters had no intent to be threatening, abusive or insulting. All that the defendants did in that case was to show pictures of an aborted foetus to police officers and one passer-by. To commit an offence under s. 5 the protest needs to be more vigorous, as in *DPP* v *Fidler and Moran* [1992] 1 WLR 91, where there were also shouts and threats against those attending the clinic, in addition to the display of photographs and models of dead foetuses. *Percy* v *DPP* (2002) 166 JP 93 confirms that the 'No Abortion Campaign' are unlikely to have committed an offence. Even if behaviour is held to be insulting, this must be balanced against the right to freedom of expression under Article 10 of the European Convention of Human Rights.

PC Kent cannot use the powers under s.14 of the Public Order Act 1986, to impose conditions upon public assemblies against the 'No Abortion Campaign', because there are only 12 of them. Section 16 requires 20 or more persons for a public assembly.

Because of this, PC Kent could impose conditions upon the members of Women's Choice, as there are enough of them. She chooses not to do this, despite the fact that this group appears to have committed criminal offences. Unlike the 'No Abortion Campaign', they are using insulting words, which seem intended or likely to cause their opponents to fear immediate personal violence: *R* v *Horseferry Road Magistrate ex parte Siadatan* [1991] 1 All ER 324. So s. 4 would be satisfied and so would the lesser offence under s. 5. It seems likely that the 'No Abortion Campaign' would experience harassment, alarm or distress, unless the courts decide that by their frequent protesting they will have become used to insulting, threatening and abusive words or behaviour, rather like the police officers in *DPP* v *Orum* [1988] 3 All ER 449.

It is possible that more serious offences have been committed. Section 1 of the Public Order Act 1986 defines riot as '12 or more persons who are present together use or threaten violence for a common purpose . . . as would cause a person of reasonable firmness present at the scene to fear for his personal safety'. There are over 12 members of Women's Choice and according to s. 7 'violence' can include violence towards property, not just people and would include the throwing of missiles. It would have to be proved, though, that at least twelve of them had a common purpose to violently attack the clinic or their opponents: *R* v *Jefferson* [1994] 1 All ER 270. This could prove difficult, so s. 2, which makes violent disorder an offence, is more likely. This is similar to riot, but only requires three participants and does not require a common purpose. The three window breakers would have committed this offence as the 'No Abortion Campaign'; the inmates of the clinic, bystanders and even the police officer would have been put in fear. Affray, under s. 3, has not been committed, as under s. 8, violence against persons is required.

PC Kent has tried to disperse the No Abortion Campaign, but as we have seen above she has no statutory power under the Public Order Act 1986. Section 42 of the Criminal Justice and Police Act 2001 allows the police to disperse persons who are outside a dwelling and 'likely to cause harassment, alarm or distress to the persons living at the residence'. The clinic is not a 'dwelling' though. PC Kent does, however, have a common law power to take reasonable measures to prevent a breach of the peace. The accepted definition, today, of a breach of the peace is an act or threat of violence against a person or their property in their presence, which puts someone in fear of violence: *R* v *Howell* [1982] 2 QB 416 and *Percy* v *DPP* [1995] 3 All ER 124. This power has been used to disperse meetings as in *Duncan* v *Jones* [1963] 1 KB 218 and to refuse to obey the reasonable instructions of a police constable is the offence of obstruction of a police officer in the execution of his duty: *Duncan* v *Jones* (ibid.)

On the facts it seems reasonable for PC Kent to assume that violence might break out, but has she acted against the wrong group? The old case of *Beatty* v *Gillbanks* (1882) 9 QBD 308 held that the Salvation Army should not be forbidden from marching through Weston-Super-Mare, just because they might be violently opposed by the rival Skeleton Army. In *Platform Arzte fur das Leben* (above), the European Court of Human Rights has ruled that this is the correct approach and that, in certain circumstances, the state has a duty to protect peaceful protesters from those who would oppose them with violence. In *Redmond-Bate* v *DPP* (1999) 163 JP 789, the defendants were women preaching from the steps of Wakefield Cathedral but, as the listening crowd were becoming hostile, the police stopped the women. Sedley LJ said that the police were wrong to do this and that 'the common law should seek compatibility with the values of the European Convention on Human Rights'. 'The question for the police officer was whether there was a real threat of violence and if so, from whom it was coming.' So PC Kent should really have taken action against the troublemakers, Women's Choice.

Processions and marches are well regulated by law and under s. 11 of the Public Order Act 1986 the organisers must give the police six day's written notice 'unless it is not reasonably practicable to give any advance notice of the procession'. It is surely arguable here that it is not reasonable to expect the 'No Abortion Campaign' to notify the police in advance as their march has, in effect, been caused by the police. Section 12 allows a senior police officer to give directions to the organisers if he 'reasonably believes that' the procession 'may result in serious public disorder, serious damage to property or serious disruption to the life of the community' or the purpose of the march is intimidation. As these directions have to be in writing, they are hardly practical in this situation. The law, in the Public Order Act 1986, makes a clear distinction between assemblies and processions, for instance there is no minimum number for processions, yet assemblies do not have to be notified to the police in advance. The facts of this problem illustrate, that there may not be a clearcut distinction between assemblies and processions, as was shown in *DPP* v *Jones* [2002]

EWHC 110, where the police illegally imposed assembly conditions on what was in fact a procession.

In conclusion, PC Kent took legal action against the wrong people, the 'No Abortion Campaign' group, who were merely exercising their peaceful right of protest. She should have taken action against the violent and threatening Women's Choice.

Q Question 2

Gotham is a small city in the North of England. As a result of government spending cuts, Gotham District Council's Education Committee became extremely short of funds, and so they decided to sell, for development, one half of the playing fields of the local comprehensive school. This caused tremendous opposition locally, and a 'Parents Action Committee' was formed. However, the sale went ahead, and work began on the site. The Action Committee at once initiated a plan of 'peaceful disruption' involving all-night vigils at the site and constant demonstrations by day. To keep its spirits up, the Action Committee plays music and sings protest songs, particularly during the night. These demonstrations were, at first, peaceful but then began to turn ugly, with the parents and building workers taunting each other. The demonstrations take place largely on adjoining common land, but tend to overflow into the road and onto the site itself. A group of more militant parents has now 'occupied' the site by lying down on it.

The Chief Constable of Gotham City is being pressed by the Council and the developers to do something about this situation. Advise him.

Commentary

This problem is designed to raise the issue of large public protests and how the law might apply to them. As well as the 'standard' old 'common law' and offences under the Public Order Act 1986 you need to consider the newer Criminal Justice and Public Order Act 1994. Although it seems that the government's intention was not to legislate directly to deal with protests as such, some of the Act's provisions are wide enough to cover such events. These create the offences of 'aggravated trespass' and the concept of a 'trespassory assembly'. Lastly the question asks the classic civil liberties question: even if offences are being committed, does this oblige the police to act?

- Police may take reasonable preventative action to prevent a breach of the peace.

- A breach of the peace is acts or threats of violence against other people or acts or threats likely to provoke violence.

- Threatening, abusive or insulting words or behaviour.

- Likely to cause harassment, alarm or distress.

- Causing a person to believe that immediate unlawful violence will be used.

- A public assembly of 20 or more persons in a public place open to the air.

- Wilful obstruction of the highway.

- Aggravated trespass — intimidate, disrupt or obstruct a lawful activity.

- The police have power to remove trespassers who have a common purpose of residing on the land.

- A rave is a gathering on land in the open air of 100 or more persons at which amplified music is played at night distressing the inhabitants.

- The Secretary of State may ban a trespassory assembly for 4 days over a 5 mile radius.

:Q: Suggested answer

The Chief Constable should be advised that his powers to deal with the parents' occupation are considerably increased by the Criminal Justice and Public Order Act 1994. First, however, it should be pointed out that the police already had both common law and statutory powers to deal with this type of matter before the 1994 Act.

If the police officers present have honestly and reasonably formed the opinion that there is a real risk of an imminent breach of the peace, both in place and time, then they may take reasonable preventative action; *Moss* v *McLachlan* [1985] IRLR 77. A breach of the peace was defined in *R* v *Howell (Erroll)* [1982] 2QB 416 as acts or threats of violence against other people or even acts or threats likely to provoke violence. *Percy* v *DPP* [1995] 3 All ER 124 confirms this interpretation. It seems clear from the parents and building workers taunting each other that a breach of the peace may occur. This entitles the police officers present to disperse the protestors or indeed, the building workers! It also gives the officers power to enter the land which may be private property; *Thomas* v *Sawkins* [1935] 2 KB 249. If the protestors refuse to leave, this would be obstruction of a police officer in the execution of his duty under s. 89(2), Police Act 1996 (*Duncan* v *Jones* [1936] 1 KB 218).

The 'taunting' could well qualify as an offence under the Public Order Act 1986. Threatening, abusive or insulting words likely to cause harassment, alarm or distress are prohibited by s. 5. If any of the words carry with them threats of violence, then it is possible that the more serious s. 4 offence is committed. This outlaws threatening, abusive or insulting words uttered with the intent to cause another person to believe that immediate unlawful violence will be used against the person threatened. Even provoking that other person to violence is covered, confirming the old case of *Jordan* v *Burgoyne* [1963] 2 QB 744.

Under the same Act, a senior police officer could exercise his power of control under s. 14 over 'an assembly of twenty or more persons in a public place which is wholly or partly open to the air'. He could place conditions on the place, duration and maximum number of the assembly. It would be an offence to disobey.

It should be noted that some of the demonstrations overflow onto the road. According to *Arrowsmith* v *Jenkins* [1963] 2 QB 561 wilful obstruction of the highway under s. 137, Highways Act 1980 can be committed even if there was no intention to obstruct traffic and even if no one was actually obstructed. The more recent *DPP* v *Jones* [1999] 2 All ER 257 indicates that minor obstructions are not an offence, but in that case the obstruction, a few people standing on a roadside verge, was very minor indeed, so *Arrowsmith* would probably still be followed.

The Criminal Justice and Public Order Act 1994 grants some new powers to the police to deal with trespass. The most obvious one here is aggravated trespass under s. 68. The parents are trespassing by being present on the old school playing fields and these fields certainly qualify as 'land in the open air'. The Act is unclear on this point so far as s. 68 is concerned, but it is usually possible to trespass on common land. The building workers are engaged in a 'lawful activity' and the parents are intending to obstruct or disrupt that activity. Actual disruption does not have to be proved; *Winder* v *DPP, The Times,* 14 August 1996. Any police officer in uniform may arrest for this offence. Under s. 69 a senior police officer could also direct them to leave. It would be an offence to fail to leave as soon as practicable.

It is also likely that the protestors are covered by s. 61 of the 1994 Act and that therefore a senior police officer may direct them to leave the land. There must be two or more parents and they are obviously trespassing. They have a common purpose in residing there. Even common land is included under this section. The other elements that need to be proved are that the occupier has taken reasonable steps to ask them to leave and that the parents have either damaged the land or used threatening, abusive or insulting words or behaviour towards the occupier's employees or agents. Alternatively the other element could be that the protestors had six vehicles with them. This seems unlikely on the facts. Damage could be merely trampling the grass down; *Gayford* v *Choulder* [1898] 1 QB 316. As we have seen earlier, the parents have almost certainly used, at the very least, abusive or insulting words to the building workers who could well be employees of the occupier. To fail to leave as soon as reasonably practicable is again an offence.

From the point of view of the Chief Constable both s. 61 and s. 68 give him the ability to 'clear' the site. It is an offence for any person who knows of the directions to return within a three-month period.

Although this protest is definitely not a 'rave', it is just about possible that it meets the definition in s. 63. They are on land in the open air. Trespass is not necessary. There might be one hundred or more of them. They are present during the night. It is doubtful though that their music is 'amplified' or of such a 'loudness and duration' as to be 'likely to arouse serious distress to the inhabitants of the locality'. The parents' musical tastes are unimportant. 'Music includes sounds wholly or predominantly characterised by the emission of a succession of repetitive beats' which means that 'ordinary' music is covered by the Act, not just rave music.

The ability to apply for a four day ban in a five mile radius under s. 70 might seem attractive to the Chief Constable. The assembly is a 'trespassory' one and probably involves 20 or more people but it seems unlikely that it is causing significant damage to land of historical, archaeological or scientific importance. 'Serious disruption to the life of the community' is just about possible but the local authority and Home Secretary would have to agree to such a ban. This seems unlikely in these circumstances.

So it is clear that the Chief Constable has a number of 'dispersal' powers at his disposal. He does not, however, have to use any of them if it seems inappropriate to him, despite the wishes of the Council and the developers. Even following the passing of the Criminal Justice and Public Order Act 1994 it would seem that *R* v *Chief Constable of Devon and Cornwall ex parte CEGB* [1982] QB 458 still applies (confirmed by *R* v *Chief Constable of Sussex, ex parte International Trader's Ferry Ltd* [1999] 1 All ER 129). There, according to the Court of Appeal, clear breaches of the criminal law were being committed by trespassers occupying a site. Despite this the Court was content to rely on the Chief Constable's discretion and would not order or advise him to do anything.

Q Question 3

Article 11 of the European Convention on Human Rights refers to the right to freedom of peaceful assembly, subject to the imposition of lawful restraints on the exercise of that right. Consider whether citizens of the UK enjoy the right to peacefully assemble or whether the lawful restraints mean that such right exists only so far as the police in the exercise of their discretion allow it.

   Discuss.

Commentary

For a number of reasons, this looks to be a fairly intimidating essay question! For a start it seems to cover what to many students would seem to be two quite separate topics, the European Convention on Human Rights and public order law. However, since the Human Rights Act 1998 came into force, on 2 October 2000, such questions will be seen as increasingly relevant. Whether the existing law measures up to these new standards could be asked of several areas of constitutional law. Fortunately, there is plenty of material with which to answer this question. A critical account of the existing public order law would just about get by. Ask yourself the question, how much freedom to protest have we really got when all the various offences and police control powers are taken into account? There are also some cases, involving the UK, which the European Court of Human Rights has already decided. The issue of police discretion seems tricky, but has been dealt with in cases as old and as well-known as *Beatty* v *Gillbanks* (1882) 9 QBD 308. Structure and argument are everything in an essay like this. Do not just write down every case that you can remember and list all the offences in the Public Order Act 1986, but select the cases and offences that you want to discuss. Only use those that advance your argument, i.e., do they reveal a respect for peaceful protest or are they unnecessarily restrictive?

- **Article 11 of the European Convention of Human Rights declares that everyone has the right to freedom of peaceful assembly.**

- **Protest must be peaceful.**

- **Processions may be prohibited if there is a threat of violence.**

- **Violence or the threat of violence is an essential constituent of breach of the peace.**

- **Restrictions on the right to protest must be clearly prescribed by law.**

- **Peaceful protest may allow obstruction of the highway.**

- **The State has a duty to protect peaceful protest.**

⌯Ọ̈ Suggested answer

Some have suggested that English law unduly hinders peaceful protest. Take, for example, the view of Geoffrey Robertson QC in *Freedom, The Individual and The Law*, 1993: 'Although the virtues of peaceful protest are frequently extolled, there is in England no legal right of peaceful assembly or procession or . . . even to hold meetings in public places'. Article 11.1 of the European Convention on Human Rights states that: 'Everyone has the right to freedom of peaceful assembly . . .'. Article 11.2 allows this right to be restricted, but the restrictions must be 'prescribed by law' and must meet one at least of the legitimate aims listed there such as, 'national security', 'public safety', 'the prevention of disorder or crime' or 'the protection of the rights and freedoms of others'. The restriction on the right to protest must also be justified as 'necessary in a democratic society'. In other words it must be genuinely designed to protect, for example, 'public safety', but must go no further than is necessary to achieve that purpose. This is known as 'proportionality'. This essay aims to explore whether Geoffrey Robertson is right, or whether English law does guarantee a right of peaceful protest in accordance with the European Convention.

It is clear that any protest must be peaceful, as the European Commission held in *Christians against Racism and Fascism* v *United Kingdom* (1980) 21 DR 138 at 148: 'Disruption incidental to the holding of the assembly will not render it "unpeaceful", whereas a meeting planned with the object of causing disturbances will not be protected by A. 11.' Therefore there seems to be nothing objectionable to the offences in the Public Order Act 1986, for an essential element of riot, violent disorder and affray is that violence or threats of violence is used, so, by definition, they are not 'peaceful' actions. Even the 'threatening, abusive or insulting words or behaviour' in s. 4 must carry with them a threat of violence or at least provoke violence. Section 5, which merely requires the 'threatening, abusive or insulting words' etc. to be likely to cause 'harassment, alarm or distress' seems more suspect, as violence is not a constituent of the offence. In *Chorherr* v *Austria* (1993) 17 EHRR 358, however, the European Court of Human Rights held that a protest that caused annoyance or agitation was not protected by Article 11. Hence, s. 5 of the Public Order Act 1986 might well be acceptable.

Some have argued that it is an undue interference with public protest to prohibit processions, under what is now s. 13 of the Public Order Act 1986. This has, however, been considered acceptable under the European Convention, if there is a likelihood of violence in the area; *Christians against Racism and Fascism* v *United Kingdom* (1980) and *Rai* v *United Kingdom* (1995) 82-ADR 134. Turning aside from the statutory provisions of the Public Order Act 1986, the ancient common law power to control a breach of the peace has often caused concern amongst civil libertarians. According to Lord Denning in *R* v *Chief Constable of Devon and Cornwall ex parte CEGB* [1981] 3 All ER 383: 'There was a breach of the peace whenever a person who was lawfully carrying out his work was unlawfully and physically prevented by another from doing it'. Other cases have preferred a tighter definition, which involve threats of harm or violence. This was expressed in *R* v *Howell (Erroll)* [1982] 2 QB 416 as 'an act done or threatened to be done which actually harms a person, or in his presence his property, or is likely to cause such harm or which puts someone in fear of such harm being done'. This was further explained in *Percy* v *DPP* [1995] 3 All ER 124, that to be conduct that was a breach of the peace, it had to involve violence, a threat of violence or carry a real risk that it would provoke violence in others.

The use of breach of the peace has been questioned three times in the European Court of Human Rights. Each time the Court has been satisfied that the restriction that breach of the peace makes upon the right to protest is 'prescribed by law'. In other words it is sufficiently well-defined for someone to be able to understand what it is they are forbidden to do. The Court has, however, preferred the definition in *Howell* and *Percy*, which stresses the need for violence to make the conduct unlawful, for 'peaceful assembly' is a right. On the facts though, the court has disapproved of the use of breach of the peace in some circumstances. In *Steel* v *United Kingdom* (1999) 28 EHRR 603, Ms Steel walked in front of a grouse shoot and Ms Lush stood in front of a JCB digger in order to hinder the building of the M11. This was an acceptable restriction upon their rights to protest as Ms Steel might have been accidentally shot and Ms Lush might have provoked violence, so their protests were not peaceful. Ms Needham, Mr Polden and Mr Cole were conducting an entirely peaceful protest, outside a sale of 'fighter helicopters', when they were arrested. This was unacceptable under Article 11, Article 10, which guarantees freedom of expression and Article 5.1, which guarantees that no one will be deprived of their liberty unless they break the law. The three had not broken English law as they had not threatened or provoked any violence and so there was no breach of the peace.

In *McLeod* v *United Kingdom* (1999) 27 EHRR 493, the police had been present when Mr McLeod entered and removed items from his ex-wife's house, because they claimed that they feared a breach of the peace. The Court held that this was unjustified, as there was in fact little or no risk of disorder or crime occurring, as Mrs McLeod was not there at the time. This was a breach of Article 8, Mrs McLeod's right to respect for her home.

Finally, in *Hashman and Harrup* v *United Kingdom* (2000) 30 EHRR 241, hunt saboteurs were bound over to keep the peace. The words used by the English magistrates were to be of 'good behaviour'. The European Court of Human Rights found this to be unacceptable, because it did not tell the protesters what it was they were forbidden to do. It was particularly difficult for them to know, because they had not been convicted of or charged with any offence. Restrictions on the right to protest must be 'prescribed by law' and this lacked any clear definition.

So, in summary, the European Court has not found breach of the peace unacceptable, as properly defined, but has just required it to be used properly, to restrict violent protest only. The English courts have also been moving tentatively towards accepting a right of peaceful protest on the public highway. Completely peaceful assemblies, protests and demonstrations have often fallen foul of s. 137 of the Highway Act 1980, because it is a criminal offence to obstruct the highway. Cases such as *Arrowsmith* v *Jenkins* [1963] 2 QB 562, have held that the only lawful use of the highway is for passage and re-passage, so a public meeting in the street was an obstruction. Other cases, such as *Hirst* v *Chief Constable of West Yorkshire* [1987] 85 Cr App R 143, have taken a slightly more lenient line, that very minor protests, which cause no real obstruction, can be tolerated. Some judges have been willing to go further and find that a right of peaceful assembly on the highway might exist. The Lord Chancellor, Lord Irvine, gave tentative support for such an idea in *DPP* v *Jones* [1999] 2 All ER 257 and felt that, if necessary, the common law should develop in order to conform to Article 11. Lord Hutton was confident that such a common law right already existed and cited Lord Denning's spirited dissent in *Hubbard* v *Pitt* [1976] 1 QB 142, where he defended the 'right to demonstrate and the right to protest on matters of public concern', 'provided that everything is done peaceably and in good order'. Otton J in *Hirst* (1987) was also quoted in support of the same idea. Importantly, the House of Lords in *DPP* v *Jones* (ibid.) also accepted that the peaceful protest, of 21 people on the grass verge of the A344 at Stonehenge, was not only not an obstruction of the highway, but also not a trespassory assembly under the Criminal Justice and Public Order Act 1994. The English courts seem to be gradually getting into line with the rulings of the European Commission, in *Rassemblement Jurassien et unite Jurassiene* v *Switzerland* (1979) 17 DR 93 and the European Court of Human Rights, in *Platform Arzte fur das Leben* (1988) 13 EHRR 204, where it was held that there is a *right* to hold meetings in public places.

The *Platform* case also made clear that the state does not merely have a duty to permit peaceful protest, in certain circumstances there may be a duty to protect peaceful protesters from those who would oppose them with violence. Even the English courts have occasionally endorsed this approach and asserted that the authorities should not merely take the easy way out and prevent those with an unpopular message from speaking, for fear of the possible reaction. In *Beatty* v *Gillbanks* (1882) 9 QBD 308, it was held that the Salvation Army should not be forbidden from marching through Weston-Super-Mare, just because they might be opposed by the Skeleton Army. In a modern version of this case, the police were not permitted to stop women preaching from the steps of Wakefield Cathedral just because some of their audience were hostile: *Redmond-Bate* v *DPP* (1999) 163 JP 789

It might be apparent from the contrasting cases given above, that the police have many difficult decisions to make. Do they permit free speech or step in to prevent a possible outbreak of public disorder? The English courts have usually been most unwilling to interfere with police discretion. In *R* v *Chief Constable of Devon and Cornwall ex parte CEGB* [1982] QB 458, even though the Court of Appeal seemed confident that criminal offences were occurring, they were unwilling to instruct the police to act. Similarly, in *R* v *Chief Constable of Sussex ex parte International Trader's Ferry Ltd* [1999] 1 All ER 129, the House of Lords were unwilling to interfere with the police decision to protect live animal exports from protesters on only two days a week, despite a strong argument that this infringed the free movement of goods under Article 34 of the European Community Treaty. Article 11 of the European Convention on Human Rights explicitly allows for the balancing of conflicting interests and, indeed, the few decisions of the European Court of Human Rights in this area do not seem any more willing to 'overrule' the decisions of the police than the English courts. Perhaps all the English courts need to do is to try and be a bit more consistent and not forget the basic principle that peaceful protest should be permitted.

Further reading

Barnett, H. *Constitutional & Administrative Law*, 4th edn (Cavendish, 2002), ch 27, part 1.

Bradley, A. and Ewing, K. *Constitutional & Administrative Law*, 13th edn (Longman, 2003), ch 24.

Bailey, S., Harris, D. and Jones, B. *Civil Liberties Cases and Materials*, 5th edn (Butterworths, 2001), ch 4.

Feldman, D. *Civil Liberties and Human Rights in England and Wales*, 2nd edn (OUP, 2002), ch 18.

Freedom of speech

Introduction

Freedom of speech is one of the most important civil liberties in a democratic society. It enables citizens to say or write what they like. This could include criticism of the government or other powerful institutions and discussion of alternative policies. Without free and open debate it is difficult to see how a democratic system could work.

As it is a civil liberty and not a right, we need to study the various laws that restrict free speech. One can say or write whatever one likes unless there is a law against it. Unfortunately there are a lot of laws that may need to be considered. The main areas would be obscenity, official secrets, breach of confidence and contempt of court. Other relevant laws might be blasphemy, sedition, incitement to disaffection, incitement to racial hatred and civil and criminal defamation. Different constitutional law courses will have different emphases and may concentrate on only some areas. Read the syllabus and listen to what your lecturers and tutors are telling you! If this does not work, a study of past examination papers should usually give you a clear idea of the areas that are required study.

Different lecturers will often have very different ideas of what should be studied. A traditional concern was the freedom of expression of writers and artists. This is reflected in the 'reform' of the law in the Obscene Publications Act 1959. Other laws would probably be considered such as the common law conspiracy to corrupt public morals, and the statutes regulating cinemas, theatre and videos. A more modern way of looking at this area might be to assume that the battle for artistic freedom was won back in the 1960s and 1970s and that the worry now might be whether there is sufficient control over pornographic material. A topical concern here might be paedophilia and as well as the above laws there might be a consideration of the Protection of Children Act 1978.

Other courses might be interested in the freedom of the press. The Broadcasting Acts, the non-statutory procedures for press complaints, contempt of court and defamation might well be the main focus of study.

Yet again there has been recent concern over the government's control over official information. Here one would look at not just the Official Secrets Acts but also the Public Record Acts, breach of confidence and the Spycatcher trials. The convention of Ministerial Responsibility can also play a role in controlling the flow of information. See **Chapter 6**, Prime Minister and Cabinet and the *Scott Report of the Inquiry into the Export of Defence Equipment and Dual-use Goods to Iraq and Related Prosecutions*. When John Major became

Prime Minister he announced that he was in favour of open government and a White Paper of this name was issued in 1993 (Cm 2290). This scheme relied on voluntary disclosure, but the Labour government, elected in 1997, promised a legally binding Freedom of Information Act which was enacted in 2000.

Now that the Human Rights Act 1998 is in force, the courts of Britain will have to take account of the European Convention on Human Rights, when establishing the meaning of case law and interpreting Acts of Parliament. Article 10 guarantees a right to freedom of expression. For some time, English courts have been considering Article 10, in their attempts to make sense of conflicting case law in the various areas of law that affect freedom of expression. Examples would include *Derbyshire* v *The Times* [1993] AC 534, which concerned libel and *A-G* v *Observer, The Times (Spycatcher)* [1990] AC 109, which involved the equitable doctrine of breach of confidence. The general tendency has been to conclude that English case law usually conforms to the demands of Article 10. There has also been a slight change, in favour of liberalising the law to uphold freedom of expression. For example, in the *Derbyshire* case it was concluded that a corporate body, such as a local authority, had no legal personality to sue for libel, free speech being more important. So, with the Human Rights Act 1998 now in force, the courts should not have too many problems *if* they are correct in their belief that English law usually meets the requirements of Article 10 anyway! (See **Chapter 7** for more on human rights.)

It is unlikely, nowadays, that any constitutional and administrative law course would attempt to cover all of the possible aspects of freedom of expression. So our suggested answers only try to cover the main and, we hope, most likely areas.

Q Question 1

Humbert, who lives in Alphaville, is interested in computing and child pornography. He obtains from his computer images of young children engaged in sexual activity. These he prints out and exchanges with his friends. He also exchanges video recordings dealing with similar subject matter. He is arrested by the police and prosecuted.

In his defence, he wishes to argue that his sexual desires are incurable and that looking at such pictures is beneficial in that it satisfies those desires. He also wishes to argue that some of the computer images are of artistic merit. Eminent psychiatrists and art experts are willing to give evidence on his behalf.

Two days before his trial, the local newspaper, *The Alphaville Record* publishes an article under the headline, 'Hanging is Too Good for Humbert' and reveals that he has previously been convicted for sexual offences. The editor defends publication as in the public interest.

Advise Humbert and the editor of *The Alphaville Record*.

Commentary

This is a fairly typical problem designed to raise most of the main issues on obscenity law. The cases are interesting in themselves and fairly easy to remember. All that is needed is to apply them to the facts. In common with many questions on obscenity the student would also be expected to know about other laws which cover roughly the same area. There are quite a number of them and it is hard to predict which ones would come up in a particular question. So it is best to have a general idea of most of these laws. The examples here are the Protection of Children Act 1978, the Video Recordings Act 1984 and perhaps conspiracy to corrupt public morals.

Another common tactic is to expect students to be aware of fairly obscure changes in the law, here those made in the Criminal Justice and Public Order Act 1994 will need to be mentioned.

It is hard to make a problem question about obscenity long enough, so it is not unusual to include another area of law in the question. Here it is contempt of court. Again it would be hard to devise a full problem question on contempt. There are only so many points that could be raised.

- **Obscenity is a tendency to deprave and corrupt.**

- **Those who are likely to read, hear or see the 'obscene' article.**

- **Expert evidence on artistic merit is allowed.**

- **Offence to possess indecent electronic data.**

- **Freedom of expression can be restricted for the protection of morals.**

- **Contempt is a substantial risk that the course of justice will be impeded or prejudiced.**

- **A discussion in good faith of public affairs is not contempt.**

:Q: Suggested answer

The first offence that springs to mind is that Humbert might have contravened the Obscene Publications Act 1959. Section 1 makes it an offence to publish an obscene article.

Publishing includes any form of distribution. It is not necessary to show that Humbert did this for gain, for distributing or circulating is enough according to the Act. Even if this was not the case, an 'exchange' might well be held to be for gain. 'Article' includes video cassettes according to *A-G's Reference (No. 5 of 1980)* [1980] 3 All ER 816. Whether obscene material stored on a computer was an 'article' was open to doubt until the Criminal Justice and Public Order Act 1994 (schedule 9, para 3) made it clear that the transmission of electronically stored data was covered by the 1959 Act.

The test for obscenity is also set out in s. 1, Obscene Publications Act 1959. It is that the article is obscene 'if its effect . . . is, if taken as a whole, such as to tend to deprave and corrupt persons who are likely, having regard to all relevant circumstances, to read, hear or see' it. This test has eluded precise definition. *R v Secker and Warburg* [1954] 2 All ER 683 stated that the material being merely shocking and disgusting was not enough. The famous, though unreported, case concerning the book, *Lady Chatterley's Lover* in 1960 suggested that it meant 'to make morally bad, to pervert, debase or corrupt morally'. The old case, *R v Hicklin* (1868) LR 3 QB 360 mentioned 'exciting impure or libidinous thoughts'. It is not necessary to show that anyone was actually depraved or corrupted, merely that the material has that tendency.

The statutory definition above also demands that the likely audience is taken into account. If it is children, obscenity is more likely to be proved; *DPP v A & BC Chewing Gum* [1968] 1 QB 519 and *R v Anderson* [1972] 1 QB 304. Here though, although the material concerned children, they are most unlikely to be the 'target' audience. This is likely to be adults. Humbert cannot argue that they are likely already to be paedophiles and so incapable of further corruption. The argument that the 'audience' for pornography is already corrupt has not succeeded; *R v Anderson* [1972] 1 QB 304; *DPP v Whyte* [1972] AC 849.

The vague definition of obscenity may not be a problem. The jury will decide. Expert evidence is not permitted to help them on this issue unless the type of obscene material is outside the normal experience of adults. Expert evidence was allowed upon the effects of cocaine in *R v Skirving* [1985] QB 819 and the effects of horrific pictures upon children in *DPP v A & BC Chewing Gum* (1968). There seems no justification for this type of expert evidence in this case, as the 'target audience' for the material are adults.

Section 4 of the 1959 Act does, however, permit expert evidence upon 'artistic merit' (*R v Anderson; Lady Chatterley*). If the material can be shown to be for the 'public good' it is not obscene. The jury decide first whether material is obscene and then, if it is, whether considerations of public good outweigh this and if publication is desirable. More general arguments and evidence that pornographic material has therapeutic effects has never been permitted; *DPP v Jordan* [1977] AC 699 and *A-G's Reference (No. 3 of 1977)* [1978] 3 All ER 1166.

On balance I consider that Humbert's computer images and videos will be judged to be obscene. If this is not so, there are other offences that could be considered. Mere possession of an 'indecent' photograph is an offence under the Protection of Children Act 1978. The prosecution must prove that Humbert had 'knowledge' of what he possesses, but on the facts here that does not seem too difficult; *Atkins v DPP* [2000] 2 All ER 425. Section 84, Criminal Justice and Public Order Act 1994 makes very clear that 'photographs' include both the electronic data and the print-out. There is no defence of public good. Similarly there is no such defence to the common law offence of 'conspiracy to corrupt public morals'; *Shaw v DPP* [1962] AC 220. Paedophile 'rings' have been dealt with under this offence. Lastly it is highly unlikely that Humbert's videos have been given a classification under the Video Recordings Act 1984 by the British Board of Film Classification. This is particularly so, since the Board was urged to have 'special regard' to videos dealing with 'human sexual activity' in s. 90, Criminal Justice and Public Order Act 1994. It is a criminal offence merely to supply such a video, punishable by imprisonment.

The Human Rights Act 1998 may not help him very much. Under section 2, a British court must 'take into account' decisions of the European Court of Human Rights. This Court has consistently allowed contracting States a 'margin of appreciation' in the area of obscenity law, because they cannot find an agreed European standard of morals in domestic law of these States. So the Court has refused to say that obscenity laws infringed the Article 10 right to Freedom of Expression in both *Handysides* v *UK* (1976) 1 EHRR 737 and *Muller* v *Switzerland* (1991) 13 EHRR 212.

The Alphaville Record is almost certainly guilty of contempt of court. Under s. 2(2), Contempt of Court Act 1981 there needs to be a 'substantial risk that the course of justice will be seriously impeded or prejudiced'. The publication of previous convictions has long been held to be contempt; *R* v *Odhams Press* [1957] 1 QB 73. The sproceedings are clearly 'active' because Humbert has been arrested (s. 2(3)).

There is a defence under s. 5 that the risk of prejudice is purely incidental to a discussion in good faith of public affairs'. A passing mention in a newspaper article about a forthcoming trial might benefit from this section: *A-G* v *English* [1983] 1 AC 116. Here, though, the main purpose of the article seems to be to discuss Humbert, his trial and his previous convictions. It is a clear contempt. The Contempt of Court Act 1981 was enacted to bring English law into line with the European Convention on Human Rights, following Britain's defeat in *Sunday Times* v *United Kingdom* (1979) 2 EHRR 245. So, the Human Rights Act 1998 is unlikely to make a difference to the editor's case.

Indeed, it could be argued that the editor obviously knows about the trial and is deliberately trying to interfere with the administration of justice. This intentional contempt is not covered by the Act (s. 6), but remains as a common law offence; *A-G* v *Hislop* [1991] 2 WLR 219. It would be treated most seriously by the courts if, as would be likely here, the Attorney-General brought a prosecution against the editor.

In conclusion both Humbert and the editor face conviction. In a strange way the contempt might help Humbert. If convicted, he might be able to appeal successfully on the grounds that the contempt meant that he did not receive a fair trial; *R* v *Taylor* [1993] 98 Cr App R 361.

Q Question 2

Jane is a civil servant working for the Ministry of Defence. Because of the nature of her work she had signed the Official Secrets Act on commencing her employment. During the course of her work Jane comes across a document indicating that a

British company is selling artillery shells to the government of Fantasia. She knows that this is contrary to British law and contrary to the stated policy of Her Majesty's government. Jane asks a more senior civil servant what she should so. He tells her that the Secretary of State for Defence knows all about it but the matter is to be kept secret.

Jane is still concerned that the law is being broken so she hands over a copy of the document to a journalist who works for the *Sentinel* newspaper. That journalist discovers that there is a D-notice relating to arms sales to Fantasia. He and his editor decide to publish the document anyway.

The government learns about the proposed publication and wants to stop it. It also wishes to punish the parties responsible.

Advise the government.

Commentary

The problem with this sort of question is that at first glance it might seem unclear which area of constitutional law is relevant. The inspiration for the question is fairly obviously the 'Arms to Iraq' scandal, but it is not about the main concerns there of ministerial accountability and public interest immunity. Reading the rubric carefully, what you are actually asked to do with the facts given, is often helpful. Here it tells you that we are looking at the laws protecting government information.

The Official Secrets Act should immediately spring to mind, but so should breach of confidence, even though it is now several years since the Spycatcher trials. As will be seen from the suggested answer there are a few other bits and pieces of law that come in handy for questions like this.

Although this is a problem question, this sort of area is more often examined by means of an essay. The same material could be 'recycled' to answer an essay. With an essay, though, you would be expected to be critical rather than analytical as with a problem.

- Communicating to an enemy information that is prejudicial to the safety and interests of the State.

- Disclosure of defence information that is damaging to British defence.

- Disclosure of information relating to international relations that is damaging to British international relations.

- Knowing receipt of such information.

- The document belongs to the government.

- Damages can be recovered for breach of contract.

- Breach of confidence can be restrained to protect national security.

·Q· Suggested answer

The most obvious avenues for the government to explore are the Official Secrets Acts 1911 and 1989, but there are other possibilities. A civil action, perhaps for breach of confidence, might be possible and as Jane remains a civil servant, she is subject to Civil Service discipline.

Jane has signed the Official Secrets Act. This is a common procedure, but has no legal effect. All it does is warn her that she is in the sort of job that may be subject to the Act. Despite the reforms of 1989, s. 1, Official Secrets Act 1911 remains in force. Breach of this is a serious offence and can be committed by communicating to an enemy information which may be 'prejudicial to the safety and interests of the state'. Jane might well argue that she has not communicated to an enemy and that her actions are not 'prejudicial to the safety and interests of the state', *Chandler* v *DPP* [1964] AC 763 indicates that only the government can decide what is in the interests of the state. In *R* v *Ponting* [1985] Crim LR 318 Clive Ponting, another civil servant, tried to argue that he was helping the state by revealing to an MP information that ministers were hiding from Parliament. This is the 'whistle blower' argument: he has a duty to expose wrongdoing. In *Ponting* the court ruled that this argument was unacceptable, as in *Chandler*, only the government of the day could rule on what was 'in the interests of the state'. Despite the ruling the jury acquitted Ponting. For this reason, it is unlikely that the government would use s. 1 against Jane or the journalist, who would also be liable.

The old s. 2 of the 1911 Act was replaced by the Official Secrets Act 1989. Geoffrey Robertson QC described it in *Freedom, the Individual and the Law*, 1993 (p. 168) as replacing 'a blunderbuss with an armalite rifle'. The Act is meant to focus only on those areas where the Crown is genuinely concerned with the revelation of official information. As a Crown servant Jane is definitely affected by the Act. At first it seems that she has committed an offence under s. 2 because she has disclosed 'defence' information. 'Defence', as defined in s. 2(4)(b), includes 'weapons' but only those used by the armed forces of the Crown. Foreign armed forces are not included. Maybe it is possible that foreign weapon sales come under subsection (d), the more general 'defence policy'. Not only this but the prosecution must prove that disclosure of information is 'damaging' to British defence. It is difficult to see how this could be so. Damage to British interests abroad is also mentioned in s. 2 and might be easier to prove on our facts. There is also a 'did not know' defence in the Act. Jane, would perhaps claim that she did not know that this was defence information, as defined by the Act. It would be hard for her to claim that she did not know that it was 'damaging'.

Another government possibility is s. 3 of the Act which protects information relating to 'international relations' in a similar way. Conceivably arms sales to a foreign country might well be connected to foreign policy matters. Again damage to British interests would need to be shown.

Chandler v *DPP* (1964) suggests that the courts would accept the government's view upon what was 'defence', 'international relations', or 'the interests of the United Kingdom abroad'.

It was hoped that the courts would take a more liberal line under the 1989 Act and allow defendants, such as Jane, to put forward their own evidence on what was damaging to the country's defence or international relations. In *R* v *Shayler* [2003] 1 AC 247, however, the defendant claimed that he had tried to reveal the wrong-doings of the security services and that this was in the public and national interest. He also argued that the Official Secrets Act 1989 was incompatible with Article 10 of the European Convention of Human Rights, because it infringed his right to freedom of expression.

The House of Lords did not agree. They followed decisions of the European Court of Human Rights, where the needs of 'national security' were deemed to outweigh freedom of expression: *Engel* v *Netherlands (No. 1)* (1976) 1 EHRR 647 and *Klass* v *Germany* (1978) 2 EHRR 214.

Shayler's 'whistle-blower' argument also fell on stony ground. *R* v *Ponting* [1985] Crim LR 318 had stated that a civil servant, concerned about wrongdoing, should report their worries to their superiors, not the press. The House of Lords suggested that Shayler should have told his Secretary of State. A minister may authorise the disclosure of 'secrets' under s. 7 of the 1989 Act. It seems, on these precedents, that Jane will be convicted under the 1989 Act.

The journalist too, commits an offence if he knowingly receives the information and knowingly passes it on (s. 5). This the *Sentinel* newspaper seems determined to do. It is necessary, however, for the information to contravene the foregoing provisions of the Act for this to be an offence. As we have seen, it is by no means clear that it is 'defence' or 'international relations' information. The journalist also has a 'not damaging' defence.

Under s. 8 it is a specific offence for a Crown servant like Jane to retain the actual document 'contrary to her official duty'. Again, though, for the offence to be committed it has to relate to 'defence' or 'international relations'.

The government has other measures that it could utilise against Jane. The 'D-notice' is just a non-statutory warning issued by a committee of members of the media, civil servants and the military. It is not an offence to ignore the notice. Civil injunctions can be sought to prevent breach of the Official Secrets Act, as occurred in the Zircon Affair of 1986–7. As such an injunction would probably be issued ex parte, the government might be successful in obtaining it. The court would await the full trial before looking into the finer legal points.

There is possibly a very simple way to recover the document. The document and copies of it are personal property that belong to the government. It could simply sue in tort for its return. This occurred in a rather similar case to our facts, *Secretary of State for Defence* v *Guardian Newspapers* [1984] Ch 156. Sarah Tisdall, a civil servant, had handed a document about cruise missiles to *The Guardian* newspaper. Section 10 of the Contempt of Court Act 1981 allows a journalist to protect his sources, but not if it is an issue of national security. This might well be such an issue and the document's return would be ordered.

Jane, as a civil servant, would be subject to dismissal for breach of contract. If the newspaper paid her, the fee could be recovered as damages according to *A-G* v *Blake* [2001] 1 AC 268.

The most flexible remedy that the government has, is to seek an injunction for breach of confidence. It is clear that Jane has an obligation of confidence as a civil servant. The government would need to show that it was in the public interest to prevent disclosure: *A-G* v *The Observer, The Times (Spycatcher)* [1990] AC 109. Damage to the security services was the reason for non-disclosure in that case. Here, though, Jane, wishes to reveal breaches of the law. It is permissible to reveal criminal wrong-doing, even if it is a breach of confidence: *Cork* v *McVicar, The Times*, 31 October 1984. The court did not extend this approach to the revelation of government wrongdoing in *Attorney General* v *The Observer, The Times* [1990] AC 109. A civil servant, such as Jane, should report their worries to their superiors and not the press.

It is possible though, that the entry into force of the Human Rights Act 1998 might help Jane. Decisions of the European Court of Human Rights have emphasised the importance of freedom of expression. Although the Court found the law on breach of confidence acceptable in *Observer* v *UK* (1991) 14 EHRR 153, they thought that the 'Spycatcher' injunction should have been lifted earlier, as the material was already in the public domain. Now, under s.12 of the Human Rights Act 1998, the courts of the UK must have special regard to freedom of expression. In *Attorney General* v *The Times* [2001] 1 WLR 885 the newspaper was about to publish extracts from a book by, Tomlinson, a former MI6 officer. The court allowed this as the material had already been published elsewhere. It was up to the government to prove that there was a need to restrict Freedom of Expression 'in the interests of national security'. The newspaper did not have to prove that the material was already in the public domain, the government had to prove that it was not.

Jane's problem is that her material is not already in the public domain. I would suggest that the court is more likely to follow the approach in *Shayler* (above) and issue an injunction to protect national security. The *Sentinel* would also be injuncted and all other newspapers that could reasonably be expected to know about the injunction would also be bound: *Attorney General* v *Newspaper Publishing* [1999] 2 WLR 994. So, in conclusion, Jane risks conviction under the Official Secrets Act 1989, damages for breach of contract and an injunction forbidding her disclosures. The Human Rights Act 1998 does not seem to have allayed the courts' fears about endangering national security.

Q Question 3

'In a democracy, people should have information about the workings of government. Without it, they cannot call their representatives to account and make informed use of their rights as citizens and electors.'

(Cm. 7285 White Paper on reform of the Official Secrets Act 1911.)

Consider whether a Freedom of Information Act would give people more information about the workings of government.

Commentary

Freedom of information legislation has been much in the news, because the incoming Labour government promised such an Act in their election manifesto of 1997. The authors of this book have long memories and they can recall that the previous Labour government of 1974 to 1979 also considered such legislation. That is the origin of the quotation above, but, as usual in constitutional and administrative law, it is not necessary to be familiar with the source of a quotation in order to answer. If you read the question it is perfectly straightforward; would a Freedom of Information Act be a good thing?

There has been a long-running campaign to introduce such an Act, and the Freedom of Information Act 2000 finally became law after making very slow progress through Parliament. Campaigners for freedom of information want more rights of access to information than any government, of any political persuasion, is likely to concede. The Act has been much criticised, particularly because of the large number of exemptions to the right of information contained within it and, also, because of the considerable powers that the government has retained to decide what those exemptions should be. Therein lies valuable material for your essay! The suggested answer below is slightly more ambitious, in that it attempts to set a Freedom of Information Act in the context of the various powers that the government has to control the flow of information. Here you could show your knowledge of legislation such as the Official Secrets Acts, which you might have revised or studied anyway. Another possibility would be to try and compare the British Act with similar legislation in other countries. That would, however, require a reasonably detailed knowledge of that foreign legislation.

- The Public Records Acts allow the release of some government documents.

- The Official Secrets Act 1911 prevents the release of information for a purpose prejudicial to the safety and interests of the State.

- The Official Secrets Act 1989 protects information relating to security and intelligence, defence, international relations and criminal investigations.

- Breach of confidence protects government information.

- A voluntary Code of Practice promotes the release of government information.

- The Freedom of Information Act 2000 requires public authorities to publish information.

- The public may request information from a public authority.

- But there are many exemptions.

- Government ministers have a strong role in exempting information.

- Appeal to the Information Commissioner.

∶Ọ̈∶ Suggested answer

The Home Office's 1999 consultation paper on freedom of information starts by stating that:

> Freedom of information is an essential component of the government's programme to modernise British politics. This programme of constitutional reform aims to involve people more closely in the decisions which affect their lives.

While this may be true, the government does not plan to repeal the laws that successive governments have used to control government information.

The Public Records Act 1958 allows public access to some historical government documents. Each government department decides upon which of its files needs preserving for historical reasons. Normally these are released after 30 years and contain much interesting material, such as the minutes of Cabinet meetings. However some material is never released, such as security and intelligence, civil and home defence atomic energy and the personnel records of civil servants. Other material is retained for periods in excess of 30 years. For instance tax documents are kept back for 75 years and census material for 100 years. Decisions on retention are taken by the Lord Chancellor, but at least the Freedom of Information Act will replace that with its general statutory scheme for access, complete with an appeal mechanism.

The Official Secrets Act 1911 can always be used in a serious case, for s. 1 remains and makes it a serious offence to obtain or communicate any document or information 'for a purpose prejudicial to the safety or interests of the state'. *R v Ponting* [1985] Crim LR 318 held, in the case of a whistle-blowing civil servant, who wanted to reveal documents about a controversial military act to an MP, that only the government could decide what was in 'the safety or interests of the state'. The Official Secrets Act 1989 was a reform, but the crucial areas of information, that a government would wish to keep secret, are still protected by criminal sanction. These are security and intelligence, defence, international relations and criminal investigations. The D Notice committee, which warns journalists not to investigate certain areas, for fear of prosecution, also still exists, as does the practice of 'signing' the Official Secrets Act, which serves a similar warning function for individuals.

Failing this, a government could always use the civil remedy of breach of confidence to restrain, by injunction, government employees, ex-employees and those they pass the information to, such as newspapers and publishers, from betraying confidences. The most spectacular example of this was the protracted litigation against the ex-security agent Peter Wright's book, 'Spycatcher' in the late 1980s and early 1990s, culminating in the House of Lords' decision *A-G* v *Guardian (No. 2)* [1990] 1 AC 109, where the injunctions were only lifted because the information was, by now, so well known that to continue them would be pointless. Governments have not tired of pursuing such actions for in *A-G* v *Blake* [2000] 4 All ER 385, an ex-member of the Secret Intelligence Service had been sued for breaching his contractual obligation, not to reveal what he had learnt from his employment. The House of Lords decided that Blake would have to account (i.e., restore) the profits made from the book, that he published about his career.

Legal proceedings against Blake actually began in 1991, under the previous Conservative government of John Major. At the same time he was proclaiming his belief in 'Open Government'. This started with the release of hitherto secret information, such as the names and composition of the various Cabinet committees, the guidelines for ministerial behaviour 'Questions of Procedure for Ministers' (now known as the Ministerial Code) and some details about M15 and M16. Later on a Code of Practice was introduced which, for instance, required government to routinely release far more information than previously. A Code of Practice was chosen, rather than a legally binding system, because the government claimed that they did not want to damage the convention-based system of Ministerial Responsibility, under which ministers voluntarily release information in parliamentary statements, answers to MPs' questions etc. The more cynical might think that the government preferred a system where the courts would not be able to order them to release information. Under the Code, an applicant might make a 'reasonable request for information' although a charge reflecting 'actual costs' could be made. Unlike, say, the US Freedom of Information Act 1966, copies of the actual document themselves would not be released, just the information that they contained. If the request was refused there was an appeal mechanism, first to the department concerned, then to an MP and finally to the Parliamentary Commissioner for Administration. As is common with such systems in other countries, there were a great number of categories of information exempt from disclosure, ranging from defence to commercial confidences. This system exists to this day and requests for information can even be made over the Internet!

In the year 2000, a Freedom of Information Act was enacted to replace this voluntary Code of Practice. Although this will make requests for information enforceable in court and there are some improvements in access to information, the problem of numerous exemptions still remains.

First, the government wants to promote a 'change of culture within the public sector' and wants all 'public authorities' to voluntarily publish far more information.

Public authority is broadly defined, to mean any body or office exercising a public function and includes those providing services of that nature to the public authority. There is a list of public authorities in the Freedom of Information Act and all must draw up a publication scheme. It is anticipated that this would include things like schools: admission criteria and how priorities on hospital waiting lists are determined, which are matters of concern to the general public, not just to those interested in politics.

Otherwise any person can request information from a public authority. The public authority has a duty to confirm or deny whether they hold the information or not. If they do they must provide it, although a small fee may be charged. The applicant may even express a preference about whether they want the information to be provided as a copy of a document, a digest or summary or whether they just want to inspect it. There are a number of grounds upon which the public authority can refuse to supply the information, such as that it is already available, about to be published, would be too expensive or the request is 'vexatious', e.g., the applicant has made repeated requests for the same information.

The main criticism of the Act is that there are a large number of exempted categories of information where there is no duty to disclose. Apart from this obvious criticism, the different exemptions are differently defined, which may cause confusion amongst the public. For instance, there is no duty to disclose information relating to security and intelligence agencies or national security, nor is there even any duty to confirm or deny that the requested information exists. There are similar exemptions for any information relating to the Queen, Royal Family or Royal Household, including the conferring of honours. The usual formula, though, is that refusal can be justified only if disclosure 'would, or would be likely to, prejudice' certain specified interests such as defence, international relations, relations between Scotland, Northern Ireland, Wales and the rest of the UK, the economic or financial interests of the country, law enforcement and trade secrets. Other exemptions lack the 'prejudice formula' and cover things like legal professional privilege, breach of confidence personal data, endangering a person's physical or mental health etc.

Another problem is the strong government role in these exemptions, when the government is the very organisation which may be trying to conceal information. Government ministers certificate whether information has been supplied by a security or intelligence agency and whether it is a threat to national security. Communications between government ministers, Cabinet communications and advice from civil servants on policy formulation are all exempted information. What is more, a government minister can also give an opinion that information should be withheld because it could prejudice the convention of collective responsibility, inhibit the free and frank provision of advice or prejudice public affairs. Lastly, and most controversially, a Secretary of State can add to the list of exempt information, merely by using delegated legislation. This could even be retrospective, so a government confronted with an unwelcome request for information could, presumably, change the law so that they did not have to release the information. Parliament would, however, have to agree to this delegated legislation, as the Act requires the affirmative resolution procedure.

Fortunately, the Freedom of Information Act comes complete with a fairly robust enforcement system. First, the public authority needs to provide an internal complaint procedure. Then the applicant can apply to the 'Information Commissioner', an independent official created by the Act. Either the applicant or the public authority has an appeal to an Information Tribunal, with further appeals on a point of law to the High Court and then upwards to the Court of Appeal and House of Lords, if necessary. It may be noted that the Tribunal can only question a Minister's national security certificate on a judicial review basis. This Information Commissioner will also have pretty impressive enforcement powers and she will be able to investigate, obtain search warrants and order the release of information. The penalty for defying her or lying to her could be proceedings in the High Court for contempt of court.

When compared to freedom of information legislation in other countries, such as the US Freedom of Information Act 1966, or the Australian or Swedish equivalents, the same problem of exemptions occurs. The British Act, in comparison, does seem to have rather a lot of exemptions and they are rather widely drawn. The government also seems to have undue power to widen the scope of these exemptions. A strong Information Commissioner would help to counteract this and it is to be hoped, in the post-Human Rights Act 1998 era, that courts dealing with the inevitable appeals will interpret the Act in a way that promotes freedom of expression. For the moment, however, we will have to wait, because the Freedom of Information Act does not come fully into force until 30 November 2005.

Further reading

Bradley, A. and Ewing, K. *Constitutional & Administrative Law*, 13th edn (Longman, 2003), ch 23.

Bailey, S., Harris, D. and Jones, B. *Civil Liberties Cases and Materials*, 5th edn (Butterworths, 2001), chs 6, 7 and 8.

O Hoad, Phillips and Jackson. *Constitutional and Administrative Law*, 8th edn (Sweet & Maxwell, 2001) chs 25 and 26.

Administrative law:
extra-judicial redress

Introduction

This chapter covers a variety of topics which could be included in constitutional and/or administrative law courses, though not all courses will include all of them, particularly since the growth of judicial review has rendered other methods of redress of less interest to lawyers. But, where they are included, they provide students with relatively straight-forward subjects for examination answers. What will in each case make an adequate answer into a good one is the quality of the arguments advanced and the drawing from those arguments of a soundly based and well reasoned conclusion.

Q Question 1

The processes for the making of delegated legislation are not satisfactory. Parliament grants excessively wide powers to the administration, and then fails to scrutinise adequately the way those powers are used.

Explain and discuss. What reforms would you suggest to improve the scrutiny of delegated legislation?

Commentary

This question addresses two areas, the way Parliament delegates powers to the administration and the way Parliament watches over the making of the subsequent orders, regulations and statutory instruments. The answer will need to be based on an explanation of the place of delegated legislation within the administrative system, though there is no need for a lengthy discussion of the merits and defects of it in principle. The student needs to identify reforms which will address the defects identified in the earlier part of the answer, and justify them by argument.

- Scrutiny of enabling Act.

- Henry VIII clauses.

- Affirmative resolution.

- Negative resolution.

- Joint Committee on Statutory Instruments.

:Q: Suggested answer

The delegation of legislative powers by Parliament to the administration has long been a feature of the British administrative system. Although such delegation has been criticised as inherently improper, and contrary to the doctrine of separation of powers, it is now accepted as essential. Parliament could not possibly enact all the laws necessary in the complex, modern welfare state; it has difficulty coping with the current amount of primary legislation. A proper distinction has to be drawn between matters of policy and principle, requiring Parliament's full attention, and matters of technical detail, which can safely be left in the hands of the administration. Delegated legislation may be accepted as conceptually satisfactory, but still subjected to criticism on grounds of inappropriate use or inadequate supervision.

There are no constitutional limits on the power of Parliament to delegate legislative powers to the administration, because of the doctrine of parliamentary supremacy, except that Parliament may always revoke any delegation it has made. Parliament has granted the administration extremely wide powers; the Emergency Powers (Defence) Act 1939 permitted the government to make regulations for 'public safety, the defence of the realm, the maintenance of public order and the efficient prosecution of the war'. It is difficult to imagine any subject not covered by such a provision.

Control over the extent of delegation is in the hands of Parliament when it passes the enabling Act, but a government with a secure majority in the House of Commons can be sure in most circumstances of obtaining whatever delegated powers it wants. Indeed, Parliament may easily fail to realise the implications of an enabling Act. There is general agreement that parliamentary scrutiny of legislation is unsatisfactory, especially where pressures of time lead to the imposition of guillotine motions, leaving some provisions of a Bill unexamined by committee. Whether regulations are subject to affirmative or negative resolution may appear to be a mere technical detail, but, as will be seen, is in fact of major importance.

The only specific machinery for the scrutiny of enabling legislation is in the House of Lords. The select committee on the scrutiny of delegated powers was set up in 1992. It examines enabling legislation when it is introduced into the House of Lords, considers the justifications offered by the government for seeking such powers, and then reports to the Lords in time, normally, for the committee stage of the Bill. It performs the very useful function of drawing to the Lords' attention any delegation it considers excessive or undesirable. This forces the government to offer a public justification of its proposals, and has on occasion helped to force the government to accept amendments to the legislation. It is significant that this valuable addition to parliamentary scrutiny of legislation is in the House of Lords, where the government cannot rely on the passive obedience of its back-bench MPs. It would clearly be desirable for the House of Commons to establish some such committee, or for a joint Lords and Commons committee to be set up, but the potential for government embarrassment is likely to prevent the acceptance of any such proposal. Reliance will have to continue to be placed on the vigilance of individual MPs in standing committees instead.

The most controversial form of enabling provision is the so-called Henry VIII clause, which permits the government to make delegated legislation which amends other primary legislation. This is regarded by many as constitutionally improper, on the grounds that the amendment of parliamentary legislation should only be conducted by Parliament itself. It can, however, be justified where the draftsmen have been unable to assure themselves that all possible clashing legislation has been suitably amended. It is also possible to justify the provision in the European Communities Act 1972 which authorises the government to use delegated legislation to implement European Community laws as they are made, including amendments and repeals of earlier UK statutes. Schedule 2 of the 1972 Act imposes restrictions on the use of this power, and in any case the EC law will have passed through, and been scrutinised during, the EC's own legislative processes. The Human Rights Act 1998 contains a Henry VIII clause, presumably to protect the government where a statute has been found to be in breach of human rights. Rather than having to persuade Parliament to pass amending legislation through the full legislative process, a minister can use delegated legislation to make a remedial order. In cases of extreme urgency, the order can take effect before Parliament approves it. As such orders are, by definition, intended to improve the protection of human rights, they have attracted less criticism than other forms of Henry VIII clause. Very serious concern was expressed in Parliament during the passage of the Deregulation and Contracting-Out Act 1994, which gave ministers unprecedented powers to make orders which amend or repeal previous legislation, if the minister considered this would relieve business of an unnecessary burden. But the government was able to ensure the passage of the Act with only minor amendments to the procedural safeguards on the making of such orders, demonstrating the limited control that Parliament can actually exercise at this stage over a government with a working majority.

Turning to examine the scrutiny of the delegated legislation itself, it is normally the practice that delegated legislation has to be laid before Parliament, though there is no obligation to include such a requirement in any enabling Act. There are various procedures which may be selected; the instrument may simply have to be laid, or laid in draft, and Parliament may or may not have an opportunity to vote on it. Parliament's greatest opportunity for control arises where the instrument is subject to affirmative procedure, that is, it has to be approved by a vote of each House, in draft or in its final form, before it can come into effect. This means that the government has to find time for debates in both Houses, though in the Commons most measures are debated in a standing committee rather than on the floor of the House. The provisions of the Parliament Acts 1911 and 1949 do not apply, so the House of Lords retains its veto, though it has only ever used it once in modern times. The Wakeham Commission proposed that a reformed second chamber should lose this veto, replacing it with power to delay delegated legislation for three months. It is possible for the enabling Act to demand the approval of the Commons only, and this is normal for taxation matters, over which the Lords have almost no control. Affirmative resolution procedure is generally regarded as satisfactory and many commentators would like to see it more widely used.

It is far more common, however, for enabling Acts to impose the negative resolution procedure, which is governed by the Statutory Instruments Act 1946, s. 5. The instrument is laid before Parliament, either in draft, or after the department has made it. During the next 40 days, either House may pass a 'prayer' that it be annulled, forcing the government to withdraw it. The main defect of this procedure is that a prayer will only be debated if time is made available by the government, which it will be reluctant to do. In recent years, only a handful of instruments subject to negative resolution procedure have been debated at all. To improve this, the House of Commons procedure committee suggested in 1996 that a sifting committee should be set up to examine all instruments laid before the House. It would have power to recommend which instruments subject to negative resolution should be debated, and could also recommend which instruments subject to affirmative resolution were so non-controversial that they could be approved without debate. This would seem a desirable reform, but the Government rejected it. In 2003 the House of Lords decided to set up its own sifting committee to perform this function. A suggestion that a joint committee should be established was rejected by the government, on the ground that it wanted to see how the Lords committee worked. If it is seen to be useful, there may be pressure to introduce what would be a useful reform.

Under both the affirmative and negative procedures, Parliament has no power to amend delegated legislation, unless such a power is granted by the enabling Act. This is an unfortunate rule, as it means the House has to vote against an entire instrument if it is unhappy with just one aspect of it. The instrument will then have to be withdrawn and a new instrument laid, with the whole procedure repeated. As both Houses of Parliament are permitted to amend primary legislation, it is difficult to justify a different rule for secondary legislation. A change to the rule would make parliamentary scrutiny more effective and would ultimately save parliamentary time.

The negative resolution procedure would be even less effective if it depended solely on the vigilance of individual MPs, as the sheer volume of delegated legislation makes it impossible for them to check on all proposals. Since 1973, a joint committee on statutory instruments, drawn from both Lords and Commons, has assisted MPs and Lords in this task. It examines all statutory instruments laid before Parliament and all other general statutory instruments. It can draw the attention of Parliament to the instrument on various grounds concerned with the procedure and legality of the instrument, though not its substantive merits. These grounds include: that it imposes a charge, is retrospective, attempts to exclude review, may not be intra vires, makes an unusual or unexpected use of powers or that there has been delay in its laying or publication. The committee will be given an explanation by the department of its proposals; it can call witnesses from the department if it thinks it necessary.

The committee, a hard-working body, issues reports after each of its weekly meetings, but all too often it is impossible for it to report in time for Parliament to make use of its reports. The 40 day period for prayers against instruments is not extended to allow for scrutiny by the joint committee, though such a provision would clearly be desirable. However, the committee still performs a useful task, ensuring that departments have to justify their proposals; where obvious defects are identified, it is always open to the department to withdraw the instrument itself for amendment and improvement, rather than risk disapproval by Parliament or later legal action on grounds of ultra vires.

An interesting development occurred in relation to the Deregulation and Contracting Out Act 1994, now replaced by the Regulatory Reform Act 2001. These Acts have given ministers wide powers to make orders modifying previous legislation. Such orders have to be laid in draft and approved by both Houses, with the period for parliamentary scrutiny extended to 60 days. The House of Commons set up a select committee, now the Regulatory Reform Committee, which examines proposed orders in detail. If the committee approves the proposal, it is voted on in the House of Commons without debate, but if it rejects the proposal, a full debate must be held. In practice, governments have withdrawn any orders rejected by the committee rather than trying to force them through. The House of Lords uses its delegated powers scrutiny committee to perform the same function. A similar procedure has been adopted to deal with remedial orders under the Human Rights Act 1998. These are referred to the Joint Committee on Human Rights, which may recommend approval or rejection of an order. These new procedures have improved parliamentary scrutiny of some of the most far-reaching enabling powers held by the government, but it would be desirable if other powers were more closely examined in this way.

Although traditionally primary legislation has received much more attention from Parliament, scrutiny of delegated legislation is just as important, as it too creates the law of the land, conferring rights and obligations on citizens. Parliament cannot be said to perform this function satisfactorily, though the blame for this lies primarily in the level of executive dominance, particularly over the House of Commons. But the more extensive the powers delegated to ministers, the more essential it is that

Parliament should not neglect scrutiny of its use. The price of freedom is indeed eternal vigilance.

Q Question 2

'In Britain, Parliament is the place for ventilating the grievances of the citizen . . . It is one of the functions of the elected Member of Parliament to try to secure that his constituents do not suffer at the hand of the Government.'
White Paper on the Parliamentary Commissioner for Administration, 1967.

How important is Parliament as a means of redressing citizens' grievances? How effective are MPs in performing this task?

Commentary

This question requires the student to explain why MPs have this role, how it fits into the constitution and what MPs can actually do in practice. It is hardly possible to attempt any quantitative assessment, but any relevant statistics will be useful. The student can usefully make some comparisons with other methods of redress and explain how they interrelate.

• **Closer ties between MP and constituency.**

• **Access through MPs' surgeries, websites and correspondence.**

• **Writing to and buttonholing ministers.**

• **Parliamentary Questions, adjournment debates and ombudsmen.**

☼ Suggested answer

One of the stock remarks of that traditionally irascible British citizen, Disgusted of Tunbridge Wells, has always been, 'I shall write to my MP about this!'. Every day, MPs receive numerous letters, calls and e-mails from their constituents, and almost every week they set aside times for surgeries in their constituencies where voters can meet them in person. This demonstrates clearly how much this function of MPs is a deep-seated part of the British constitution.

The role of the MP, from as far back as the Middle Ages, has always included bringing the concerns of the constituent to the attention of the authorities, though the unreformed electoral system often meant that the MP had only a patron to please, rather than a wide electorate. But as the system was reformed in the nineteenth century, with extensions to the franchise and redistribution of seats, more MPs had to take account of their constituents' concerns. By 1900 it was common practice for MPs to take up individual grievances, though there were still MPs in safe seats whose contact with their constituencies was minimal.

Over the last 50 years, however, there appears to have been a considerable increase in the involvement of MPs in the redress of individual grievances. Various factors have contributed to this. The growth of the welfare state and the intervention of the government in new areas have increased the occasions for grievances to arise. All citizens have dealings with public bodies which may give rise to problems; taxation, social security and health are obvious examples.

The electorate is increasingly articulate, educated and willing to express dissatisfaction, rather than suffering injustice passively. There has been a growth in campaigning groups, in areas such as the environment, who are likely to try to gain the ear of the local MP. It also appears that MPs have changed their attitudes towards their constituency duties. It has been suggested that, feeling that their influence at Westminster has been reduced by the rigidity of the party system, MPs seek the satisfaction of assisting individual constituents as a replacement for the loss of opportunity to influence government policy. In selecting and reselecting candidates, local parties take account of the level of local commitment shown by those seeking nomination.

A further relevant factor is that many more MPs can now be described as career politicians, hoping to remain in Parliament long enough to gain a front bench position. Such MPs are likely to take much more trouble to cultivate their constituency reputation, in the hope of securing a personal vote as a cushion against party unpopularity. It is important to note that the first past the post electoral system, with its single member constituencies, provides a strong incentive for MPs to take up individual cases, unlike some other systems. Although assisting constituents does not guarantee that they will vote for that MP, no MP dare risk offending a constituent by refusing to help. Many MPs are at pains to ensure that the local media are informed of their successes on their constituents' behalf.

The description of Parliament as the place for ventilating grievances is constitutionally justified as an aspect of the doctrine of ministerial responsibility. The MP is entitled to demand information from ministers and to call ministers to account. The strength of the party system now means that Parliament can rarely overthrow the government, but ministers are still under an obligation to satisfy MPs as to their conduct and that of their departments. Of course, MPs deal, on their constituents' behalf, with other organisations as well, but underlying even these is the possibility that, if such organisations are misbehaving, the minister could be expected to intervene with improved regulation. Although ministerial resignation has become a rarity, ministerial accountability on a daily basis remains an active element in the constitution.

There is some evidence of the increasing scale on which people contact their MPs, for assistance and information, as well as to let off steam. In the 1960s, MPs each received between 25 and 75 letters a week; by the 1980s this had risen to 20 to 50 letters every day. These were followed up by MPs writing over 15,000 letters a month to ministers; one minister claimed to send 300 replies to such letters every week. These figures demonstrate how extensive the use of MPs is, and contrasts markedly with the 2,000 or so applications for judicial review made each year. The issues raised by constituents will vary according to the social make-up of the constituency. In poorer areas, council housing and welfare benefit problems will predominate; in wealthier areas, health, transport and education issues will be more common. Most initial contact from constituents is by correspondence, though significant numbers attend an MP's surgery in person. Many MPs now have personal websites, and invite contact by e-mail.

It appears that MPs will very rarely decline to take up a matter on behalf of a constituent, though most adhere strictly to the convention not to take up a matter raised by any other MP's constituent. Only if a complaint appears totally ill-founded, or if some other means of redress is clearly more appropriate will the MP refuse to become involved. The most usual course of action for an MP who takes up a complaint is to write to the appropriate ministry, agency or other organisation. Civil Service practice ensures that MPs' letters are given priority over other business, and are dealt with at a higher level in the official hierarchy. Where an individual citizen may be fobbed off with a standard letter from a junior official, the MP's intervention will at least provoke a prompt response from someone more senior, even the minister in person. In many cases this may achieve the desired result without further action. If the constituent's complaint was of delay in the administration, the MP will normally be able to speed up the process; if the constituent wanted a decision reviewed, the MP's involvement will ensure a second look is taken.

Most MPs will leave it up to the constituent to decide whether the initial response is satisfactory, but will be willing to take further steps if the constituent is still aggrieved. This may take the form of further correspondence. or more informally, speaking to the minister perhaps in the corridor or voting lobby in Parliament. Failing this, the MP may arrange a formal meeting with the minister to press the case. If all these methods fail, the MP may invoke the formal procedures of the House of Commons. Foremost among these is the parliamentary question, put down for oral or written answer. This will elicit a public response from the minister which will be on the record. It is likely to be most effective where the matter is of a kind to attract attention. Parliamentary questions can be used to embarrass the government by asking a question in abstract terms and then raising the constituent's grievance as a supplementary question. If this still achieves no result, the MP may seek to raise the issue as an adjournment debate; there is a ballot among MPs for the opportunity to choose the topic. By this stage the MP's chances of forcing the government to act will be dependent on the subject having attracted some media attention, or being taken up by one of the political parties.

If the grievance needs thorough investigation, the MP may refer it to the Parliamentary Commissioner for Administration, or another appropriate Ombudsman, though MPs seem reluctant to do this unless the constituent suggests it. Once such a reference is made, the matter is out of the MP's hands, though the MP will probably claim some of the credit if there is ultimately a successful result.

It is very difficult to assess the effectiveness of the MP in obtaining redress, but it appears that they are most effective in dealing with relatively minor and uncontroversial matters which can be disposed of by correspondence. Most government departments and other public bodies will feel able to make a concession or admit a mistake in the relative privacy of a letter. But once the matter has come out into the open, and entrenched positions have been adopted, it becomes very difficult for the MP to force a change of mind on a reluctant government. Only if there is a substantial media campaign, or an investigation by an Ombudsman, can a determined authority be forced to concede defeat.

MPs, however, have some great advantages as redressers of grievances. Their services are free and easily accessible; many MPs take great pains to advertise their surgery times and other means of contact in the local media. Most are assiduous in taking up grievances, and often the mere fact of receiving a letter from an MP, rather than from an ordinary citizen, will induce the authority to give a favourable response. Further, the MP's services are equally useful whether the constituent is asking for the correction of an error or the more favourable exercise of a discretion, where no legal redress would be available. Legal action for judicial review has the advantage of being able to produce a decisive and binding result, but it is limited in scope, and carries financial penalties if unsuccessful.

Although some traditionalists resisted innovations like the introduction of Ombudsmen on the grounds that they would diminish the role of the MP in the redress of grievances, it would seem that neither Ombudsmen, nor the growth of judicial review, have prevented the role of the individual MP from developing and expanding. MPs are clearly continuing to provide a useful and popular means of redress for the aggrieved citizen.

Q Question 3

How effective has the Parliamentary Commissioner for Administration been in providing redress for citizens aggrieved by acts of maladministration?

Commentary

This is a fairly straightforward question. The answer requires as a basis a description of the jurisdiction, powers and practices of the PCA. To produce a good answer, the student needs to cite some examples of the PCA's work, and to make explicit the criteria against which effectiveness is being judged. Any comparisons with Ombudsmen from other states will enhance the answer.

- Power over central government.

- Exclusions.

- Relationship with judicial review.

- The MP filter.

- Maladministration defined.

:Q: Suggested answer

The office of Parliamentary Commissioner for Administration (PCA) or Ombudsman was introduced into the UK in 1967, because of concern that existing methods of redress were inadequate. Following the example of Scandinavian states, it was hoped that an Ombudsman would provide a simple and understandable means by which citizens' complaints could be dealt with. Since 1967, the idea of redress through Ombudsmen has spread widely through both the public and private sectors in the UK, but some disappointment has been expressed that the PCA, the most senior Ombudsman with the most important area of jurisdiction, has not been more effective.

The PCA's powers of investigation cover most government departments and very many non-departmental government bodies. It appears to be accepted practice that as such bodies are created they are brought within the PCA's jurisdiction, though there may inevitably be some time lag. There are, however, various matters specifically excluded from the PCA's remit by Sch. 3, Parliamentary Commissioner Act 1967. Some of the exclusions can be justified on the grounds that alternative methods of redress are available. The National Health Service has its own Commissioner, though the post has always been held concurrently with that of the PCA. Other exclusions are open to criticism, particularly the exclusion of contractual and other commercial transactions entered into by the government. Governments use contracts as an instrument of policy and their maladministration could easily cause injustice. In recent years there has been an increase in the contracting out to the private and voluntary sectors of services traditionally performed by the government itself, and it is clearly undesirable if this process is excluded from investigation. Personnel matters in both the military and civil services are also excluded from the PCA's jurisdiction, in spite of the fact that sensitive issues may arise. The introduction of a formal appeal machinery for the dismissal of civil servants has alleviated this problem, but in many other countries, complaints from civil servants form an important part of the Ombudsman's work.

A further limitation on the PCA's powers is found in s. 5(2) of the Act, which forbids her to investigate matters which the aggrieved person could have taken to a tribunal, or brought before the ordinary courts, unless she considers that it was not reasonable for the person to have used that remedy. It seems acceptable that, where a specific statutory remedy has been provided, such as the tribunals dealing with taxation or social security, the individual should be expected to use it. There is more difficulty where the remedy is not specific, and those who drafted the 1967 Act cannot have anticipated the huge growth of judicial review. The PCA seems to take the view that it is generally reasonable for a person to use her services rather than seek judicial review, given the cost and uncertainty of that method of redress. It is important to note that the PCA's services are free to the complainant, whether the complaint is upheld or not. There is inevitably some overlap between the roles of courts and PCA. For example, the PCA criticised the heavy-handed treatment by HM Customs and Excise of travellers with too many cigarettes; in *R. (Hoverspeed)* v *Customs & Excise Commissioners* [2002] EWCA Civ 1804, [2003] 2 All ER 553, the courts found the treatment constituted a breach of EU law on the free movement of goods and persons. If legal action is started after the PCA has received a complaint, he may drop his investigation, as he did with complaints about the discriminatory treatment of widowers by the Inland Revenue.

The aspect of the PCA's powers that has always caused most controversy is the fact that, unlike virtually every other Ombudsman in the world, she cannot accept complaints directly from the public. Instead, they must be referred to her by an MP. This system was imposed partly because of fears that the PCA would be overwhelmed by the number of complaints, and partly to help preserve the traditional method of redress through Parliament. But it has acted as a severe limitation on the availability of the PCA as a method of redress. The number of complaints referred by MPs has rarely exceeded 2,000 in any year, and many of these are rejected as outside the PCA's jurisdiction. The PCA does try to ensure that all MPs are aware of her services and understand her powers, but this does not seem to be effective. In any case, MPs prefer to deal with constituents' complaints themselves, as they will then get credit and, they hope, votes at the next election.

The lack of direct access creates a circular problem. There is little point in the PCA embarking on any large-scale publicity campaign, when any matters referred directly to her would have to be sent back, and complainants advised to contact their MP. Few people have heard of the PCA and fewer still would suggest to their MP that the PCA might be used. Research indicates that the MP will rarely make the suggestion of reference to the PCA if the constituent does not raise it. The PCA therefore remains underused. Many critics have argued for the abolition of the MP filter, and a recent Cabinet Office paper supported this view. There is the further issue that, if the number of complaints increased substantially, the PCA's staff would have to be expanded, with a consequent increase in public expenditure, always unpopular with governments. When direct access to the Commission for Local Administration was introduced, the number of complaints shot up from 3,000 to 12,000 a year, and the same would certainly happen with the PCA.

The PCA's function is defined in s. 5(1) of the Act as being to investigate complaints of 'injustice in consequence of maladministration'. The term 'maladministration' was deliberately not defined in the Act, though Richard Crossman gave some examples during the passage of the Bill: 'bias, neglect, inattention, delay, incompetence, ineptitude, perversity, turpitude, arbitrariness and so on'. The Act did, however, make it clear that the PCA was not to reconsider the merits of discretionary decisions taken without maladministration (s. 12(3)); she was not providing a means of appeal against decisions which people did not like.

There were initial concerns that the first PCA was taking too narrow a view of maladministration. He was encouraged by the Select Committee to extend his definition to include both bad decisions, that is, decisions appearing at first glance to be unreasonably perverse, and bad rules, that is, rules which produced excessively harsh results in practice. Most cases concern defects in the way decisions are made and unfair treatment of individuals. Common examples are delay, giving incorrect or misleading advice, failing to inform people of their rights and unfairness as between individuals.

The process of investigation is generally seen as painstaking and thorough. The PCA has power to demand all government papers, with the exception of Cabinet papers, which may be withheld by the Cabinet Secretary with the Prime Minister's approval. The PCA has all the powers of a court to summon witnesses and take their evidence on oath if necessary, and can order the production of documents. She is not bound by the Official Secrets Act, Crown privilege or public interest immunity. It is therefore possible for the PCA to go deeply into the decision-making processes of the government and uncover what lies behind the public façade. It would be quite impossible for an individual MP to do this. A striking example is the PCA's investigation into the Barlow Clowes affair, where the Department of Trade and Industry had failed to exercise its regulatory powers properly. This complex investigation resulted in the production of a 120,000 word report detailing a history of maladministration lasting 13 years.

The only problem with the thoroughness of the PCA's investigations is that it makes them slow, averaging over one year, though this is partly explained by the fact that only complex cases get through the MP filter; MPs manage the straightforward cases themselves. As a former PCA has pointed out, the mere fact that a reference to the PCA has been made may induce a government department which knows that it has not behaved properly to offer immediate redress, thereby avoiding an adverse finding. Only the debatable cases will need full investigation.

The PCA has the power to make recommendations, but has no power to force the government to follow them. However, as a general rule, the government will comply with the recommendations even if reluctant. In the Barlow Clowes case, the government disputed the PCA's finding of maladministration but none the less accepted the obligation to compensate the investors, at a cost of £150 million, by far the largest sum ever paid out on the PCA's recommendation. The PCA only succeeded, however, in obtaining compensation for a few of those whose properties had been blighted by delays in choosing and building the Channel Tunnel rail link. In general, it is politically very difficult for a government to reject what is seen, by Parliament and the country, as an independent, impartial and thorough assessment of the complaint.

If difficulties do arise in persuading the government to accept the PCA's recommendations, the matter may be taken up by the Select Committee on the PCA which monitors the PCA's activities and the government's response to them. The existence of this committee increases the effectiveness of the PCA by ensuring that any failure to follow the recommendations is followed up. The relevant minister or the permanent head of the department is likely to be asked to appear before the committee to explain and justify the failure and the committee will not hesitate to issue an adverse report. In some countries, Ombudsmen do have the power to enforce their decisions, but such a power is rarely used.

In evaluating the overall effectiveness of the PCA, the first point to make is that the PCAs have succeeded, over the last 30 years, in obtaining redress for many hundreds of people who would probably have had no chance of redress in any other way. Those matters which are investigated are dealt with thoroughly and impartially and it is never suggested that the PCA has failed to get to the bottom of the problem and find out the truth. Dissatisfaction is concentrated on the issue of access; the limits on the PCA's jurisdiction and the MP filter have been the subject of sustained and cogent criticism, though reform seems as unlikely as ever. It is perhaps hardly fair to criticise the PCA, not for the cases she deals with, but for those which never reach her because of the obstructions placed in their way.

The hopes of those who initially advocated the introduction of a British Ombudsman may not have been entirely fulfilled, but the PCA has become one essential part of the machinery for redressing the grievances of individual citizens. Even the growth of judicial review during the last 30 years has not removed the need, in Britain as in many other countries, for a citizen's defender in this form.

Q Question 4

Because of global warming, it is considered likely that sea levels around the UK coast will rise, making existing sea defences inadequate. The government has decided that, in certain vulnerable areas, no further attempts will be made to protect them from flooding. Instead, a scheme will be established to pay compensation to property owners as their land becomes unusable. The government seeks your advice as to whether it would be desirable to establish a tribunal to deal with disputed claims for compensation. It also seeks advice on how any such tribunal should be operated.

Advise the government.

- Tribunals as judicial bodies.

- Tribunals distinguished from courts.

- Membership.

- Procedure.

- Appeals or judicial review.

Commentary

The underlying material for answering this question is the standard material on the advantages and disadvantages of tribunals. But it gives students a good opportunity to display and apply that material. For a good answer, a critical assessment of tribunals will be needed.

:Q: Suggested answer

There are three reasons why the government would find it wise to set up some machinery for dealing with this matter. First, there are bound to be disputes about eligibility and allegations that mistakes have been made in the initial administrative assessment of such claims. Any attempt to have such disputes dealt with by a purely administrative machinery is likely to be unpopular as it will not be seen to be sufficiently impartial. Secondly, at a more theoretical level, the scheme gives people an entitlement to compensation if they fulfil the relevant criteria. This makes disputes about entitlement judicial rather than administrative in nature. The doctrine of separation of powers, which though not rigidly adhered to in the UK is still influential, requires such disputes to be dealt with by a judicial body, whether court or tribunal. Thirdly, any failure by the government to set up some specific machinery for these disputes will not keep the matter out of the hands of the courts. Dissatisfied applicants may seek judicial review, which is available in respect of any decisions made by public bodies under public law, unless specifically excluded by Parliament. The government should note the case of *Anisminic v Foreign Compensation Commission* [1969] 2 AC 147, which demonstrates how difficult it is to draft an exclusion clause which will be effective where the courts are determined that it shall not be. Because the process of judicial review is slow, inconvenient for the applicant and uncertain in its application, the government would be wise to reduce, though not eliminate, its incidence by providing a specialised means of dealing with these disputes.

It is therefore necessary to decide whether disputes should be dealt with by a tribunal or by the ordinary courts. A tribunal, like a court, can be defined as an independent, impartial body with power to make decisions binding on the parties by the application of legal rules to facts established by evidence. The distinction between courts and tribunals lies in terminology rather than substance. The term 'court' is generally used where the body has a general jurisdiction over a wide range of cases, whereas 'tribunal' refers to a body with a limited, often very specific jurisdiction. Both courts and tribunals are, as the Franks Committee asserted in 1957, part of the judicial system; the term 'administrative tribunals' is misleading and should not be used.

If these disputes were to be referred to an ordinary court, they would have to be dealt with by the ordinary judges, whereas a tribunal could be staffed by persons with particular expertise. Tribunals often consist of three people, a legally qualified chair and two lay members with appropriate qualifications and experience. If this format were adopted, it would be particularly useful to have a qualified surveyor as one member of the tribunal. A further advantage would be that the members of the tribunal, by specialising in dealing with this particular group of claims, would develop a particular expertise and experience, which should enable them to deal with cases more quickly and efficiently.

If the number of claims is substantial, a group of tribunals may be needed. According to the Council on Tribunals, the best system of organisation is the presidential system, where the tribunals are under the supervision of a president, who is responsible for organising, co-ordinating and monitoring the work of the tribunals. The appointment of members of the tribunals is generally in the hands of the relevant government department, which has raised concerns as to the impartiality and independence of tribunals. But, under the Tribunals and Inquiries Act 1992, s. 5, the Council on Tribunals may make general recommendations about membership. Further, the Lord Chancellor is responsible, under s. 6 of the Act, for the appointment of the legally qualified chairmen of many tribunals, and, by s. 7, his consent is necessary for the dismissal of tribunal members. This in many ways assimilates the position of tribunal members to that of magistrates, so that concerns about independence and impartiality are no greater than those which can be expressed in relation to the courts. It is generally considered that tribunals' independence should be symbolised, wherever this is practicable, by their sitting in premises separate from the relevant government department.

The government's main concern in practice is likely to be the relative cost of using a tribunal or a court. If there are only a few cases, the expense of establishing a tribunal will hardly be justified, but if there are many, it will certainly be cheaper to refer them to a tribunal. The tribunal members may be part-time or occasional appointees, so cheaper than the full-time High Court or Circuit judge, and there is no need for the elaborate trappings traditionally associated with the higher courts.

The procedures of tribunals are designed to be as simple, straightforward and informal as possible. The Council on Tribunals, which is consulted over the making of tribunals' procedural rules, endeavours to reconcile the desire for simplicity with the need for a procedure to be fair to all parties. But it has proved very difficult in practice to develop a procedure simple enough to enable the average lay person to appear unrepresented. This leads to consideration of a major issue. The government's choice may well be powerfully influenced by the realisation that legal aid is not available for representation before the majority of tribunals. The only exceptions are the Lands Tribunal and Employment Appeal Tribunal, which are virtually equivalent to the High Court, and the Mental Health Review Tribunals, where by definition the applicant's ability to represent him or herself may be impaired. The government can therefore feel quite justified in establishing this new tribunal and refusing to extend legal aid to it. This is likely to leave most applicants with no choice but to attempt to represent themselves, whereas, if these cases were dealt with by a court, applicants would have the chance of seeking legal aid, albeit subject to a stringent means test.

Because they are used to hearing unrepresented applicants, tribunals take a more active part in the proceedings than the traditionally passive judge, and will do what they can to help. For example, they may suggest issues the applicant and the witnesses might like to talk about. The formal legal rules of evidence will not be applied, and witnesses will be encouraged to tell their story in their own words, rather than being tripped up by awkward questioning. But problems will inevitably arise where the inexperienced and inarticulate are trying to represent themselves. It is particularly difficult to avoid the appearance of unfairness where one side is represented, either by a lawyer or an experienced official, and the other is not. Many people, including the Council on Tribunals, have argued that legal aid should be extended to all or most tribunals, but this is most unlikely in the current climate of financial stringency.

If the disputes are referred to the ordinary courts, there is a risk that, because they will have to take their turn with other litigation, cases may suffer considerable delays, which is in itself a cause of injustice. One of the main reasons for establishing tribunals has been to ensure that cases are dealt with more promptly. There have, however, been problems of delay even within tribunal systems, where the number of cases has increased beyond the capacity of the tribunals to cope. An adequately funded tribunal system should still be able to deal with cases more quickly than the courts could, particularly if the procedures adopted are straightforward.

If the disputes are referred to the ordinary courts, then it will be natural to apply the normal procedure for appeals to the Court of Appeal and, with leave, to the House of Lords. If a tribunal is established, it will be necessary to decide what form any appeal should take. The government might take the view that no appeal should be provided, relying instead on the inherent jurisdiction of the High Court to hear cases by way of judicial review. It could be argued that, as the most likely grounds of complaint would be error of law and breach of the rules of natural justice, both of which are well-established grounds of review, that will provide adequate redress. But given the complex procedures involved in judicial review, it might be quicker and cheaper, for both applicant and government, to provide an appeal to the High Court on point of law. A strict time limit could be imposed to make sure appeals are made promptly. It is unlikely to be necessary to set up an appellate tribunal to hear appeals on both fact and law; this is only essential where there are a large number of tribunals whose decisions could diverge without an overall tribunal to give definitive rulings.

In conclusion, it appears that the establishment of a tribunal may be the most satisfactory way of dealing with these cases. The Franks Committee report in 1957, and its rapid implementation enhanced the reputation of tribunals and the quiet but effective work of the Council on Tribunals has ensured that a good standard is maintained. There is now little feeling that tribunals provide only second class justice.

Further reading

DELEGATED LEGISLATION

Bradley, A. and Ewing, K. *Constitutional & Administrative Law*, 13th edn (Longman, 2003), ch 28.

Wade, W. and Forsyth, C. *Administrative Law*, 8th edn (OUP, 2000), ch 3.

REDRESS BY MP

Rawlings, R. *The MPs' Complaints Service* (1990) 53 MLR 22.

OMBUDSMEN

Giddings, P. 'The Parliamentary Ombudsman', in *The Law & Parliament*, G. Drewry and D. Oliver (eds) (Butterworths, 1998).

Bradley, A. and Ewing, K. *Constitutional & Administrative Law*, 13th edn (Longman, 2003), ch 29A.

Wade, W. and Forsyth, C. *Administrative Law*, 8th edn (OUP 2000), pp 87–112.

TRIBUNALS

Bradley, A. and Ewing, K. *Constitutional & Administrative Law*, 13th edn (Longman, 2003), ch 29D.

Wade, W. and Forsyth, C. *Administrative Law*, 8th edn (OUP, 2000), ch 24.

Administrative law: judicial review

Introduction

This chapter covers one of the most important growth areas of the law. Some courses have found it impossible to include it within the general constitutional law course and have hived it off into a separate administrative law or public law course. These questions are designed to cover all the aspects likely to be included in a general, rather than a specialised course.

This subject lends itself particularly well to problem questions, and is for that reason popular with examiners seeking to give a more legal slant to what might otherwise be an excessively political subject. Students will need to demonstrate their legal skills in identifying and applying the appropriate case law.

The diagram opposite provides a template for answering problem questions on judicial review. It is most unlikely that any one question will raise all the issues identified, or all the grounds of review. Questions 2, 3 and 4 of this chapter are typical in raising a limited number of issues. But examination questions, unlike seminar questions, do not come with a convenient heading identifying the topic, such as 'questions on natural justice'. So, if you are not sure which issues are being raised, working through the questions on the diagram will help. It will also ensure that you do not miss out on the extra marks that may be available for, e.g., discussing the applicant's locus standi, or identifying the appropriate remedy.

Q Question 1

The twentieth century saw both the decline of administrative law to virtual extinction, and its revival and development to unprecedented heights.
  Discuss. Why has the development of administrative law been so erratic?

Commentary

The basis of the answer to this question will be a description of the way administrative law, particularly judicial review, has developed over the century, illustrated with the appropriate

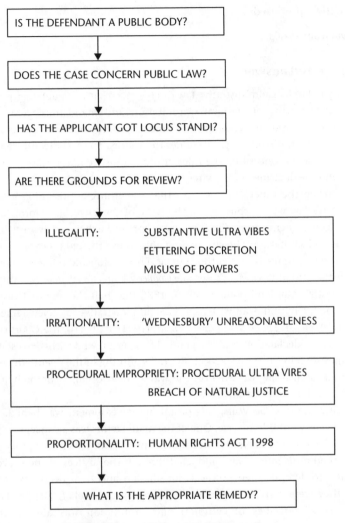

IS THE DEFENDANT A PUBLIC BODY?

DOES THE CASE CONCERN PUBLIC LAW?

HAS THE APPLICANT GOT LOCUS STANDI?

ARE THERE GROUNDS FOR REVIEW?

ILLEGALITY: SUBSTANTIVE ULTRA VIBES
              FETTERING DISCRETION
              MISUSE OF POWERS

IRRATIONALITY: 'WEDNESBURY' UNREASONABLENESS

PROCEDURAL IMPROPRIETY: PROCEDURAL ULTRA VIRES
                        BREACH OF NATURAL JUSTICE

PROPORTIONALITY: HUMAN RIGHTS ACT 1998

WHAT IS THE APPROPRIATE REMEDY?

Tackling problems on judicial review

cases. What will make the answer a good one will be the discussion of the reasons for its erratic progress. There are no cut and dried answers on this; the student's answer will be judged on the way the arguments are presented and the evidence marshalled in support.

- **Historical prerogative and other remedies.**
- **Initial development of ultra vires and natural justice.**
- **Decline in review during and after the Second World War.**

- Alternatives proposed.

- Revival from 1960s.

☼ Suggested answer

The history of English administrative law can be traced back through many centuries. The prerogative writs of certiorari, prohibition and mandamus were originally developed in the Middle Ages, but first came to prominence with the growth of a more effective administrative system under the Tudors. The seventeenth century sees the first precedents concerning the rules of natural justice (*Baggs Case* (1615) 11 Co Rep 93b) and the doctrine of ultra vires (*Hetley* v *Boyer* (1614) Cro Jac 336).

It was during the nineteenth century that something approaching a system of administrative law was established, in the wake of the Victorian reforms of central and local government, and official intervention in such areas as health, factory conditions and sanitation. The courts were able to use the old prerogative remedies against the new administrative authorities, and to develop and refine the concepts of natural justice and ultra vires, in cases like *Cooper* v *Wandsworth Board of Works* (1863) 14 CB (NS) 180. Maitland pointed out in 1888 that half the reported cases in the Queen's Bench Division dealt with aspects of administrative law. New remedies also became available; in *Dyson* v *Attorney-General* [1911] 1 KB 410, the Court of Appeal confirmed that a declaration could be granted to a person who wished to establish the unlawfulness of administrative action. By the beginning of the twentieth century, it seemed that English law was well on the way to developing a comprehensive and effective system of administrative law.

But during the next 50 years, this promising development was halted; in some respects the law went into reverse. One of the main factors was a conceptual problem about judicial and administrative decisions. Until the nineteenth century reforms, much local administration was conducted through the justices of the peace, and it was natural to describe their power as jurisdiction and their decisions as judicial, whether they were convicting a thief or allocating poor relief. The availability of the prerogative remedies of certiorari and prohibition was also described as being dependent on the decision challenged being judicial. This presented no problems as long as the courts were willing to define decisions as judicial whenever they affected individual rights. But, during the 1920s and 1930s, the courts started to distinguish between judicial and administrative decisions more strictly, confining the definition of judicial decisions to those where Parliament had imposed some kind of judicialised procedure. As a consequence, the rules of natural justice were no longer applied to decisions affecting individual rights where these were classified as administrative; see *R* v *Metropolitan Police Commissioner ex parte Parker* [1953] 1 WLR 1150.

Over the same period, the courts showed some antipathy to the very idea of administrative law, perhaps under the influence of Dicey, who was critical of the French idea of a special body of rules governing the conduct of the administration, assuming that it would give them too much protection. The term *'droit administratif'* was used almost as a term of abuse! Perhaps, as a further effect of this, academic lawyers paid little heed to the subject, and it was not taught except as a minor part of constitutional law.

What was perhaps most unfortunate in these developments was that the courts abdicated their responsibility for protecting the rights of the individual at the very time when the government's activities put those rights most at risk. A notorious example is the case of *Liversidge* v *Anderson* [1942] AC 206, where the Secretary of State had the power to detain persons without trial if he had reasonable cause to believe them to be of hostile origin or associations, a power justifiable enough in wartime. But the House of Lords, with the honourable exception of Lord Atkin, held that the reasonableness of the Secretary of State's belief was not reviewable, turning an objective power into a wholly subjective one. A similarly unfortunate ruling was made in *Duncan* v *Cammel Laird* [1942] AC 624, when the House of Lords held that the Crown had an absolute and unreviewable privilege to withhold documents in litigation, if ministers felt it was in the public interest to do so.

The courts' attitude was not surprising in wartime, but even after the war, the courts remained very reluctant to interfere in the work of the administration in any way. In *Franklin* v *Minister of Town and Country Planning* [1948] AC 87, the House of Lords refused to apply the rule against bias to an administrative decision taken by a minister, even where Parliament had imposed a quasi-judicial process. In *Smith* v *East Elloe RDC* [1956] AC 736, the House of Lords accepted as effective a clause excluding judicial review, even where bad faith was alleged. Perhaps the most likely explanation for this lies in the effect of the doctrine of precedent. It will always be difficult to convince a court that the recent precedents should be disregarded and an ancient ruling preferred. A rare example of such a decision was *R* v *Northumberland Compensation Appeal Tribunal ex parte Shaw* [1952] 1 KB 338, where the Court of Appeal revived the doctrine of error of law on the face of the record after a century of disuse, as a means of controlling the increasing numbers of statutory tribunals.

Overall, anyone surveying the condition of administrative law in the early 1960s would have found a depressing sight. Natural justice was restricted, discretionary power not subject to judicial control, and remedies constrained by ancient rules and obscurities. As a consequence, few applicants considered the risks of litigation to be worthwhile, causing the law to fall yet further into decline. It was generally assumed that the law could not offer a means of controlling the administration, and attention turned to other methods, such as the reform of tribunals and inquiries after the Franks Committee report in 1957, and the introduction of an Ombudsman. Some even advocated the importation of the French system of *droit administratif*, and the establishment of an English *Conseil d'Etat*.

But, to the surprise of many, the English courts showed themselves to be capable of reviving this moribund area of law. In *Ridge* v *Baldwin* [1964] AC 40, the House of Lords attacked the dichotomy of judicial and administrative decisions, restoring the rule that decisions affecting the rights of subjects were subject to natural justice, even if Parliament was silent on the need for a hearing. This was followed by a stream of cases, extending the right to a fair hearing even into areas which had always been characterised as administrative. Other precedents were reversed. In *Conway* v *Rimmer* [1968] AC 910, the House of Lords removed the Crown's power to withhold documents in litigation, replacing it with the power of the court to grant public interest immunity. In *Anisminic* v *Foreign Compensation Commission* [1969] 2 AC 147, the House of Lords found a way of defeating the express exclusion clause which had been held effective in *Smith* v *East Elloe RDC* (1956), and in so doing extended the courts' powers to review errors of law. In *Padfield* v *Minister of Agriculture* [1968] AC 997, the House of Lords rejected the idea of the unfettered and unreviewable administrative discretion.

Why did the courts change the law so radically and so unexpectedly?

One important factor was certainly a change in judicial personnel, with judges used to Diceyan orthodoxy being replaced by others with a less restricted outlook. One of the most influential was Lord Reid, who came to the House of Lords from Scotland, where administrative law had never fallen to such a low ebb. Lord Denning also played a significant part, as he did in so many branches of the law. Some credit is also due to academic lawyers, such as S. A. de Smith and Sir William Wade, whose publications and research into administrative law established it as an important academic subject. It is possible that the courts may have felt that, if the law was not reformed, they would lose out to other methods of redress, such as the Parliamentary Commissioner of Administration, who was introduced in 1967. Such statutory reforms also demonstrated that governments were willing to contemplate improved methods of redress, and the courts would not be risking political controversy if they joined in.

Once the process of revival began, there was no shortage of litigants seeking redress for what would once have been inescapable injustices. Within a few years, a new body of precedents had been built up, and cases decided between 1910 and 1960 are almost always viewed with suspicion. To consolidate this new law, procedural reforms were introduced on the advice of the Law Commission; see the Supreme Court Act 1981, s. 31.

The overall effect has been a huge expansion in the role of judicial review, which now shares with criminal justice the highest profile and the most media attention. From October 2000, its importance was recognised by the formal establishment of the Administrative Court as a specialised section of the Queen's Bench Division. Few other branches of the law can show such dramatic changes. It is to be hoped that the courts will maintain their role of protecting individual rights against abuse at the hands of the administration, as they have during the last 40 years.

Q Question 2

Under the (imaginary) Radiation Protection Act 1993, any person wishing to use radioactive materials must obtain a licence from the Radiation Protection Agency (RPA). On receipt of an application, the RPA must consult any organisation which it considers to be representative of those affected, and must publish notice of the application in the national and local press, and in any other way it considers desirable. The RPA must allow three months for the submission of comments and objections, which should include the name and address of the sender. After considering all representations submitted to it, and giving the applicant a hearing, the RPA may grant or refuse a licence.

The Sulphurous Chemical plc applied for a licence to use radioactive materials in its factory in Coketown. The RPA published notice of the application in three national and two local newspapers, and put up a small notice in the Coketown public library. The RPA wrote to the Coketown Borough Council and the Cokeshire County Council asking for comments. It received a reply only from the Coketown Borough Council. The RPA made no attempt to consult the National Union of Chemical Workers, which represented the majority of Sulphurous Chemical's employees.

The RPA received many objections, including several from an unknown and unidentified group calling itself the Green Anti-Nuclear Faction; the RPA threw these away. A petition signed by 25,000 inhabitants of Coketown was presented the day after the three month submission period had expired, but the RPA refused to accept it.

After completing its consideration and giving Sulphurous Chemical a hearing, the RPA granted the licence.

Consider the validity of the licence.

Commentary

This question is concerned with judicial review, primarily though not exclusively with procedural ultra vires. The student will need to identify and explain the general principle involved, the distinction between mandatory and directory procedural requirements. It is then simplest for the student to work through the problem point by point. Although some issues raised in this type of question may bear a sufficient resemblance to decided cases to be straightforward, others will require the student to argue by analogy. Where issues are debatable, the student will be assessed on the quality of the argument, whichever conclusion is reached. Refer back to the diagram on page 151 for advice.

- **Distinguish mandatory and directory conditions.**

- **Notice of application.**

- Consulting representative organisations.

- Challenge by judicial review.

- Locus standi.

⚙ Suggested answer

The validity of this licence can be challenged by judicial review, because, as laid down in *O'Reilly* v *Mackman* [1983] 2 AC 237, it concerns the activities of a public body in matters relating to public law. The grounds of challenge mostly concern procedural defects in the way the RPA dealt with the application.

In dealing with procedural defects, the courts have to balance the need to ensure that statutory procedural safeguards are carefully observed against the risk that trivial procedural defects are used as a pretext by objectors seeking to halt or delay an unpopular scheme. To do this the courts have generally drawn a distinction between mandatory and directory procedural requirements. A mandatory requirement is one which is regarded as so essential that failure to observe it justifies treating the decision reached as invalid. A directory requirement is one whose non-observance will not invalidate the decision. In *London & Clydeside Estates* v *Aberdeen District Council* [1980] 1 WLR 182, Lord Hailsham LC suggested that these two categories should not be regarded as the only two alternatives, but as the extremes of a range of possibilities. An example of a more subtle approach can be found in *Coney* v *Choyce* [1975] 1 WLR 422, where various detailed publication requirements were only partially complied with. The court held that it was mandatory that there be substantial compliance with the requirement of publication, but that the exact details were merely directory.

It is possible for statute to specify the precise consequences of failure to comply with procedural requirements, but in practice this rarely occurs. It is therefore left to the courts to decide retrospectively whether the failure has invalidated the decision. This area of the law is criticised as uncertain, but some guidance may be obtained from decided cases.

The RPA is required by the Act to publish notice of the application 'in the national and local press'. They published it in three national and two local newspapers. In *Bradbury* v *Enfield London Borough Council* [1967] 1 WLR 1311, the court held that giving notice was to be construed as a mandatory requirement as it was essential for the protection of the rights of the individual citizen. But in that case there was a complete failure to give notice. In *Coney* v *Choyce* substantial compliance was held to be sufficient. It could be argued here that there has been substantial compliance. The size of the petition is evidence that there was widespread awareness of the application. In *Coney* v *Choyce* it was considered material that all those affected had become aware of the proposal in spite of the defects in the publication. The RPA is given a discretion to publicise the application 'in any other way it considers desirable'. It could be argued that one small notice in the library is hardly sufficient. But any challenge would have to be on the ground of 'Wednesbury' unreasonableness; see *Associated Provincial Picture Houses* v *Wednesbury Corporation* [1948] 1 KB 223. It is unlikely that the courts would consider this to be beyond the limits of a reasonable exercise of discretion.

The RPA is required to consult 'organisations which it considers to be representative of those affected'. Consultation is generally held to be a mandatory requirement, as it is a means of protecting the interests of those affected; see *R* v *Secretary of State for the Environment ex parte Association of Metropolitan Authorities* [1986] 1 WLR 1. The consultation of the Coketown Borough Council seems to have been satisfactory. But in *Agricultural Training Board* v *Aylesbury Mushrooms Ltd* [1972] 1 WLR 190, sending a letter which went astray, and failing to make further inquiries was held not to amount to adequate consultation. If the RPA has made no attempt to follow up its letter to the Cokeshire County Council and check that it indeed has no comment to make, it will be considered to have broken a mandatory requirement.

The RPA's failure to consult the National Union of Chemical Workers could be challenged as an unreasonable use of discretion, as in *Secretary of State for Education* v *Metropolitan Borough of Tameside* [1977] AC 1014; no reasonable authority could have failed to consider the Union representative of those affected.

The RPA is required to consider 'all representations submitted to it', but it throws away the objections from the Green Anti-Nuclear Faction. The only possible justification for this is the provision in the Act that objections should include the name and address of the sender. This requirement could be classed as mandatory if it is essential for the conduct of the administration. In *Chapman* v *Earl* [1968] 1 WLR 1315, the failure of a tenant to indicate the proposed rent in an application to a rent tribunal was held to be a breach of a mandatory requirement. However, requirements imposed merely for the convenience of the administration are likely to be classified as directory only. In *Jackson Developments* v *Hall* [1951] 2 KB 488, the requirement that the tenant supply the landlord's name to a rent tribunal was held to be directory. In this problem, the objectors' failure to identify themselves hardly seems of sufficient importance to be treated as breach of a mandatory requirement. Their objections should therefore have been considered.

The petition is rejected because it is submitted one day late. Time limits will be held to be mandatory where they are essential in establishing legal rights and obligations. In *Howard* v *Secretary of State for the Environment* [1975] QB 235, the statutory time limit of 42 days for appealing against an enforcement notice was held to be mandatory, because it determined the legal powers of the local authority. But if no such compelling reasons exist, time limits will be treated as directory. In *James* v *Minister of Housing and Local Government* [1966] 1 WLR 135, a local authority was held to be entitled to make a planning decision after three months, though regulations imposed a limit of two months. In this problem, as the RPA will be spending some time considering the application, there seems no reason to treat the time limit for receipt of representations as mandatory.

An application for judicial review to challenge the validity of the licence under the Supreme Court Act 1981, s. 31 and Part 54 of the Civil Procedure Rules could be made by any person with locus standi, that is, with a sufficient interest in the matter. Cokeshire County Council and the National Union of Chemical Workers would clearly have a sufficient interest, as would members of the Green Anti-Nuclear Faction, if willing to identify themselves. In R v *Secretary of State for the Environment ex parte Greenpeace* [1994] 4 All ER 352, Greenpeace was held to have locus standi, as a pressure group with local members, to challenge the licensing of the THORP nuclear plant. It could further be argued that any of the inhabitants of Coketown who had signed the petition would have locus standi. In R v *Inland Revenue Commissioners ex parte National Federation of Self-Employed & Small Businesses* [1982] AC 617, Lord Diplock referred to the desirability of 'a single public-minded taxpayer' being able to challenge the validity of unlawful administrative action.

The most appropriate remedies in this case would be a quashing order to quash the licence, or a declaration that it was invalid. It would, however, be open to Sulphurous Chemical plc to make a further application for a licence.

Q Question 3

Under the (imaginary) Social Services Act 2000, all residential homes for the elderly must be licensed by the local authority. Unsatisfactory homes will be refused a licence and closed down, but there is a right to appeal against the refusal of a licence to an Appeal Tribunal.

Mrs Danvers applied to the Cokeshire County Council for a licence for the Manderley Home. The application was referred to the Social Services Committee, which instructed Rebecca, one of its employees, to investigate the suitability of the Home. Rebecca visited the Home, posing as someone looking for accommodation for an elderly relative. After completing her researches, Rebecca produced a report recommending that a licence be refused, because the kitchens and bathrooms were not cleaned properly and few of the staff had the appropriate professional qualifications.

The Committee considered the report and then invited Mrs Danvers to a meeting to discuss her application. She came to the meeting accompanied by her husband, a solicitor, but he was asked to wait outside. At the meeting, she was handed a copy of Rebecca's report and asked to comment on it. She asked for an adjournment so she could consult her husband, but the Committee refused. She denied the allegations in the report and invited the members of the Committee to visit the home and talk to the residents. The Committee declined to do so and, after deliberating in private, refused the licence.

Mrs Danvers appealed to the Tribunal, which gave her a hearing, but refused to hear evidence from the staff of the home or allow her to cross-examine Rebecca, who gave evidence in person. The Tribunal confirmed the original decision. Mrs Danvers has now discovered that the wife of the Chair of the Committee is a member of the board of a charity which campaigns for better care for the elderly.

Advise Mrs Danvers.

Commentary

This problem raises a number of issues relating to judicial review, principally concerning natural justice. Such a problem may appear at first sight rather long and daunting, but if you have a reasonable understanding of the issues it is actually quite straightforward. It is best tackled as advised earlier by working systematically through the facts of the problem, picking up each issue as it arises, explaining the law on that point, citing the relevant authority and then applying the law to the problem. You may, if you wish, introduce your answer by a few general remarks on the topic, though this answer does not. What you should not do is to attempt to answer this, or any other problem, by writing an essay. It is the ability of the student to select from the material they have learnt just those points that are relevant which marks out the competent student.

- Challenge by judicial review.

- Has she a right to a fair hearing?.

- Notice of charges.

- Legal representation.

- Evidence.

- Real possibility of bias.

:Q: Suggested answer

As Mrs Danvers has exhausted the statutory procedure, she will have to use judicial review if she wishes to challenge the refusal of a licence. Both the Council Committee and Tribunal are clearly public bodies and her grounds of challenge derive from public law, making judicial review the appropriate procedure to use. She must apply to the Court *ex parte* for Administrative permission to make an application for judicial review promptly and in any event within three months of the Tribunal's decision. As the person directly affected by the decision she has locus standi.

It appears that Mrs Danvers will have grounds for arguing that there has been a breach of the rules of natural justice, but she must first establish that she was entitled to a fair hearing. In *Ridge v Baldwin* [1964] AC 40 it was held that natural justice applied whenever a decision affected the rights of the individual, and it was made clear in *Re HK* [1967] 2 QB 617 that this applied even if the decision was of an administrative nature. By imposing a requirement that a licence must be obtained for an activity which could previously have been carried on without restriction, the law is affecting individual rights and so a fair hearing must be given. This was applied in *R v Gaming Board ex parte Benaim* [1970] 2 QB 417 to the grant of gaming licences and is clearly applicable here.

At what stage in the procedure is Mrs Danvers entitled to be heard? There is no general right to be heard during preliminary investigative or preparatory processes. In *Pearlberg v Varty* [1972] 1 WLR 534, it was held that there was no right to a hearing by the Inland Revenue as they prepared a taxpayer's assessment; he would be heard at the proper time before the relevant tribunal. It is therefore acceptable for Cokeshire County Council to conduct a covert investigation. Nor is there an objection to the matter being referred to a committee, as the Local Government Act 1972 specifically authorises this form of delegation. But, before any decision is made about the licence, Mrs Danvers must be given an opportunity to state her case. For this it is necessary that she be informed of the matters which are causing concern, otherwise she cannot offer an effective defence. In *Fairmount Investments v Secretary of State for the Environment* [1976] 1 WLR 1255, a compulsory purchase decision was held to be invalid because the inspector had based his decision on defects in the building which he had noticed but had not mentioned to the parties. Here Mrs Danvers is not shown Rebecca's report in advance or even informed of its contents. The Committee could argue that she was shown the report at the hearing, but this did not allow her any time to prepare a defence. In *R v Thames Magistrates' Court ex parte Polemis* [1974] 1 WLR 1371, it was held that it was a breach of the rules of natural justice to serve a summons on a defendant in the morning and try him that afternoon as he had no chance to prepare a defence. It therefore appears that there has been a breach of the rules of natural justice.

Mrs Danvers was refused permission to be accompanied by or to consult her husband, who was presumably also her legal adviser. It appears, from *R v Maze Prison Visitors ex parte Hone* [1988] AC 379, that there is no absolute right to legal or other representation. But in *R v Home Secretary ex parte Tarrant* [1985] QB 251, the court held that an adjudicatory body must consider in each case whether to permit legal representation, and that an unreasonable refusal could invalidate the proceedings. Mrs Danvers would find it difficult to argue that she should have been represented at the hearing, but will certainly be able to show that the refusal to adjourn the hearing to allow her to read the report and seek advice was a breach of natural justice.

The Committee is obliged to hear all relevant evidence; see *R v Hull Prison Visitors ex parte St Germain (No. 2)* [1979] 1 WLR 1401. It could be argued that they should have visited the home and spoken to the residents, but in cases such as *Osgood v Nelson* (1872) LR HL 636, it has been held to be acceptable for a subordinate to collect evidence for submission to those who decide, as was done here.

The breach of natural justice committed by the Committee will render its decision invalid, and it can be argued that as a matter of logic no subsequent procedures can cure that initial invalidity. But the courts have accepted that where an appeal takes the form of a full rehearing, it can make up for any defects in the initial process; see *Calvin* v *Carr* [1980] AC 574 and *Lloyd* v *McMahon* [1987] 1 AC 625. This is however dependant on the appeal itself being conducted fairly, which is open to question in Mrs Danvers' case.

The Tribunal refused to hear evidence from the staff of the home. This seems to be a clear breach of the obligation to hear all relevant evidence discussed above, as the qualifications of the staff seem to be one of the principal issues of concern. The refusal to allow Mrs Danvers to cross-examine Rebecca is more problematical. In *Bushell* v *Secretary of State for the Environment* [1981] AC 75, the House of Lords held that, at a public inquiry into the route of a proposed motorway, the inspector was entitled to refuse to allow witnesses to be cross-examined, as this would lead to excessive judicialisation of what was basically an administrative decision. In this problem, however, the Tribunal can properly be described as a fully judicial body and it might be considered that as Rebecca gave her evidence in person, cross-examination should have been allowed.

The final substantive issue is the allegation that one member of the Tribunal was biased. It is clear that the presence of one biased person is enough to invalidate a decision. There are some forms of bias which lead to automatic disqualification; a financial interest in the decision, as in *Dimes* v *Grand Junction Canal Co.* (1852) 3 HLC 759; or direct association with a party to the case, as in *Ex parte Pinochet* [1999] 1 All ER 577. But neither of these seems applicable here. For other, more indirect, forms of bias, the courts have formulated various tests, such as looking for a 'real likelihood' or 'reasonable suspicion' of bias. In *Porter* v *Magill* [2001] UKHL 67, [2002] 1 All ER 465, the House of Lords formulated a general test for bias as follows:

> whether the fair-minded and informed observer, having considered the facts, would conclude that there was a real possibility that the Tribunal was biased.

Can it be argued that there is such a real possibility here? It is doubtful; the Tribunal's very existence is in order to improve the care of the elderly and there is nothing in the background of the Chair of the Tribunal to indicate any connection with or prejudice against Mrs Danvers.

If Mrs Danvers is successful in establishing grounds for judicial review, as seems likely, the most appropriate remedy would be a quashing order to quash the decisions of the Committee and Tribunal, though a declaration would also be a possibility. She could in addition ask for a mandatory order to compel them to reconsider her application. The award of remedies is at the discretion of the court, but there seems no reason why the court should decline to give redress. However, the court's decision will not necessarily mean that Mrs Danvers will obtain the licence she seeks. That decision will be made by the Committee and Tribunal and will be based, as it should be, on the suitability of the home she runs.

Q Question 4

As a result of local elections, the Radical Party has taken control of the Coketown District Council. It has implemented the following changes and wishes to know whether there could be any legal challenge to them. It also wishes to know who could make such a challenge and by what legal process.

(a) To revoke, with immediate effect, the licences given to Able (A), Baker (B) and Charlie (C) to sell ice creams from their vans in council owned parks.

(b) To refuse to give any more discretionary grants for the insulation of homes.

(c) To save money by refusing to put up the notices of applications for planning permission which are required by regulations.

(d) To increase the pay of its lowest paid workers to 20 per cent more than the statutory minimum wage.

(e) To pay a famous conceptual artist £100,000 to drape the Town Hall in multi-coloured fabric.

Commentary

This question raises a variety of issues relating to judicial review and must be tackled by identifying the material relevant to each part of the problem. It will be appropriate to introduce the answer by dealing with those issues which are clearly common to all parts of the question. But there is no need to write an essay on judicial review before tackling the problems and little credit will be given for doing so. The good student will look separately at each part of the problem, identify one or two relevant grounds and support them with references to cases. Putting in far-fetched suggestions, such as challenging a perfectly sensible decision on the grounds of irrationality, is likely to make the examiner think you do not really understand the law. Note also that the question specifically asks about locus standi and process, and it will be appropriate as part of this to suggest which remedy or remedies should be sought.

- Public body, public law, judicial review.

- Breach of natural justice.

- Fettering discretion.

- **Procedural ultra vires.**

- **Misuse of discretion.**

- **Unreasonableness.**

·Q· **Suggested answer**

Because the Council is a public body, its decisions can be challenged by way of judicial review. Any person who has a sufficient interest will be able to bring a case on the grounds characterised by Lord Diplock as illegality, irrationality and procedural impropriety. Such a person must apply to the Administrative Court for permission to make an application for judicial review within the three-month time limit. If permission is granted, the case will proceed to a full hearing.

(**a**) No information is given about the grounds on which the Council has acted, but it is clear from the facts given that the way the decision was made is open to challenge. A, B and C, as licence holders, have rights and under the general principle laid down in *Ridge* v *Baldwin* [1964] AC 40, decisions affecting the rights of individuals must be made in accordance with the rules of natural justice. Indeed it was specifically held in *R* v *Wear Valley DC ex parte Binks* [1985] 2 All ER 699 that contractual as well as statutory licences were protected. It therefore appears that if the revocation of the licences was not preceded by an opportunity for A, B and C to state their cases, it can be challenged. It has been held, however, that in situations of extreme urgency a decision can be made before any hearing is given. In *R* v *Secretary of State for Transport ex parte Pegasus* [1989] 2 All ER 481, it was held that an air charter company's licence could be revoked with immediate effect because of fears over public safety. If the Council's decision in this problem was provoked by, for example, fears that the ice cream posed a threat to public health, there would be no breach of natural justice, provided a proper hearing was given at a later stage. It is unlikely, however, that such urgency is needed. A, B and C clearly have locus standi as the persons directly affected by the decision and are likely to seek either a quashing order to quash the Council's decision or a declaration that it is invalid.

(**b**) The Council appears to have a discretion to make these grants. It is entitled to adopt general policies to guide it in allocating such grants, but that does not permit it to adopt a rule and refuse to depart from it. In *R* v *London County Council ex parte Corrie* [1918] 1 KB 68, the Council was held to have acted ultra vires in adopting a rule against the sale of pamphlets in parks and refusing even to consider making an exception to it. In *A-G ex rel Tilley* v *Wandsworth LBC* [1981] 1 WLR 854, the court declared invalid a council's decision never to use a statutory power to rehouse homeless families with children.

There is, however, nothing unlawful in the adoption of a policy, provided that consideration is given to each individual case. In *British Oxygen* v *Board of Trade* [1971]

AC 610, a decision to refuse the applicant an investment grant, in accordance with a stated policy, was held to be valid, because consideration had been given to the individual application. The easiest way to demonstrate that individual cases are considered is to offer applicants an opportunity to state their case either orally or in writing. The Council would therefore be well advised to adopt a procedure which shows its willingness to consider applications; it can then lawfully reject any applications which it does not feel justify a departure from its policy.

If the Council does not do so, its decision could be challenged by anyone who has applied for a grant and been rejected. Such an applicant could ask for a declaration that the Council was acting unlawfully or a mandatory order to compel them to consider the application again. It will remain within the Council's discretion, however, whether any particular grant is made or not.

(c) Because these notices are required by regulations, it appears that a refusal to display them would amount to procedural ultra vires. The consequences of a breach of procedure are normally discussed in terms of the distinction between mandatory and directory requirements. Breach of a mandatory requirement will render a decision invalid, but the courts accept that an inadvertent or even negligent failure to obey a minor procedural rule need not do so. In this problem, however, the Council has deliberately decided to disobey the law and it is most unlikely that the court would allow this. The Council's action will therefore be unlawful.

There may be some problem in identifying who would have locus standi to challenge the Council. It is unlikely that property owners or developers would wish to make any challenge, as they might be quite pleased to find that possible objectors are not being given notice of their plans. Persons living near any proposed developments would have sufficient locus standi, assuming that they can discover what is being proposed despite the lack of notices. The courts have accepted on occasion that environmental pressure groups may have locus standi; see *R* v *Secretary of State for the Environment ex parte Greenpeace* [1994] 4 All ER 352. An appropriate remedy would be a mandatory order to compel the Council to conform to the statutory procedures.

(d) The Council will have a discretion over the rates of pay it adopts and this discretion must be exercised on the basis of relevant considerations and to achieve proper purposes. In examining this problem, it is clear that the Council must take into account its fiduciary duty to its rate and tax payers, as laid down in *Roberts* v *Hopwood* [1925] AC 578 and *Bromley LBC* v *Greater London Council* [1982] 1 AC 768. In *Roberts* v *Hopwood*, excessively generous wages were found to breach that principle. The radical Poplar Borough Council had ignored such relevant considerations as the cost of living and the rates of pay agreed by collective bargaining with the trade unions. If it could be shown here that the Council had made an arbitrary decision to increase the wages, its decision might be open to challenge. If, on the other hand, the increase was part of a negotiated wage settlement, or a response to an acute shortage of workers, no objection could be made.

This decision could be challenged by a council tax payer by way of judicial review. The courts have generally accepted the locus standi of those who pay local taxes to challenge councils' activities; see *Barrs* v *Bethell* [1982] Ch 294. The most appropriate remedy would be a declaration.

(e) This final decision could be challenged on two grounds. First, as in the previous problem, it could be said to be a breach of the Council's fiduciary duty to its tax payers. Secondly, it could be suggested that it is unreasonable or irrational, within the strict test laid down by Lord Greene in *Associated Provincial Picture Houses* v *Wednesbury Corporation* [1948] 1 KB 223: 'something so absurd that no sensible person could ever dream that it lay within the powers of the authority'. It could well be argued that this scheme is an absurd extravagance, though it is possible to envisage circumstances which justify it. Many local authorities, for example, spent considerable sums on celebrating the millennium, without legal objection. Challenges based on pure unreasonableness are rarely successful, because the test is so strong, but the challenge might be successful in this case.

Any council tax payer would have locus standi to challenge this decision. There are several possible remedies; a quashing order to quash the decision; a declaration that it would be unlawful; or an injunction to stop the scheme going ahead.

Q Question 5

The divorce between public and private law, proclaimed by Lord Diplock in *O'Reilly* v *Mackman* [1983] 2 AC 237, has not been a happy addition to English administrative law. It has caused problems for litigants, without aiding the development of a coherent system of judicial review.

Discuss.

Commentary

This question deals with the complex issue of the division between public law and private law procedures. The student will need to explain the background to this development, and then examine *O'Reilly* v *Mackman* itself in some detail. The ensuing problems and how the courts have dealt with them should then be discussed. A good answer might make some reference to other legal traditions and should certainly offer suggestions as to whether the law should be reformed and, if so, how.

- After reform of remedies, abuse of process to use private law remedies.

- If judicial review is appropriate, it must be used.

- What is a public body?

- What is a matter of public law?

- Should the distinction be maintained?

:Q: Suggested answer

In the civil law tradition, the distinction between public and private law is the primary and fundamental classification of law. It is traceable back to the jurist Ulpian, writing in 200 AD, and is among the first rules mentioned in Justinian's *Institutes*; to this day it forms one of the first lessons for the student of civil law. But in English law, which developed incrementally and without a theoretical framework, the distinction between public and private law was almost unknown. Principles such as ultra vires and natural justice were applied indifferently to public and private bodies and, with the exception of the rules limiting the liability of the Crown, the same laws of tort, contract and property applied to public and private bodies. Indeed, Dicey's analysis of the rule of law depended heavily on the absence of any division. He praised the English use of private law as a means of controlling the activities of the government, and compared it favourably with the strictly separated French system of *droit administratif*.

The only area where the distinction between public and private law was important was in relation to remedies. The prerogative remedies of certiorari, prohibition and mandamus were available only against public bodies, defined by Atkin LJ in *R v Electricity Commissioners* [1924] 1 KB 171 at 205 as 'any body of persons having legal authority to determine questions affecting the rights of subjects'. But the private law remedies of injunction, declaration and damages were equally available against public and private bodies, with the exception of the immunity of the Crown from injunctions, preserved by the Crown Proceedings Act 1947, s. 21(1)(a). Litigants against public bodies therefore had a choice of remedies, but unfortunately could not combine remedies from the two groups in the same proceedings, until the introduction of the application for judicial review in 1978.

This new procedure adopted many features from the prerogative remedies, such as the need to obtain leave to make an application, and the short time limit, now set at three months. All applications for certiorari, mandamus and prohibition had to use this new procedure. Applications for injunction, declaration and damages could also use it where the case concerned matters for which the prerogative remedies were available and appropriate. In effect, if an injunction or declaration was sought against a public body, on grounds arising from public law, the new judicial review procedure was available. But the new rules did not use any conceptual terms such as 'public law'. If there was any legal principle underlying the changes, it was not openly expressed.

What was left uncertain was the boundary between those claims for injunction and declaration where judicial review procedure should be used and those where the normal High Court procedure was still applicable. Did it matter which procedure was used? The Law Commission had specifically addressed this issue and had recommended that the new procedure should not be exclusive. But when the issue came before the House of Lords, a stricter rule was adopted.

O'Reilly v *Mackman* [1983] 2 AC 237 concerned various prisoners who wished to challenge decisions taken by prison Boards of Visitors on grounds of breach of the rules of natural justice. Judicial review would clearly have been the appropriate procedure to have used, but instead they started actions by writ in the High Court for declarations, the time limit for judicial review having long since expired. The defendants successfully claimed that the actions should be struck out as an abuse of process. Lord Diplock's justification for this decision was as follows. In the days before the reform of remedies, it was justifiable for applicants to use ordinary High Court procedure rather than the prerogative orders, because of such procedural defects as the absence of discovery and the virtual impossibility of cross-examination of witnesses. But these procedures were now available under the reformed application for judicial review. On the other side, judicial review contained safeguards against the 'groundless, unmeritorious or tardy harassment' of public authorities and applicants should not be allowed to evade these. It was therefore generally contrary to public policy and an abuse of process, for an applicant to begin an action by writ which should have been brought by judicial review. If the case concerned a public body and an infringement of public law rights, judicial review must normally be used, though Lord Diplock conceded that there might be exceptions.

It therefore became essential for the first time for an applicant to identify whether the case was suitable for judicial review or action by writ. This presented two difficulties. First, judicial review is only available against public bodies, not private bodies; they do not have 'legal authority' merely rights and duties under contract. Trade unions, private employers and sporting bodies have all been held not to be subject to judicial review, though it has taken substantial litigation to establish this in some cases; see *R* v *Chief Rabbi ex parte Wachman* [1992] 1 WLR 1036 and *R* v *Jockey Club ex parte Massingberd-Mundy* [1993] 2 All ER 207. But problems arise because of the lack of any conceptual distinction between public and private bodies embodied in English law. The court found it very difficult to decide, in *Scott* v *National Trust* [1998] 2 All ER 705, whether the National Trust, a charity created and given a privileged status by Parliament, was a public or private body. The issue was most fully addressed in *R* v *Panel on Takeovers and Mergers ex parte Datafin* [1987] QB 815, and the result was pragmatic rather than theoretically based. The Panel, one of the self-regulatory bodies of the City of London's financial markets, was held to be subject to judicial review, in spite of having no legal authority or even existence! The court pointed out that it was performing a function which, if it did not perform, would have had to be performed by a public body set up for the purpose. If the Panel were held not to be subject to judicial review, its decisions could be arbitrary or unfair and no redress would be available. Subsequent decisions on bodies such as the Advertising Standards

Authority, LAUTRO, and university visitors have confirmed the impression that the courts define a body as public in order to subject it to judicial review, rather than subjecting it to judicial review because it is public. In the absence of a specific precedent, it is difficult to tell whether a body without a clearly defined status will be treated as public or private.

The second problem is identifying which issues are regarded as public rather than private law, again in the absence of a theoretical framework. In *O'Reilly* v *Mackman* itself the case was clear; the prisoners' complaint was of breach of the rules of natural justice by a statutory tribunal to which they were subjected by statute, public law in all respects. On the other hand, the rights of public employees in their work derive ultimately from the private law of contract, so judicial review is not appropriate; see *R* v *East Berkshire Health Authority ex parte Walsh* [1985] QB 152. But many cases can be characterised as either public or private depending on the perspective the parties choose to adopt. The GCHQ case, *Council of Civil Service Unions* v *Minister for the Civil Service* [1985] AC 374, was brought as a public law case, by judicial review; in this perspective it concerned a breach of the rules of natural justice by the government in the exercise of a discretionary power. But it could have been treated as a private law matter relating to the contractual right of government employees to belong to a trade union. Conversely, in *Gillick* v *West Norfolk Area Health Authority* [1986] AC 112, the plaintiff brought a private law action complaining that the advice given to doctors infringed her rights as a mother, but the case could have been defined more easily as a public law challenge to the legal validity of the advice.

Particular problems arise where liability in tort or contract is alleged to arise as a consequence of the validity or invalidity on public law grounds of some adminis-trative decision. In *Cocks* v *Thanet DC* [1983] 2 AC 286, a case decided at the same time as *O'Reilly* v *Mackman*, the House of Lords attempted to split up a claim for damages for failure to rehouse a homeless family. If the claim was that the decision that they were not eligible for rehousing was invalid, that was a matter of public law; if it was a claim that the council, having decided they were eligible, had failed to rehouse them, that was a matter of private law. This makes choosing the right procedure very difficult.

The difficulties of attempting to draw the distinctions which the decision in *O'Reilly* v *Mackman* rendered necessary have led the courts to develop the possibility of exceptions to the rule. In *Davy* v *Spelthorne Borough Council* [1984] AC 262, the plaintiff was allowed to proceed with a private law action for damages, even though it depended on establishing the invalidity of a council decision. In *Wandsworth LBC* v *Winder* [1985] AC 461, the defendant was allowed to resist an eviction order by argu-ing that a rent demand was ultra vires and void. It now seems that, provided the ultimate form of the action is suitable for an action begun by writ, the involvement of public law issues does not matter. In *Roy* v *Kensington Family Practitioner Committee*

[1992] 1 AC 624, the plaintiff was allowed to bring a private law action based on the claim that the decision to deprive him of certain payments was invalid and this was followed in *Trustees of Denis Rye Pension Fund* v *Sheffield City Council* [1998] 1 WLR 840.

A particular problem concerns the relationship between judicial review and the criminal law. It had long been accepted that the invalidity of a by-law could be subject to collateral challenge by being raised as a defence to a prosecution. But it was not clear whether this was affected by the decision in *O'Reilly* v *Mackman*. In some cases it was suggested that whether collateral challenge was allowed depended on the particular ground of invalidity, some grounds only being challengeable by judicial review. However, in *Boddington* v *British Transport Police* [1998] 2 WLR 639, the House of Lords restored the rule that any ground of invalidity could be pleaded as a defence to a criminal charge of breaking a by-law.

In the most recent cases, it appears that the courts are unwilling to reject any claim on the basis that the plaintiff has chosen the wrong procedure, unless the procedure chosen is clearly inappropriate. In *Mercury Communications* v *Director-General of Telecommunications* [1996] 1 All ER 575, the House of Lords rejected the assertion that a challenge to the validity of the defendant's ruling in a dispute between Mercury and British Telecom could only be sought by judicial review. The court stated that, as the limits of public and private law were not worked out, the procedural rules should be applied flexibly. In *British Steel plc* v *Customs and Excise* [1997] 2 All ER 366, the plaintiffs were allowed to claim repayment of taxes by a private law action in restitution. The Law Commission stated in their 1994 report on judicial review, that continuing flexibility was desirable, to be combined with procedures enabling a case to be transferred to the more appropriate court if the wrong procedure had been initiated. There would seem to be no reason why the concept of abuse of process should not be confined to those cases where a plaintiff is trying to evade a restriction which should be applied to the case, such as a time limit. A litigant who, on legal advice, opts for one of two possible procedures should not be penalised.

The problems thrown up by the decision in *O'Reilly* v *Mackman* can all be traced back to the absence of any conceptual distinction between public and private law in the English legal tradition. It has proved almost as difficult to incorporate the distinction into English law as it would be to incorporate the distinction between common law and equity into a civil law system. Although there are valid arguments for having a special procedure for judicial review cases, these should not lead to the erection of procedural barriers against litigants. It is notable how many of the cases cited have been fought to the House of Lords merely to discover by which procedure the substantive issue should be resolved, a great waste of resources. English law should perhaps stick to its traditional concern with practical remedies, rather than trying to adopt concepts which sit uneasily alongside the pragmatic historical development of judicial review.

Q Question 6

What are the main procedural difficulties facing someone who wishes to make an application for judicial review? Should any of the rules in this area be reformed?

Commentary

This is a straightforward question, requiring the student to examine just the procedural aspects of judicial review, not the substantive law. There is scope for differences of emphasis about what is included; the selection made here covers the principal issues, but other issues could properly be included. What will make for a good answer is the assessment of the law and discussion of whether reform is needed. This answer concludes with a defence of the present law, but it would be just as acceptable to conclude with criticism and calls for changes.

- The public/private divide.
- Applying for permission to sue.
- Time limit.
- Locus standi.

☼ Suggested answer

From the earliest times, when the courts developed the prerogative writs, there have been special procedures for obtaining judicial review, which have differed from those used in ordinary civil proceedings. Generally such procedures have made it more difficult to seek judicial review, because they have been imposed to protect public authorities. Whether the retention of special procedures can be justified has been widely debated. Some changes to the rules have been made, but other aspects remain problematic.

An applicant who is thinking of seeking judicial review must first of all be sure that judicial review is the appropriate procedure to use. The defendant must be a public body, not a private body. But because the conceptual difference between public and private is not a traditional part of English law, this rule may be difficult to apply, and litigants have failed through using the wrong procedure. The courts have little difficulty in identifying as private those bodies whose legal authority derives only from contract, such as trade unions and sporting bodies; see *R v Disciplinary Committee of the Jockey Club ex parte Aga Khan* [1993] 1 WLR 909. But where bodies of uncertain status perform a public function, the courts tend to classify them as public, in order to subject them to judicial review, as in *R v Panel on Take-overs and Mergers ex parte Datafin* [1987] QB 815. The applicant must also show that the case concerns issues of public, not private law, though since the case of *Roy* v *Kensington Family Practitioner Committee* [1992] 1 AC 624, the courts have taken a flexible view on this matter. It is in any case possible for a case wrongly commenced by an application for judicial review to be transferred for hearing as an ordinary civil case. There have been proposals to allow cases to be transferred into the judicial review procedure, but these have not, unfortunately, been adopted.

Having decided to use judicial review, applicants are faced with one of the main procedural hurdles. They cannot commence proceedings as of right, but must apply for permission (formerly leave). The defendant public authority will be informed, and then a judge in chambers will consider the papers and decide whether to grant permission. If the judge is minded to refuse, the request will be considered in open court, and the applicant can appeal against a refusal to the Court of Appeal. Why is permission needed? The justification offered is that attempts are made to seek judicial review in cases which are plainly hopeless, sometimes as a publicity stunt or as a last desperate throw of the dice. There would be a great waste of resources if public authorities had to defend all such cases at a full hearing. Instead, these cases are filtered out at the permission stage, and this also saves the applicant unnecessary expense. The counter-argument is that it is wrong in principle that litigation should need the permission of the court. In no other branch of the law is permission needed. An action against a public authority in tort or contract can be commenced as of right. Frivolous or vexatious claims are deterred sufficiently by the risk of liability for costs. Although every applicant with an arguable case should be granted permission, there is a danger that someone with a good case may be unable even to start proceedings. There have been cases where an applicant, having initially been refused permission, went on to win the case on its merits.

When the Law Commission examined this issue in 1994 it recommended that the permission stage should be retained as the only means of preventing a flood of hopeless cases. Many writers have criticised this finding, but public authorities are happy with it. Provided that judges are generous in their initial assessment of cases, the current law can be defended.

The next problem for the applicant is the time limit. Application must be made promptly and in any event within three months of the decision being challenged. This is a much shorter time limit than applies in normal civil proceedings, but it is justified by the need for the legal position of public authorities to be firmly settled at the earliest opportunity. Short time limits are normal in administrative law. Under Article 230 of the EC Treaty, the limit for challenging the actions of European Union institutions is only two months, a period adopted from French administrative law. The courts do have the power to extend the period for a good reason; in *R* v *Stratford on Avon DC ex parte Jackson* [1985] 1 WLR 1319, the applicant justified his delay by showing that he was waiting for a decision from the Legal Aid Board. But the court will not allow a belated application if this would cause administrative difficulties. In *R* v *Dairy Produce Quota Tribunal ex parte Caswell* [1990] 2 AC 738, the court refused to allow a challenge after two years to the way milk quotas had been allocated to farmers, as there would have been enormous problems in trying to undo previous allocations. It seems reasonable to expect applicants to be prompt and no change to this rule seems necessary.

The final issue which may cause problems for applicants is locus standi. When the Application for Judicial Review was introduced, locus standi was deliberately described in words without a previous legal meaning, as a 'sufficient interest' in the matter. The meaning of this expression was discussed by the House of Lords in *R v Inland Revenue Commissioners ex parte National Federation of Self-Employed and Small Businesses* [1982] AC 617. The applicants wished to challenge the validity of an agreement between the IRC and Fleet St casual workers about past and future payments of tax. Although the challenge failed on the facts, the House of Lords felt that only 'busybodies, cranks and other mischief makers' should be regarded as not having locus standi to seek judicial review of the actions of public authorities. Pressure groups and even 'a single public-spirited taxpayer' should be allowed to bring such cases, in order to ensure that the rule of law applies.

The effect of this decision was a general liberalisation of the rules of locus standi. The 'single public-spirited taxpayer' has brought actions for judicial review. In *R v HM Treasury ex parte Smedley* [1985] 1 QB 657, a taxpayer challenged, albeit unsuccessfully, the UK's payment of certain sums to the European Community. The locus standi of pressure groups has been generally accepted, though in *R v Secretary of State for the Environment ex parte Rose Theatre Trust* [1990] 1 QB, the judge refused to allow a pressure group formed specifically for the purpose of saving the Rose Theatre to challenge the government's decision. Other cases have been more generous. Most striking was the decision in *R v Foreign Secretary ex p World Development Movement* [1995] 1 WLR 386. The applicants were a respected voluntary organisation whose interest in challenging the use of UK aid to fund the Pergau Dam in Malaysia was purely moral. But, as the court said, if WDM did not have locus standi, no one would be able to challenge the decision, except people living in a remote area of Malaysia whose opportunity to take legal action in the English High Court is limited. It seems therefore that locus standi will not cause a problem to genuine applicants and no change to the law on this point is needed.

In conclusion, it can be argued that, although there are practical problems in bringing any type of legal action, the special rules relating to judicial review do not act as too great a hindrance to litigants. The need to obtain permission is the most contentious issue but even this can be defended. It would be a great problem for those seeking judicial review if frivolous or vexatious cases filled the courts and caused delay to genuine applicants.

Further reading

Bradley, A. and Ewing, K. *Constitutional & Administrative Law*, 13th edn (Longman, 2003), chs 30 and 31.

Turpin, C. *British Government & The Constitution*, 5th edn (Butterworths, 2002), pp 575–618.

Cane, P. *Introduction to Administrative Law*, 3rd edn (OUP, 1996) chs 1–6.

De Smith, S., Woolf, H. and Jowell, J. *Principles of Judicial Review* (Sweet & Maxwell, 1999).

Wade, W. and Forsyth, C. *Administrative Law*, 8th edn (OUP, 2000), chs 8–20.

Public authority proceedings

Introduction

The topics dealt with in this chapter are more likely to be included in an administrative law course than in a general constitutional law course, with the exception of public interest immunity, which is of such constitutional interest that it may be included where the other aspects are not. Students will need to be guided by their own examiners and syllabus.

Examples of both essay and problem questions are included. Good answers will require the student to show skills of legal analysis and application. A student who has studied or is studying tort or contract need not be afraid to bring that extra knowledge into the answer. The law may be divided into discrete subjects for the purpose of teaching and examining, but in reality it is an undivided whole.

Q Question 1

In 1999, the Home Office decided, as part of its policy of reducing the prison population, to establish hostels where long-term prisoners could spend the last year of their sentences, being gradually rehabilitated into the outside world. One of these hostels was established in Coketown. It was a converted house in a residential area, occupied by eight prisoners, who went out to work during the day, but were otherwise supervised by a warden and his staff.

Consider the liability of the Home Office in the following situations.

(a) White, Black and Gray, who live in the same street as the hostel, consider that it has reduced the amenity and value of their homes. They consider that the hostel should have been established somewhere else.

(b) Brown, who lives next door to the hostel, thinks that the choice of site for the hostel was made because he is a prominent campaigner against Home Office policies: he suspects that there is evidence of this hidden in Home Office files.

(c) The Home Office decided that prisoners convicted of violent crimes could if considered suitable, be sent to the hostel. Reg had been sentenced to 15 years for attempted murder and, because he had behaved impeccably throughout his time in prison, was due for release next year. He was sent to the hostel, obtained a

job, and apparently settled in well. But last week, on the way home from work, he
went to the pub, got drunk, and punched Green, the landlord.

Commentary

This question raises various issues relating to the liability of public authorities. It is important
for students to deal both with the general rules applicable to all public authorities and with
the special rules governing the liability of the Crown. The student will not be expected to
examine issues of tortious liability in as great depth as would be appropriate in a tort
examination, but should concentrate on those aspects peculiar to public authorities. The
question also touches on public interest immunity.

* Nuisance, subject to statutory authority.

* Misfeasance in public office.

* Public interest immunity.

* Liability in negligence for policy and operation.

·̣Ọ̈· Suggested answer

(a) White, Black and Gray will have to prove that the hostel constitutes an action-
able nuisance if they wish to obtain redress. Under the Crown Proceedings Act 1947,
s. 2, the Crown is subject to the same liabilities as any other person in respect of torts
committed by its servants or agents, and torts arising from its ownership, occupation
or control of property. But there are circumstances in which a body may be able to
plead that it has statutory authority. If a statute specifically authorises some activity
which will inevitably result in the commission of a nuisance, no action will lie. In
Allen v *Gulf Oil Refinery Ltd* [1981] AC 1001, the defendants obtained a private Act of
Parliament authorising them to construct a refinery on a particular site, from which
some nuisance would inevitably result. They were held to be immune from action,
unless they negligently operated the refinery in such a way as to increase the nuisance
beyond what was inevitable.

But this defence does not operate where the authorisation is general and the
nuisance not inevitable. In *Metropolitan Asylum District* v *Hill* (1881) 6 App Cas 193,
the plaintiff had statutory authority to build hospitals, and chose to build one in a
place where it would cause a nuisance. As it would have been possible to exercise the
statutory power without causing a nuisance, no defence of statutory authority
existed.

In this problem, it appears that the choice of site was in the hands of the Home
Office. It can be argued that the hostel could have been established anywhere,
including places where it would not have constituted a nuisance.

If therefore the interference which the hostel causes to surrounding property is sufficient to amount to nuisance, White, Black and Gray will be able to sue for damages. They will not, however, be able to obtain an injunction against the Crown to order the closure of the hostel. By the Crown Proceedings Act 1947, s. 21, no injunction may be awarded against the Crown, though a declaration may be awarded instead.

(**b**) Brown is alleging that the choice of site for the hostel was made maliciously. This would constitute grounds for judicial review, the decision being made for an improper purpose or even in bad faith. Such proceedings would be an appropriate way of getting the decision quashed but would not lead to the award of any compensation to Brown unless he can demonstrate the existence of some established form of liability.

To make a decision which subsequently proves to be unlawful does not in itself give rise to any liability. In *Dunlop* v *Woollahra Municipal Council* [1982] AC 158, the Privy Council refused to impose any liability on a local authority whose decision, based on a misunderstanding of their legal powers, was later held to be ultra vires.

Brown may be able to recover damages for the tort of misfeasance in a public office, which is designed to provide redress for the victims of malicious abuses of public power. The elements of this tort were set out in *Three Rivers DC* v *Bank of England* [2000] 3 All ER 1. The House of Lords held that liability exists where a public official, exercising power as such, either does something intended to injure a person, or does something knowing that it is unlawful and that it will probably injure the plaintiff. Brown's claim is based on the first form of this tort, intentional or targeted malice. An example is *Roncarelli* v *Duplessis* (1959) 16 DLR (2d) 689, where the defendant ordered the revocation of the plaintiff's liquor licence, because he had annoyed the authorities by his lawful activities in support of an unpopular religious sect. The defendant knew the revocation was unlawful, but chose it as a good way to make the plaintiff suffer.

If Brown can prove that the decision was in fact made with the deliberate intention of causing him injury, he will be able to recover damages. His difficulty will be to obtain proof of this.

Any attempt by Brown to obtain the documents which he thinks will reveal misfeasance may be met by a claim for public interest immunity from the Home Office. Such a claim may be based on the contents of the particular document, or on the assertion that that class of document needs, in the public interest, to be kept secret. As was made clear in *R* v *Chief Constable of the West Midlands Police ex parte Wiley* [1994] 3 All ER 420, if the Home Office does not think that the public interest would be harmed by revealing these documents, there is no obligation on it to claim public interest immunity.

The case of *Conway* v *Rimmer* [1968] AC 910 established that the decision on disclosure or otherwise rests with the court, not the government. The court has to balance two aspects of the public interest; on the one hand, the public interest in secrecy and confidentiality, and, on the other hand, the public interest in the fair administration of justice. Where necessary, the court may inspect the documents to help it decide whether disclosure should be ordered.

The Home Office may have two possible grounds for arguing that these documents should be kept secret. One is that the security of the hostel, its inmates and neighbours might be compromised if the documents were revealed. This does not appear to be very plausible, though security would generally be taken as a reasonable ground to use as a basis for secrecy. The other ground might be the confidentiality of civil service advice to ministers. It has been asserted in various cases that the candour of public officials, and hence their usefulness to ministers might be impaired if they knew their words might be revealed in later litigation. But the courts have shown themselves very unsympathetic to such claims, refusing to believe that officials, whose advice will in any case be preserved on file, will be frightened by the remote possibility of later litigation into failing to do their job properly. In *Williams* v *Home Office* [1981] 1 All ER 1151, this argument concerning candour was rejected and documents relating to penal policy revealed. In that case, inspection of the documents revealed them to be essential to the plaintiff's case, so that the court had no difficulty in holding that the public interest in the fair administration of justice prevailed.

In this problem, it may well be that the court will find it necessary to inspect the documents to discover whether they are necessary to Brown's case, because, if unnecessary, they need not be disclosed. In *Burmah Oil Co.* v *Bank of England* [1980] AC 1090, where sensitive papers were concerned, the court inspected them before deciding that their evidential value to the plaintiff was so limited as not to outweigh the genuine claim to confidentiality put forward by the Attorney-General. Brown is therefore in the hands of the court, which must perform the difficult task of balancing the two aspects of the public interest.

(**c**) The Home Office's liability to Green would have to be based on the claim that it has been in some way negligent. The basic principles governing the liability of public authorities in negligence have been laid down by the House of Lords in the cases of *X* v *Bedfordshire CC* [1995] 2 AC 633 and *Phelps* v *London Borough of Hillingdon* [2000] 4 All ER 504. Some policy decisions may be regarded by the courts as non-justiciable in public law terms and they can then give rise to no duty of care to any individual. But for other decisions, it is sufficient to establish liability using the ordinary tort principles laid down in *Caparo Industries* v *Dickman* [1990] 2 AC 605.

Applying these principles to Green's case, it is difficult to see how he could succeed in any claim based on the policy decision to create such a hostel. The choice of appropriate penal policies is one which the Home Office has to make and, in the absence of some extreme irrationality, the courts will not intervene in such a decision. Green might attempt to assert that the Home Office was negligent in choosing Reg for admission to the hostel. Such negligence would have to be established on ordinary tort principles, and this might prove difficult. It is not clear whether the court would find it fair, just and reasonable to impose a duty of care. In *Hill* v *Chief Constable of West Yorkshire* [1989] AC 53, the court held that the police owed no duty of care to members of the public in respect of the investigation and prevention of crime. It may also be difficult for Green to demonstrate sufficient proximity, though he can certainly argue that it is foreseeable that a prisoner in Reg's position will go to a pub and get drunk!

Green will have a much stronger case if he can show that the warden and staff were under instruction to keep the inmates under supervision and had failed to do so. In *Home Office* v *Dorset Yacht Co.* [1970] AC 1004, the Home Office were held to be vicariously liable for the negligence of prison officers, who had failed to keep a party of borstal boys under supervision as they had been instructed to. But if, as seems to be the case here, the whole reason for the inmates' stay in the hostel is that they are not under constant supervision, no negligence on the part of the warden and staff can be shown. It would therefore appear that Green may be unable to establish any liability on the part of the Home Office, in which case he will be left with the right to sue the probably impecunious Reg only.

Q Question 2

How far is it true to say that the Crown, when involved in litigation, is in the same position as any other litigant before the English courts? Are any further reforms to proceedings involving the Crown necessary?

Commentary

This question covers a fairly wide range of issues relating to Crown proceedings and the student will need to be careful to pick up issues which may not all have been covered under that heading. Clearly, the Crown Proceedings Act will form the core of the answer, but there are still areas where common law rules remain applicable. There are further areas where other changes to the law have had an incidental effect upon the Crown, such as Crown service, which has been affected by the development of statutory rights for workers.

- 'The king can do no wrong'.

- Normal tort liability.

- Liability to armed forces.

- Crown service.

- **Contractual liability.**

- **Procedural immunities.**

☼ Suggested answer

Until 1947, the Crown enjoyed substantial immunities from liability in English law, and benefited from various procedural advantages in litigation. These derived from historical developments. The impossibility of subjecting the king to the jurisdiction of his own courts produced the paradoxical saying that 'the king could do no wrong'; because there was no remedy for those wrongs, they did not legally exist. But an immunity which originally attached to the person of the Monarch also applied if he exercised his powers through his servants and ministers. Though the individual servant might be personally liable, the Crown remained immune. When, through the development of parliamentary government, the exercise of the Crown's power was controlled by a government, the immunity remained intact. It was therefore impossible to sue the Crown in tort, and possible to sue in contract and restitution only with the permission of the Crown, if the Attorney-General granted his fiat to a petition of right.

It was, however, possible, in appropriate cases, for the victim of a tort to sue the individual Crown servant responsible. Dicey indeed regarded this as a powerful demonstration of the rule of law, as it forced the individual to accept responsibility for his or her own actions, rather than being able to hide behind some official immunity. But as a means of ensuring adequate compensation for the victim it was seriously defective, until the Crown developed the practice of standing behind its servants and paying any damages awarded against them. Even this did not help in those circumstances where tortious liability attached to the Crown itself, perhaps as employer or landowner, and not to any individual Crown servant. The cases of *Adams* v *Naylor* [1946] AC 543 and *Royster* v *Cavey* [1947] KB 204 showed that the courts were no longer willing to co-operate in evading the effects of Crown immunity by making findings of liability against nominated defendants who were not personally liable. Statutory reform, which had been under discussion for some years, was finally introduced.

The Crown Proceedings Act 1947, s. 2 subjects the Crown to the same liabilities in tort as a person of full age and capacity in the following respects. Most importantly, it is vicariously liable for torts committed by its servants or agents; by s. 6, Crown servants are defined as those directly or indirectly appointed by the Crown and paid out of the Consolidated Fund or other Treasury-controlled moneys. To avoid any suggestion of Crown interference in the judicial system, no such liability exists in respect of those acting in a judicial capacity. The only significant limitation on this form of liability, s. 2(1), gives the Crown the right to plead any defence which the servant could have pleaded. This includes not only the ordinary tort defences but defences like Act of State, which had developed to limit the liability of Crown servants. But as the case of *Nissan* v *Attorney-General* [1970] AC 179 showed, this defence is very limited in scope.

The other forms of tortious liability imposed by s. 2 are employers' liability to employees and liability arising from the ownership or occupation of property.

The Crown is also subjected to liability for breach of statutory duty, but this is subject to two limitations. First, the statutory duty must also be binding on persons other than the Crown. The Crown Proceedings Act is concerned only to extend the ordinary forms of tort liability to the Crown, not to create new forms of liability to which only the Crown could be subject. Secondly, by a common law rule expressly preserved by s. 40(2)(f), the Crown is not bound by statutes unless the statute so provides, expressly or by necessary implication. This rule has been the subject of stringent criticism, as making it far too easy for the Crown to evade liabilities and obligations to which it should be subject. It would be preferable if the presumption were reversed, as it would then be necessary for an express provision to be included in any statute to exempt the Crown from its provisions, thus alerting Parliament to the question.

There remain some specific limitations on the liability of the Crown in tort. Under s. 40(2) the Act only applies to liabilities arising in the UK. No action could therefore be brought, for example, in respect of a nuisance committed by the British Army in Berlin; *Trawnik* v *Lennox* [1985] 1 WLR 532. This seems an undesirable rule as the doctrine of state immunity may well prevent any action being brought in the foreign state either. A major problem arose as a result of s. 10, which exempted the Crown from liability for injuries caused to one member of the armed forces by the negligence of another, if the injury was classed as pensionable. After sustained criticism of this rule, the Crown Proceedings (Armed Forces) Act 1987 amended s. 10 by imposing liability on the Crown for such 'friendly fire' incidents. The amendment, however, did not have retrospective effect. In *Matthews* v *Ministry of Defence* [2003] UKHL 4, [2003] 1 All ER 689, it was argued that the continuing exemption for pre-1987 injuries was a breach of the right to a fair trial under Article 6 of the European Convention on Human Rights. But the House of Lords held that this was a substantive bar to action, not a procedural one, so Article 6 did not apply. In the 1987 Act, the Crown reserved the right to revive its immunity in case of war or emergency, but in recent conflicts it has not done so. It has in any case been held in *Mulcahy* v *Ministry of Defence* [1996] 2 All ER 758 that in battle conditions no soldier owes a duty of care to his fellow soldiers, nor does the Crown, as employer, owe any duty of care to military personnel in active combat.

The final issue in relation to tort liability is the provision in s. 40(1) which excludes the possibility of any action in tort against the Monarch in his or her personal capacity. Although this could be criticised, it is perhaps an appropriate way of preserving the Monarch's dignity. It is in any case difficult to imagine any circumstances in which the Monarch would have the opportunity to commit torts in person — perhaps a bite from a royal corgi? In any such case compensation would no doubt be paid ex gratia.

Turning to liability in contract, the Crown Proceedings Act 1947, s. 1 simply states that actions which could formerly have been brought by petition of right can now be brought as of right. Actions in contract against the Crown are now therefore straightforward, with the exception of actions against the Monarch in person which would have to use the old petition of right procedure.

The only area of contractual liability which has given rise to any substantial amount of litigation is the law of Crown service. At common law, Crown servants, both civil and military, were employed at the pleasure of the Crown and could therefore be dismissed at any moment, regardless of any terms in the contract; see *Dunn* v *R* [1896] 1 QB 116. This rule remains in the case of military personnel, whose engagement is not contractual at all; see *Mitchell* v *R* (1890), noted at [1896] 1 QB 121. But for civil servants, the law has been transformed by the extension to them of most of the statutory provisions governing employment. Civil servants are now entitled to redundancy payments, to compensation for unfair dismissal and to protection from racial and sexual discrimination. Although their common law rights remain limited, these are in general insignificant compared with statutory rights. Some categories of Crown servants continue to be governed by special rules, such as prison officers who are subject to strict disciplinary codes. The Crown's treatment of its employees has given rise to some disputes, such as the *GCHQ case* [1985] AC 374, but on the whole its behaviour compares satisfactorily with that of most large employers.

As far as other contractual litigation is concerned, few cases ever come to court. The Crown prefers to settle disputes by negotiation or arbitration, especially where sensitive matters, such as defence procurement, are involved. The Crown's freedom of contract is now constrained by the EU rules on public procurement. These are intended to ensure that there is a single Europe-wide market in the supply of goods and services to states, rather than preference being given to national contractors. There have been suggestions in some cases that the Crown may be entitled to certain immunities in contract, but the Crown does not seem to assert these. Most sweeping was the suggestion in *Rederiaktiebolaget Amplutrite* v *R* [1921] 3 KB 500 that the Crown cannot by contract fetter its future freedom of action in matters affecting the welfare of the state. Taken literally, this would entitle the Crown to break any contract it has entered into, but it is doubtful that such a wide proposition can be supported. Indeed, it can be argued that in the case itself there was no actual contract, so the remarks were merely obiter. The Crown has in any case sufficiently wide statutory powers, especially in emergencies, to make such a common law doctrine unnecessary.

Another limitation on the contractual power of the Crown was suggested by the case of *Churchward* v *R* (1865) LR 1 QB 173, where a contract was awarded to Churchward on condition that moneys were voted by Parliament. When Parliament voted against the payment, the contract necessarily fell. It was argued that this made all government contracts dependent on money being voted by Parliament, but this was refuted by the Australian case of *Attorney-General of New South Wales* v *Bardolph* (1934) 52 CLR 455, where the state was held liable even in the absence of a specific vote of money, provided that the contract was a proper one and was covered by a general vote of funds. It remains possible, under the doctrine of Parliamentary supremacy, for Parliament to forbid payments under a contract, and that would be legally effective. It is not, however, the practice of the Crown to bankrupt its contractors by refusing to pay its debts.

The Crown Proceedings Act preserves certain procedural immunities. By s. 25(1) awards of damages against the Crown cannot be enforced by the usual machinery of execution or attachment but this is no real problem. The Crown will always be able to pay damages awarded against it and, on the rare occasions when it does not wish to do so, as in *Burmah Oil* v *Lord Advocate* [1965] AC 75, it will procure the passage of legislation to reverse the decision. More serious is the provision in s. 21(1) that the courts cannot grant an injunction, specific performance or an order for the delivery up of land against the Crown. It was long thought that this would prevent the award of an injunction against a Crown servant acting in his or her official capacity. But in *M* v *Home Office* [1994] 1 AC 377 the House of Lords, acting under the influence of European Community law, held that the Act did not preclude the grant of an injunction against a particular Crown servant, even a government minister. So although the Crown is not subject to this coercive remedy, its servants who carry out its tasks are so subject. This case demonstrates the willingness of the courts to restrict the immunities and privileges of the Crown, which is further illustrated by the historic decision in *Conway* v *Rinuner* [1968] AC 910, which removed the Crown's absolute right to withhold evidence.

The remedy of declaration has always been available against the Crown as a final remedy. But no such thing as an interim declaration existed; see *International General Electric Co.* v *Commissioners of Customs and Excise* [1962] Ch 784. Recent reforms to the Civil Procedure Rules have, however, authorised the courts to award interim declarations in interlocutory proceedings, a valuable reform.

Such immunities as do survive do not seem to cause too many problems for litigants, particularly as the Crown does not seek to rely on the more extreme privileges suggested in the cases. But there needs to be continuing vigilance to ensure that the rule of law is observed and the Crown subjected to the proper degree of liability.

Q Question 3

To what extent has English law developed special rules to govern the liability in negligence of public authorities? Do you consider the law on this subject to be satisfactory?

Commentary

This question raises an issue which has given rise to a good deal of litigation and a lot of debate among academic lawyers. There are many different opinions as to what the law should be. As usual, it does not matter so much what opinion you express as how well you express it. Some students may be studying or have studied tort, and so would be able to give a more sophisticated discussion of the tort issues involved than is given here. It is important to remember that, though the law is divided into separate topics for teaching purposes, it is not divided in reality.

- One law of tort for all.

- Relevance of public law principles.

- Imposing a duty of care.

- Finding negligence.

- Liability for omissions.

:Q: Suggested answer

Because English law did not traditionally distinguish between public and private law, the ordinary principles of tort liability were developed to apply to public and private bodies alike. In *Mersey Docks and Harbour Board Trustees* v *Gibbs* (1866) LR 1 HL 93, it was held that public bodies enjoyed no inherent immunity from liability in negligence. The only exception related to the Crown, which was immune from tortious liability until the Crown Proceedings Act 1947. The Act expressly made the Crown liable 'as if it were a private person' so confirming the general principle that there is just one law of tort.

There are few problems in applying the law where the activities alleged to have been conducted negligently are of a type common to both public and private bodies. Liability for careless driving, dangerous premises or unsafe working practices is the same for public and private defendants. But difficulties may arise where the claim arises out of the exercise by a public authority of statutory powers of a type which private individuals do not have. Complaints about the exercise of such powers are principally dealt with by judicial review. This may provide adequate redress where the authority's action can be halted or reversed, by remedies such as injunction or certiorari. But to claim compensation it is necessary to establish liability in tort. In *Dunlop* v *Woollahra Municipal Council* [1982] AC 158, the plaintiff established that the Council's decision was ultra vires and had it quashed, but he was unable to obtain any compensation, because he could not establish any form of tort liability.

What then is the relationship between judicial review and tort liability? Is it necessary to prove breaches of both laws or is tort liability alone sufficient? These questions have been addressed by the House of Lords in several cases, but their judgments have not always been consistent. In *Anns* v *Merton LBC* [1978] AC 728, the court drew a distinction between claims based on the negligent operation of statutory powers, for which tort liability alone needed to be proved, and claims based on policy decisions made by the public authority. In this situation, it would be necessary to prove that the policy decision was unlawful in public law terms before there could be any question of going on to establish liability in tort. This decision provided a rough test but was rendered problematic by the difficulty of deciding where the line between policy and operation could be drawn in practice.

The House of Lords returned to the problem in *X* v *Bedfordshire* CC [1995] 2 AC 633, a group of cases in which public authorities were alleged to have been negligent in the exercise of their child care and education powers. Rather than applying the *Anns* v *Merton LBC* distinction between policy and operation, the court held that some policy decisions, such as how to allocate limited resources, are regarded as non-justiciable in the context of judicial review. Cases like *R* v *Secretary of State for the Environment ex parte Nottinghamshire CC* [1986] 2 AC 240 had established that the courts would not be willing to challenge the political judgments of public authorities in such areas. That being so, the House of Lords felt that such policy decisions could not give rise to a duty of care to any individual. This decision must be correct, as it is inevitable that decisions on the allocation of what are always limited resources must mean that some individuals do not receive benefits or services which they might otherwise have received. Legal action by one disappointed claimant could only be satisfied by creating another dissatisfied claimant who would have an equally valid claim.

For claims falling outside this non-justiciable area, whether regarded as policy or operational, the House of Lords felt that there was no need to invoke principles of public law. Rather, the cases should be dealt with on the basis of the normal principles of tort liability laid down in *Caparo Industries* v *Dickman* [1990] 2 AC 605. These principles require the court to start by deciding whether it is just and reasonable to impose a duty of care. Public authorities were keen to argue that for policy reasons it would not be just and reasonable to impose any duty of care on them when exercising their statutory responsibilities, so that cases could be disposed of at an early stage and litigants deterred from pursuing actions against them. The courts were initially sympathetic to this view. In *Hill* v *Chief Constable of West Yorkshire* [1989] AC 53, the House of Lords held that the police owed no duty of care to members of the public in respect of the prevention and investigation of crime; any other decision would have lead to resources being taken away from policing and given to the victims of crime, probably creating more victims in consequence. Similarly, in those of the *X v Bedfordshire CC* cases which concerned the immensely difficult question whether or not to take a child into care on suspicion of abuse, the court held that it would not be just and reasonable to impose a duty of care on social service departments, as such decisions are normally taken after discussion with all the agencies concerned.

As a result of these precedents, it became common for public authorities to apply to strike out claims in these areas before the facts were established. In *Osman v United Kingdom* (1998) 5 BHRC 293, the European Court of Human Rights ruled that striking out a claim in this way was a breach of Article 6 of the European Convention on Human Rights. This decision was widely criticised as revealing a misunderstanding of the legal process. But the European Court of Human Rights re-visited the issue in *Z v United Kingdom* [2001] 2 FLR 612, a case brought by one of the unsuccessful claimants in *X v Bedfordshire CC*. This time the court held that to strike out a claim after considering whether it is just and reasonable to impose a duty of care is not a breach of Article 6, as that very consideration is the fair trial to which the individual is entitled.

There have been many cases in which the courts have found it just and reasonable to impose a duty of care, especially where the claim is based on the failure of a public authority to put into effect the decisions it had made. In *X v Bedfordshire CC* itself, the court imposed a duty of care on education authorities which had taken responsibility for dealing with pupils' problems but had failed to do so. Similarly, in *Barrett v Enfield LBC* [1999] 3 All ER 193, the court imposed a duty of care on an authority which, having rightly decided that a child needed to be taken into care, failed to ensure that he was properly cared for. But the court emphasised how difficult it was for them to deal with these cases when only the preliminary issue of whether to impose a duty of care was before them, and none of the facts were established.

The House of Lords returned to this question in *Phelps v London Borough of Hillingdon* [2000] 4 All ER 504, a group of cases alleging that education authorities had failed to identify and deal with pupils' problems, such as dyslexia. The local authorities had argued that policy considerations, such as the complexity of any litigation and the danger of a flood of vexatious claims, should preclude the imposition of a duty of care. But the House of Lords held that a duty of care should be held to exist; genuine claims should not be rejected out of hand. Instead, the court felt that policy considerations would only be material at the later stage of deciding whether the duty of care had been breached, and this would only be done once the facts had been established by evidence.

This decision makes it far more likely that cases will go forward to trial, but it does not necessarily mean that claimants will be successful. The courts are well aware that public authorities make attractive defendants; they have plenty of money and will not evade the payment of any damages awarded against them. But the courts do not wish to impose excessive financial burdens on public authorities, and have emphasised that negligence must be proved to the high standard of professional negligence laid down in *Bolam* v *Friern Hospital Management Committee* [1957] 1 WLR 582.

Although all the above cases were dealt with using just tort principles, it seems to be possible that, in limited circumstances, public law principles may remain relevant in establishing liability. An example is the case of *Stovin* v *Wise* [1996] AC 923, where the local authority had a statutory power to remove obstructions adjoining the highway, but had not removed the obstruction in question, for reasons which were perfectly acceptable in public law terms. The House of Lords held that no liability could arise unless the failure to remove the obstruction was unlawful in public law terms, which it was not. If the danger created by the obstruction were so great as to make the failure to remove it unlawful or unreasonable in public law terms, tortious liability would have been properly imposed. But as the authority was entitled to do nothing, its omissions could not create liability. In any situation where an authority has a positive duty to act, however, only tort principles will be applicable.

In conclusion, the courts face difficult problems in dealing with actions in negligence against public authorities. There is constant pressure from litigants who choose to sue public authorities even in situations where someone else (with less money) is primarily liable. One thinks of the borstal boys in *Home Office* v *Dorset Yacht Co* [1970] AC 1004, the negligent builder in *Anns* v *Merton LBC* [1978] AC 728 or the careless driver in *Stovin* v *Wise* [1996] AC 923. Recent cases show the courts trying to steer a careful course between offering the victims of negligence appropriate compensation, and keeping vexatious claims out of court. The law in this area is likely to show further development.

Q Question 4

Consider the following situations in the light of the doctrine of public interest immunity.

(a) Smith was employed by Proton plc in their factory making nuclear warheads for Britain's missile defence system. He was killed in an explosion in the factory. His widow wishes to establish that the defective design of the warheads, or of the system for making them, caused the explosion, and so recover damages from Proton plc.

(b) A charity wishes to seek judicial review of the Home Office's plan to lock up young offenders in secure training centres. It believes that civil servants in the Home Office research department advised the Home Secretary that the scheme would make the offenders more delinquent, not less. The Home Office says all advice to ministers is confidential.

(c) Farmer Giles was shocked to receive a visit from animal welfare inspectors from the RSPCA, who said they had been informed that he was keeping veal calves in illegal crates. This accusation was wholly untrue. When Giles tried to discover the source of the accusation, the RSPCA said that it was their policy never to reveal the identity of their informants, in order to encourage people to inform them of caes of cruelty to animals.

Commentary

As the question makes clear, its principal concern is the doctrine of public interest immunity. It is therefore appropriate to begin with a brief introductory paragraph explaining what public interest immunity is and how it developed, though it would be wrong in such a problem question to write a detailed history. In each part of the question, the student needs to identify briefly the subject matter of the litigation and the parties to it, but the bulk of the answer should be devoted to PII. Because it is a matter for the discretion of the court whether the claim to PII is upheld in any case, the student will be assessed not on the correctness or otherwise of the final conclusion, but on the quality of the arguments deployed, and the depth of knowledge of decided cases.

- **Court to decide claims to PII.**

- **Public interest in secrecy.**

- **Public interest in fair litigation.**

- **Claims to PII from any source.**

☼ Suggested answer

The doctrine of public interest immunity (PII) is intended to ensure that documents are not revealed in the course of litigation if it is not in the public interest that they should be revealed. Originally such a claim could only be made by the Crown and was therefore known as Crown Privilege. In *Duncan* v *Cammell Laird* [1942] AC 624, the House of Lords laid down the unfortunate rule that any claim made by the Crown had to be accepted by the courts, but in *Conway* v *Rimmer* [1968] AC 910, this rule was reversed, and the courts themselves took the responsibility of assessing whether or not it would be in the public interest for the documents to be disclosed.

(**a**) In this problem, Mrs Smith will be suing her late husband's employers, Proton plc, for negligence in failing to provide him with a safe system of work. She will therefore need the plans of the warheads and of the manufacturing system in order to identify the defects which gave rise to the explosion. But the Ministry of Defence is certainly going to claim that it would be against the public interest for these plans to be disclosed. That claim may be made in spite of the fact that the ministry is not a party to the case. Because of the adversarial nature of English legal proceedings, disclosing the documents means revealing them to the parties, their solicitors and barristers as well as to the judge. The possibility of hearing the case in camera does not eliminate the danger of the documents getting into the wrong hands.

In *Conway* v *Rimmer* (1986), the House of Lords laid down that, in deciding whether documents should be disclosed or not, two aspects of the public interest had to be balanced. Firstly, there was a public interest in ensuring that no harm was done to the national interest by disclosing documents which should be kept secret. But secondly, there was a public interest in ensuring that the conduct of litigation was not frustrated. The court distinguished between claims based on the contents of the particular documents and those based merely on the class to which the documents belonged. Contents claims would generally be much stronger than class claims. As a consequence of the Scott Inquiry into the Matrix Churchill affair, the government announced that it would no longer make class claims, but only claims based on the contents of particular documents. If necessary, the court could inspect the documents to identify the strengths of the arguments for and against disclosure.

Applying these principles to the case of Mrs Smith, it seems very probable that her chances of establishing liability will be almost completely dependent on access to the documents, which, if they do reveal design flaws, will virtually prove her case by themselves. The litigation will be frustrated if she cannot gain access to them. But the arguments against disclosure are particularly powerful. The PII claim will be based on the contents of the documents themselves, and it is hardly possible to dispute an assertion that it would pose a grave threat to national security if the plans of the nuclear deterrent fell into the wrong hands, or if designs indicating how to build a nuclear warhead came into the possession of terrorists. Inspection of the documents is not likely to be necessary to convince the court that these are genuine state secrets. Comparison may be made with *Duncan* v *Cammell Laird* (1942) where the Admiralty was clearly justified in wishing to keep secret the plans of its latest submarine.

There is no doubt that the courts do have the power to order the disclosure even of documents as sensitive as these in the interest of justice, but it is doubtful whether they would do so in this case.

(**b**) The charity's appliction for judicial review may be based on the unreasonableness of the Home Office's decision or on the failure to take relevant considerations into account. Under the principle laid down in *Conway* v *Rimmer* (1968) it will be for the court to decide whether the public interest in confidentiality or the public interest in the fair conduct of litigation should prevail.

It appears that the Home Office's objection to the disclosure of documents in this case is based not on the contents of the particular documents, but on the claim that documents containing advice to ministers are a class which need to be kept confidential. The justification for this claim has been explained as the danger that officials might be deterred from being completely candid in their advice to ministers if they knew that such information might one day be revealed to the world through its use in litigation. But the courts have generally been unsympathetic to such assertions. In *Conway* v *Rimmer* (1968) such an argument was advanced in respect of the reports prepared by police officers on the conduct of a probationer, but the court rejected it. They pointed out that any such report would be protected by qualified privilege, so the official would have nothing to fear provided the report was honest. This point was also raised in *Williams* v *Home Office* [1981] 1 All ER 1151, where the court ordered the Home Office to disclose various documents including advice to ministers on the development of penal policy, rejecting the argument that the candour of public servants might be hindered by the remote chance of later disclosure in litigation. It would therefore appear that, unless some other, stronger argument for non-disclosure is presented to the court, the court may feel that the case for secrecy has not been made out.

Turning to the other side of the balance, the court will need to be satisfied that the disclosure of the documents is necessary for the fair conduct of the litigation. In *Air Canada* v *Secretary of State for Trade* [1983] 2 AC 394, this was interpreted as meaning that the applicants must show that it is very likely that the documents sought do contain material supportive of their case; applicants cannot embark on 'fishing' expeditions by demanding any document whether or not they have any grounds for thinking it material evidence. But once the applicants have passed this threshold, it may well be appropriate for the court to inspect the documents, because if they do not in fact assist the applicants' case, there is no need to order disclosure.

In this problem, the applicants seem to have good grounds for suggesting that the documents from the research department will assist their case, by demonstrating that relevant considerations were ignored. The court may feel that this is sufficient to justify an order for disclosure, given the weakness of the opposing case, or may feel it better to inspect the documents before coming to a conclusion. Only if the documents fail to support the applicants' case at all is it likely that disclosure will be refused.

(**c**) Before *Conway* v *Rimmer*, the term Crown privilege demonstrated clearly that claims for non-disclosure could be made only by the Crown. But in *Rogers* v *Home Secretary* [1973] AC 388, the claim was made by the Gaming Board which, though a public body, was not a government department. The House of Lords stated that claims based on the public interest could be made by any interested party, not just the Crown. This was applied in *D* v *NSPCC* [1978] AC 171, where the defendant, a charitable voluntary organisation, with a recognised status in the protection of children, was held able to claim PII in respect of certain confidential information. It would therefore be open to the RSPCA to raise an issue of PII in this case.

The basis of their claim is the need to offer complete confidentiality to informants who might otherwise be reluctant to contact them. Such claims have been accepted by the courts as being in the public interest. The case of *Rogers* v *Home Secretary* (1973) concerned confidential information supplied to the Gaming Board about an applicant for a gaming licence. The court accepted that, in the sometimes murky world of gaming, informants needed to be given an absolute guarantee of confidentiality. In *D* v *NSPCC* (1978) the charity was held to be justified in claiming that confidentiality served the vital function of encouraging people to report suspected child abuse.

Whether the court would feel that the same justification applied in the case of cruelty to animals is not clear. But such activity can be criminal and the RSPCA is active in prosecution, so it seems that they could assert a public interest in the enforcement of the law. To obtain information about such organised cruelty as cockfighting or badger-baiting might well require promises of complete confidentiality for informers.

To set against this is the public interest in the fair conduct of litigation. Clearly Giles will be unable to bring proceedings for defamation against the informant if he cannot discover who the informant was, and this may seem unfair, particularly as the defamation may even have been malicious. But the court may feel, as they did in *D* v *NSPCC* (1978) that this is a price worth paying for the better protection of the vulnerable.

Further reading

Bradley, A. and Ewing, K. *Constitutional & Administrative Law*, 13th edn (Longman, 2003), ch 32.

Cane, P. *Introduction to Administrative Law*, 3rd edn (OUP, 1996), chs 12, 13 and 15.

Wade, W. and Forsyth, C. *Administrative Law*, 8th edn (OUP, 2000), chs 21 and 22.

Harlow, C. *Compensation and Government Torts* (Sweet & Maxwell, 1982).

Index